PICNICS

Picnics

And other outdoor feasts

Claudia Roden

Grub Street • London

For Simon, Nadia and Anna and for Jill, with love

This edition published in 2012 by
Grub Street
4 Rainham Close
London
SW11 6SS
www.grubstreet.co.uk
email: food@grubstreet.co.uk
Twitter: @grub_street

Text copyright © Claudia Roden 1981, 2012
Copyright this edition © Grub Street 2012
Illustrations by Linda Kitson
Jacket design Sarah Driver
First published in 1981 by Jill Norman Ltd

British Library Cataloguing in Publication Data
Roden, Claudia
Picnics and other outdoor feasts. – New ed.
Outdoor cookery 2. Picnicking
Title
641.5'78

ISBN 978-1-908117-44-1

Printed and bound in India

CONTENTS

ACKNOWLEDGEMENTS

This book was drawn from many people's experiences of cooking out-of-doors. The most pleasant part of working on it for me was sharing their memories, capturing their ideas and recording their knowledge. I cannot name everyone who helped me and added a part of themselves, and although some have been acknowledged in the text, I take the opportunity here of expressing my gratitude to all of them.

Of those who gave professional information, I thank especially James Marks, Frank Odell and Brian Lee of the barbecue trade, Paul Breman who gave advice about drinks and Kumar Chowdhary, father of a family very dear to my own, who revealed the secrets of the tandoor at his Akash Restaurant.

I am particularly indebted to three friends: Sami Zubaida, whose kitchen was the setting of many joyful gastronomic events and who read the manuscript in draft and made many suggestions; Clint Greyn, who lent his experience as a camping gourmet; and Barbara Maher, whom I cannot thank enough for her enthusiastic involvement, her much appreciated advice and her constructive criticism.

I owe an affectionate debt to Elizabeth David who first inspired me to write, and to Jane Grigson whose scholarship has brought a new dimension to cookery writing, for it is from them that I have learned the ways and joys of the trade. I am especially grateful to Jane for the literary picnics she brought to my attention and to Maxime Rodinson, the French Orientalist, for historical references.

I have looked for ideas and information in many cookery books. The principal ones are listed in the bibliography.

I am very happy with Linda Kitson's collaboration. Her illustrations fill me with delight and I am particularly touched by her decision to do some of the drawings in Egypt, a land close to my heart.

I thank my children Simon, Nadia and Anna, who have gracefully eaten their way through the recipes, for their patience and their willingness to taste everything.

Finally, my greatest debt is to my first publisher Jill Norman who fostered the idea of the book and encouraged and guided me. She has been sympathetic and deeply involved in every stage, and it has been a pleasure to work with her.

I am very happy that Anne Dolamore is reissuing the book in this new edition.

PREFACE

For the better use of *Picnics*.

This book is divided broadly into four sections which represent four aspects of cooking and eating outdoors. The first, about meals to serve in the garden, whether tea, luncheon or party fare, relies on easy access to the kitchen. The second, about foods to be prepared in the kitchen and transported, is the principal and largest section. It deals with unusual as well as traditional picnic fare, from soups and sandwiches, cold meats and fish, pies, salads and dips, to desserts and drinks. The third is about barbecuing. The last, for travellers, includes provisions and impromptu meals as well as more elaborate ones. There are ideas for freshly caught fish, details of primitive ways of cooking and descriptions of equipment. Each section also contains some special menus such as those for Indian and Japanese meals.

Many dishes are suitable for different kinds of events, and recipes can be taken from one section, combined with those from another and used for a different occasion. The index had been planned to be helpful in making these selections.

Flexibility is intended in using the book just as improvisation is encouraged in cooking. Browse through the whole book for inspiration, for that is its nature.

In ample space under the broadest shade,
A table richly spread in regal mode,
With dishes piled and meats of noblest sort
And savour – beasts of chase, or fowl of game,
In pastry built, or from the spit, or boiled,
Gris-amber-steamed; all fish, from sea or shore,
Freshet or purling brook, of shell or fin
And exquisitest name, for which was drained
Pontus, and Lucrine bay, and Afric coast,
Alas! how simple, to these cates compared,
Was that crude apple that diverted Eve!
And at a stately sideboard, by the wine,
That fragrant smell diffused, in order stood
Tall stripling youths rich-clad, of fairer hue
Than Ganymede or Hylas; distant more
Under the trees now tripped, now solemn stood,
Nymphs of Diana's train, and Naiades
With fruits and flowers from Amalthea's horn,
And ladies of th' Hesperides, that seemed
Fairer than feigned of old, or fabled since
Of fairy damsels met in forest wide
By knights of Logres, or of Lyonese,
Lancelot, or Pelleas, or Pellenore.
And all the while harmonious airs were heard
Of chiming strings or charming pipes; and winds
Of gentlest gale Arabian odours fanned
From their soft wings, and Flora's earliest smells.
Such was the spendour; and the Tempter now
His invitation earnestly renewed:–

  'What doubts the Son of God to sit and eat?
  These are not fruits forbidden'

JOHN MILTON
Paradise Lost

INTRODUCTION

Everything tastes better outdoors.

There is something about fresh air and the liberating effect of nature which sharpens the appetite and heightens the quality and intensity of sensations. It is enough to see the contented expression of someone sitting at a sunny outdoor café to realize it. The sense of smell especially is extraordinarily keen and every little perfume from a nearby blossom or resinous bark adds to the flavour of the most banal sandwich filling.

Brillat-Savarin gives his support to a well-worn cliché when he describes a picnic party: 'Seating themselves on the green sward, they eat while the corks fly and there is talk, laughter and merriment, and perfect freedom, for the universe is their drawing room and the sun their lamp. Besides, they have appetite, Nature's special gift, which lends to such a meal a vivacity unknown indoors, however beautiful the surroundings.'

Visions of paradise have always been of the great outdoors, of trees laden with luscious fruit and rivers flowing with milk and honey, and many, like Milton, have been moved to eloquence by the first dining room of man.

My own experience of the Garden of Eden was in the Seychelles islands. The smell of pork roasting on a fruit-wood fire and the Indian Ocean Creole mixture of garlic, spices and chillies frying in coconut oil still fill me with sudden bursts of happiness, summoning as they do the primeval forest, the tropical climate mitigated by the sea breeze and the waters so clear that you could see the multicoloured fish and the shells and corals rocking gently on the white sands at the bottom.

Every day at noon, after a morning swim, I scrambled between clumps of fern and granite rocks up the hill slopes, lured by the smell of cooking which wafted round the lush vegetation. Light clouds of smoke rose beside corrugated iron-roofed huts nestling behind rocks and between coconut palms. They emanated from burning husks over which large heavy pots were sitting firmly on sturdy grills, the local outdoor kitchen arrangement.

Whiffs from ripe mangoes and pawpaws, still hanging on trees, mingled with the smell of bananas simmering in coconut milk and the fermenting juice of sugar cane. It was difficult to tell if the scent of vanilla came from the fragile pods dangling on their climbing stalks or from the sweet potato and yam pudding in the pot.

Scents became confused with colours and sounds. A hundred shades of green were pierced by scarlet flowered flamboyants and pale mauve bougainvillaeas. The gentle bubbling of the daube and the crackling of the fire were accompanied by the rustling of palms and the chattering chorus of little red cardinals, warblers and sunbirds.

Lunch was prepared in the open, for all to see. Exchanges were shouted about the contents of the pots which were fondly watched over by the women. To constant giggling and laughter I accepted every invitation to taste. I tried a peppery fish soup, the contents of which had been found caught in the twisted bamboo trap now resting by the fire. A coconut fallen not far away had provided the liquor for the breadfruit daube. Black fresh-water prawns, caught in the stream by a little boy, were turning red on dying embers. A sweet potato melted in the ashes. Indian Ocean Creole food, amid the trees and the birds, was an assault on all the senses; I had to hold my breath to eat. Today the smell is still in my nostrils, the taste still on my tongue.

The pleasures of outdoor food are those that nature has to offer, as ephemeral as they are intense. A bird will sing his song and fly away, leaves will flutter and jostle the sunlight for a brief second sky, flowers and scents have each their small parts to play in the perfect happiness of those enchanted moments. They serve, as Jean Jacques Rousseau said, to 'liberate the soul'.

My adventure in what has been called 'the last paradise on earth' is long past, but still, whether I have a sandwich with my family beneath a tree of rustling leaves on nearby Hampstead Heath, or breakfast in the garden watched over by an inquisitive squirrel, the food and the drink taste much better than they do indoors, and that too is a little bit of paradise.

Despite our grey and drizzly weather, picnics have become a British institution. Forever endearing is the romantic nostalgia and sublime recklessness with which people continue to indulge in the national passion at great social events like Henley Regatta and Glyndebourne, the Chelsea Flower Show, Goodwood and Ascot and on Epsom Downs on Derby Day. Race meetings, agricultural shows, sports days and regattas see thousands of enthusiasts eating their lunch in rain and snow. City parks on chilly spring days are full of office workers at lunch-time. Glorious weather or not, bank holidays bring crowds to Hampstead Heath, and every summer scores of people set off with hampers and picnic baskets to the sea, the woods or the fields. The more energetic make picnics occasions of activity, devoted to watching birds, sketching, hunting for fossils or collecting wild flowers, shells and pebbles. There are rowing and climbing expeditions, pony trekking, mushroom gathering, strawberry picking, and learned societies on architectural, archeological or botanical outings often combine their scientific research with a little joyful revelling.

Georgina Battiscombe says in *English Picnics* (1951) that the English picnicker is a hardy species, above the vagaries of the weather. It does require stoicism to defy fate and bring out knives and forks at the risk of being rained and blown upon. But it is also true that the gastronomic rigours of British hotels and restaurants are usually worse than those of the British climate, and there seems to be a particular, grim, English pleasure in a cold, wet, uncomfortable picnic. Jane Grigson has remarked that often, the success of a picnic depends on disaster. Judging by the abundance of catastrophes described with glee in English diaries and fiction, it must be so. Stories abound of rain and umbrellas blown away, of wet, wasp-infested fields, of pots fallen in the fire, and soggy bread. Even John Betjeman in *Trebetherick* writes nostalgically:

> Sand in the sandwiches, wasps in the tea,
> Sun on our bathing-dresses heavy with the wet,
> Squelch of the bladder-wrack waiting for the sea,
> Fleas round the tamarisk, an early cigarette.

All things taken into account, it is not surprising that eating outdoors has had an uneven history in England. Coming in and out of fashion as pilgrims' wayside snack, hunting feast and garden party, alfresco eating was at its most popular in Victorian times.

In their heyday, picnics were great social events, opportunities for matchmaking and introductions, with music and singing and kettles boiling for tea and fashionable ladies in bonnets, with sketchbooks, watercolours and pencils to hand. Remarkable, as all things Victorian, for their size and solidity, they were perfectly planned. Nothing was forgotten, with menus immensely varied and quantities to feed an army. The profusion of foods set in gelatine in highly decorative moulds bore tribute to this by-product of the Industrial Revolution and to the sophisticated and decorative tastes which had arrived with the fugitive cooks of the French Revolution. Until then the fare had remained the same since the Middle Ages when English and French picnics were as similar as were the manners and social habits of the two countries. The picnic outside Valenciennes, described by the fourteenth century French poet Froissart in *Espinette Amoureuse*, 'Lo! a place made for our pleasant repose; here let us break our fast! Then with one accord we brought out the meats, pasties, hams, wines and bakemeats and venison packed in heather', might have been a May-time picnic in the meadows of Kent or Surrey.

Mrs Beeton's picnic menus, lavish and extravagant as they were, followed the same tradition. Here is a bill of fare for forty persons in her *Book of Household Management*:

A joint of cold roast beef, a joint of cold boiled beef. 2 ribs of lamb, 2 shoulders of lamb, 4 roast fowls, 2 roast ducks, 1 ham, 1 tongue, 2 veal and ham pies, 2 pigeon pies, 6 medium sized lobsters, 1 piece of collared calveshead, 18 lettuces, 6 baskets of salad, 6 cucumbers.

Stewed fruit well sweetened and put into glass bottles well corked, 3 or 4 dozen plain pastry biscuits to eat with the stewed fruit, 2 dozen fruit turnovers, 4 dozen cheese cakes, 2 cold cabinet puddings in moulds, a few jam puffs, 1 large cold Christmas pudding (this must be good), a few baskets of fresh fruit, 3 dozen plain biscuits, a piece of cheese, 6 lbs of butter (this of course includes the butter for tea), 4 quartern loaves of household bread, 3 dozen rolls, 6 loaves of tin bread (for tea), 2 plain plum cakes, 2 pound cakes, 2 sponge cakes, a tin of mixed biscuits, $1/2$ lb of tea. Coffee is not suitable for a picnic, being difficult to make.

It was these Victorian picnics, with their formal rituals, and their cold lamb, roast chicken, veal and ham pies, puddings and jellies, which the English transported all over the world and which became a favourite pastime and a remembered feature of colonial life. In Calcutta and Madras, Jamaica, Aden and Egypt (where I saw them) the English entertained each other in their gardens, the desert and the wild countryside like their relatives at home, only with considerably more pomp. In the early days of the Empire picnics were often stately, formal affairs which required arranging. Servants were sent ahead with tents and provisions to start preparations, but the fare was the same as it was back home. No one, it seems, took any notice of the large saucepans bubbling with curries for the 'idle and unintelligible' servants. Nor had they much interest in the culinary ways of the high caste natives they met at shoots and hunting expeditions. The little morsels pierced by skewers roasting over dying embers in their Arab protectorates, and the spare ribs glistening in their sweet and sour sauce in Hong Kong also went unnoticed. Ironically it has taken more than a century for all these things to appear in suburban English back gardens at sunny weekend lunches. Indian tandoori chicken, spare ribs and kebabs have become party favourites with the new-found fashion for barbecues. And when we plan a 'déjeuner sur l'herbe', it is jambon persillé and poulet en croûte which summon idyllic visions immortalized by Tissot and Manet, Renoir and Léger.

Our own traditions are left to the specialist food stores such as Harrods and the Army & Navy who take pride in making up their own hampers for the great social events of Epsom, Ascot, Lords, Henley and Glyndebourne. Traditional wicker baskets are packed with every requirement for a picnic; besides the food we find condiments, champagne or wine and fruit juices, cutlery, plates, glasses, table napkins and corkscrew. Sadly, Jacksons who have provisioned yachts, tennis, boating excursions and shooting parties – also, when required, hiring out musicians and servants – since the nineteenth century, have now closed down. The usual contents of these hampers are combinations of pies (chicken and ham, game or pork), cold meats (roast chicken, ham and beef), seasonal salads, cheeses, biscuits, rolls and butter, fresh fruit and fruit salad or strawberries and cream. The more expensive offer smoked trout or smoked salmon and caviare or fresh Scotch salmon with mayonnaise and cucumber.

Now that foreign ways have crept into our lives, it is from those for whom the dining room, as well as the kitchen, are still of necessity outdoors, whose facilities are primitive and weather propitious, that we can learn the techniques and tricks of cooking in the open. From the travellers of the past and the nomads of the present we can find out about the best lunch in the pocket, about the dried salt fish which comes to life when plunged in water and the live one grilled in a parcel of leaves. The seafarer of old has also much to teach the sailing enthusiast about potted meats and pickles and preserves.

We are also learning to take advantage of wild foods, for food which you do not have to pay for has a special attraction. And when it comes as Nature's bounty, as those who know the pleasures of fresh berries, wild fruits, good game and the delicacy of fish caught in a cold mountain stream will tell you, it is even more attractive. There is the fun of the hunt, the pleasure in foraging, the promise of unexpected flavours which are no less engaging for being hazardous, all of which bring an intimacy with Nature. Whichever way you cook them, there is little to beat the special flavour of mushrooms gathered in fields, except perhaps the watercress discovered by chance in a stream, eaten with nuts and oranges, the wild sorrel found in rock crevices or on the dark, barren floors of conifer woods, the thistle dressed in oil and lemon and served with yoghurt, or the cockles winkled out from the sand after the tide has gone out and fried the same night with bacon. Who has had elderflower, stirred into beaten egg, fried by the tablespoon and eaten with plenty of sugar? I have heard ecstatic accounts of mussels cooked in a pail on the beach, of game birds encased in clay, gipsy fashion and baked in the open fire. Few things have been as tasty or as much fun. Whether a snail or a berry, there is something unforgettable about food which has not been reared or grown for eating and which has just happened to be there. Memory clothes it with very special virtues. It is like manna, the food which the Israelites found and ate during their sojourn in the desert between Egypt and Canaan. It seems probable that it was a sweet, resinous substance which exudes from the desert tree, *Tamarix manifera*, when it is punctured by the insect *Gossyparia mannipara*. It can be ground or pounded like meal, boiled and made into cakes, but it has none of the other properties attributed to what was called the 'grain of heaven' and the 'bread of the mighty', and one would imagine the Jews must have grown very weary of it. Nevertheless, the memory of this food was expanded in Jewish tradition into the regular diet of all Israel and was endowed with marvellous features. It was said to have fallen on the ground like frost, white and sweet, but never on the Sabbath, and to have melted when the heat of the morning sun reached it. It was wonderful in every way, like our wild mushrooms and strawberries and the fish which grows larger in our memories.

Planning the menu for an outdoor meal, whether it is an elaborate banquet prepared at home the day before, a camper's cook out, a sailor's luncheon or an improvised meal put together with what there is in the larder, is one of the most creative parts of the affair.

The choice of food is wide. It lies between what is easily transportable and holds well, what can be eaten cold or easily kept hot, and what can be cooked on the spot. A wide range of equipment makes it possible to transport most things and there are many types of cooking arrangements. Every type of canapé may be served at a cocktail party on the terrace, all the great dishes of the world may be offered under the marquee at a wedding party, and with a little effort, almost everything can be cooked at camp. But this book is mainly concerned with the casual and unpretentious cooking most suited to the carefree and relaxed atmosphere of outdoor eating. It has drawn on the experience of friends and acquaintances who have enjoyed or are addicted to the pleasures of eating outdoors. Traditions of other lands have been explored and foreign ways have been made ordinary, as indeed they are.

The object of the book is to inspire those who like to eat well and who love to be out among the trees. It is for those who travel all over the world, who camp and sail and caravan, who enjoy good food and cannot always afford the prices of restaurants and prefer to pack a picnic meal or cook on the spot. It is not a primer, nor a textbook; nor is it a cooking school and it assumes a certain knowledge of basic cooking skills.

In the belief that the last thing one wishes in field or boat is strict measures and dogmas, I have allowed myself and readers a certain freedom from standard recipes and precise measurements. Without scales and measuring equipment you can forget the arbitrary measures which have been forced on to an old art whose principal quality is the personal touch.

True gastronomy is making the most of what is available, however modest. It has little to do with following recipes. And the leisurely atmosphere of holiday cooking is the best time to learn to trust your own taste and common sense, to weigh with eyes and hands, to feel and taste and dream a little. I have given precise measures only where they are required and when the preparation is likely to be done in the kitchen. Otherwise I have given enough information for a moderately accomplished cook, with encouragement towards self-assurance.

You may decide simply to plan around one special dish with cheese and fruit to follow, or make it a grander affair with three or four courses: a simple first dish such as a chilled soup, a nobler second one, cheese and a light dessert. For a larger party it is best to have a variety of dishes as for a buffet, or it may just be some good sandwiches with a hearty wine to wash them down.

Mrs Beeton has a word of advice:

Watch carefully not to provide too much of one thing and too little of another; avoid serving plenty of salad and no dressing; two or three legs of lamb and no mint sauce; an abundance of wine and no corkscrew; and such like little mistakes. Given a happy party of young people, bent on enjoyment, these are trifles light as air, which serve rather to increase the fun than diminish it. But, on the other hand, the party may not all be young and merry; it may be very distasteful to some to have to suffer these inconveniences.

The easiest way to arrange that there should be nothing wanting, is to make out a menu, adding all the little etceteras. It is advisable to estimate quantities extravagantly, for nothing is more annoying than to find everything exhausted and guests hungry.

If the party is very large, and resources and efforts are to be pooled, it is best to plan the menu together. Whatever it is to be, it is worth remembering that appetites are sharper in the open air and it is advisable to estimate generous quantities. Whether it is a wayside snack or an elegant luncheon, an open air meal should always be an occasion for good food.

Author's Note

The recipes in this book are intended to provide six servings except where otherwise specified.

Olive oil when listed always means extra virgin except for use in deep frying.

EATING IN THE GARDEN

TEA ON THE LAWN

An illustration in a Cairo schoolbook of my childhood showed a daintily set tea-table on a well-mown lawn. Tea-caddy, silver teapot, cream and milk jugs, sugar bowl, slop basin with silver strainer and fine bone china service were laid out on a light Chantilly lace cloth. They symbolized the mystique of Englishness. The text, as I remember it, may well have originated from *Lady Sysonby's Cook Book* (1935) in which she says:

> A tea table without a big cake in the country in England would look very bare and penurious. The ideal tea table should include some sort of hot buttered toast or scone, one or two sorts of sandwiches, a plate of small light cakes, and our friend the luncheon cake.
> Add a pot of jam or honey, and a plate of brown and white bread and butter – which I implore my readers not to cut too thin – and every eye will sparkle, and all those wishing to follow the fashionable craze of slimming will groan in despair.

A note follows that this little foreword was written before the days of austerity.

Tea drinking came into fashion in the middle of the eighteenth century as an outdoor activity. On Sunday afternoon Londoners flocked to tea-gardens situated in open country on the fringes of the city to take tea and bread and butter and to be entertained with illuminations, firework displays, concerts and promenades. The Vauxhall, the Ranelagh, Cuper's and Marylebone Gardens were very large parks with shrubs, flowers, pools, fountains and statues. There were arbours covered with creepers and set into the hedges for the tea drinkers. And if it rained people could shelter under the rotunda and continue to enjoy the concerts. By the beginning of the nineteenth century their popularity had waned. But the habit of drinking tea in the afternoon had become a national institution honoured and observed by the middle classes and the aristocracy. Though it has now somewhat fallen into disuse, to be served tea in the garden is still one of the joys of England.

❧ About tea

In the past it was usual to offer a choice of China and Indian tea and two pots were prepared. It is still very pleasant to be given the choice. Almost all teas that you can buy are already blended, but you can improve on them by adding a specially fragrant one, or you can create your own blends by trying and tasting.

Indian teas, generally thick, rich and heavy, full bodied with a good colour and fragrance, may be served with milk or lemon and they may also be mixed with China teas.

Delicately fragrant, China tea is sometimes scented with dried flowers. Jasmine petals are left in the blend, but larger petals of gardenia, orange blossom and roses are removed when the tea has absorbed their scent. Not everyone likes Lapsang Suchong with its smoky flavour and tarry tang. Earl Grey is a varying blend which sometimes also includes Darjeeling. Its fragrant flowery aroma derives from the oil extracted from the zest of bergamot fruit. Most people prefer to have China tea without milk or sugar and rather weak.

❧ Sandwiches

English tea sandwiches are dainty affairs. They should be cut very thin with a sharp knife, trimmed of crust or not, and cut in half or in four. Day-old bread, white or wholemeal, makes cutting easier. Butter lightly and fill generously. To keep them any length of time before serving wrap in a damp cloth, polythene bag or aluminium foil and keep in a cool place.

An anchovy filling that keeps. Chop or pound anchovy fillets and beat in about twice the amount of butter. A little finely chopped parsley or minced black olives or capers may be added as well as chopped hard-boiled eggs. An old-fashioned commercial alternative is Patum Peperium otherwise known as Gentleman's Relish, which still comes in its original elegant white pot

Cucumber. Peel the cucumber, slice very thinly, sprinkle with salt and allow the juices to be drawn out for at least an hour. Dry on paper towels if you like, lay on buttered bread with a squeeze of lemon and a little freshly ground pepper, and cover. Alternatively, spread the cucumber slices with thick double or sour cream mixed with finely chopped parsley or chives.

Tomato. Scald tomatoes, peel and remove the seeds. Chop or mash the pulp with a fork, adding a little salt and pepper, and if you wish a sprinkling of oil and vinegar. You may like to sprinkle a little Worcestershire sauce, or a light powdering of cayenne pepper and sugar on top.

Sardine. Bone and mash a tin of sardines with salt and pepper and lemon juice. Or beat in a small pot of cream cheese or a mixture of cottage cheese and sour cream. Garnish with chopped parsley or watercress.

Mushroom sandwiches are old English favourites. Slice raw mushrooms on to buttered brown bread. Season with salt and pepper and lemon juice. Alternatively, you may sauté in a little butter, drain and moisten with cream.

Ham. A good old-fashioned way is to shred or chop it. Season the butter lightly with salt and pepper and mustard and garnish with a lettuce leaf.

Cress. Wash and dry before pulling the leaves off stems. Cut small with scissors and season lightly with salt and pepper, olive oil and vinegar.

Chicken. Boil the chicken (see p.22-3) and shred or chop it. Moisten with thick cream, season with salt and pepper and garnish with lettuce or watercress.

Egg. Mash hard-boiled eggs with butter, salt and pepper, a squeeze of lemon and if you like some finely chopped spring onions or chopped pickles.

৯ Rolls

Thin slices of bread and butter, spread with a filling and rolled up tightly make an elegant tea-table feature. Slice the rolls with a very sharp knife or leave them whole. Prawns, smoked salmon (with cream cheese and brown bread) and asparagus make excellent fillings. Serve with lettuce and watercress.

৯ Sweet sandwiches

As children in Egypt we were amazed to see our English school friends mashing bananas with thick cream and putting them into a sandwich topped with a very thin layer of strawberry jam. Other sweet concoctions with local exotic ingredients were a layer of honey sprinkled with chopped sultanas, dates and walnuts, a paste of ground almonds or brown tahina with honey, or honey covered with the heavy cream made from rich buffalo milk. Mashed halva is another delightful tea-time legacy of colonial days.

৯ Mrs Leyel's sandwiches

Mrs Leyel, who believed that there was 'as much art in preparing sandwiches as in preparing a French menu', devoted much space to them in *The Gentle Art of Cookery*. Her secret was to use plenty of butter and to grate, shred or chop all meats rather than leave them in slices. Here are some of her combinations:

Chicken and chopped almonds with cream seasoned with salt and pepper and paprika.
Chicken and ham with mayonnaise covered with slices of cucumber.
Salmon mashed with butter, or moistened with cream, seasoned with salt, pepper and Worcestershire sauce, covered with cucumber slices dipped in French dressing and finely chopped parsley.
Pounded shrimps and mayonnaise sprinkled with salt, pepper and lemon juice.
Cheese pounded to a paste with butter, seasoned with a touch of tarragon vinegar and made mustard.
Chopped olives and cream cheese.
Chopped hard-boiled eggs mixed with mango chutney, one teaspoonful for each egg, and some watercress.

Cooked flaked smoked haddock mixed with cream and finely chopped
parsley, seasoned with salt and cayenne.

They will easily make a substantial high tea.

🐦 Cinnamon toast

Cinnamon toast is something special. Cut the bread into fairly thick
slices and toast one side only. Butter the untoasted side liberally and
sprinkle each piece with ground cinnamon and brown sugar. Brown
under the grill and serve very hot. Cut into fingers if you like.

₰ Apple sponge cake

I have eaten this refreshing sponge cake in my friend Barbara Maher's garden, which conveniently backs on to mine. It is one of many delicious recipes I sampled while she was compiling her book on cakes.

150 g (5 oz) castor sugar, 150 g (5 oz) plain flour, 150 g (5 oz) melted cooled butter, 6 egg whites, 6 egg yolks, zest of lemon, 350-450 g (3/4 lb) Bramley or Cox's apples.

Prepare a Genoese sponge mixture: sift the flour two or three times, whisk the egg whites to form stiff snowy peaks, beat in half the sugar and gently fold in the rest using a large metal spoon, taking care not to lose any air. Lightly fork the egg yolks in a separate bowl and fold them and the lemon zest into the egg whites. Next carefully fold in the sifted flour and finally the melted butter. Pour just less than half the mixture into a greased, floured and sugared 26 cm (10 in) springform or savarin mould. Place in a pre-heated 180°C/350°F/Gas 4 oven for about 10 minutes to set the mixture; this prevents the fruit from sinking to the bottom. Peel, core and slice the apples (not too thin or they harden as they cook). The quantity can vary depending on the depth of the tin you use. Take the set cake from the oven and gently lay the prepared fruit all over. There is no need to sugar them as the mixture is already sweet enough. Cover with the remainder of the Genoese mixture and return to the oven. Bake for a further 45 minutes, or until it has browned well, shrunk from the sides of the tin, and a skewer comes out dry when plunged into the centre. (Bear in mind that the more fruit there is the longer it will take to cook.)

Most fruits, apart from citrus, are suitable for this recipe: pears, rhubarb, gooseberries, grapes, plums, even strawberries and all are delicious.

₰ Date and nut cake

My mother discovered this cake in South America and calls it 'torta di datiles i nueces'. It is very rich and moist.

250 g (8 oz) dried pitted dates, 1 teaspoon bicarbonate of soda, 350 g (12 oz) self-raising flour, 200 ml (7 fl oz) milk, 250 g (8 oz) butter, 250 g (8 oz) sugar, 6 eggs, 1/2 teaspoon salt, 1 tablespoon cinnamon, 175 g (6 oz) walnuts (coarsely chopped).

Chop the dates coarsely and put them in a bowl. Add bicarbonate of soda and dredge with 50 g (2 oz) flour. Cover with boiling hot milk and let the mixture cool, stirring occasionally.

Cream the butter and sugar well, beat in the eggs one by one, then stir in the rest of the flour gradually with the salt. Add the cinnamon, the date and milk mixture and the walnuts. Turn into a buttered and floured 21 cm (8 in) cake tin or two smaller ones and bake in a pre-heated medium 190°C/375°F/Gas 5 oven for about an hour (45 minutes if you are using small tins).

❧ Strawberry teas

A popular summer entertainment in the early nineteenth century was for guests to pick strawberries for themselves. Jane Austen describes a party collecting round the strawberry beds in *Emma*.

> . . . and Mrs Elton in all her apparatus of happiness, her large bonnet, her basket, was very ready to lead her way in gathering, accepting, or talking. Strawberries, and only strawberries, could now be thought or spoken of. 'The best fruit in England – everybody's favourite – always wholesome. These the finest beds, and finest sorts. Delightful to gather for one's self – the only way of really enjoying them. Morning decidedly the best time – never tired – every sort good – hautboy infinitely superior – no comparison – the others hardly eatable – hautboys very scarce – Chili preferred – white wood finest flavour of all – price of strawberries in London – abundance about Bristol – Maple Grove – cultivations – beds when to be renewed – gardeners thinking exactly different – no general rule – gardeners never to be put out of their way – delicious fruit only too rich to be eaten much of – inferior to cherries. Currants more refreshing – only objection to gathering strawberries the stooping – glaring sun – tired to death – could bear it no longer – must go and sit in the shade.' Such, for half an hour, was the conversation.

Few things are as welcome as strawberries and cream at tea-time, especially if they are home grown.

Hull and wash the strawberries briefly. Drain well. Serve in bowls, whole or cut in half if very large. Pass round the sugar in a dredger and a bowl of cream, whipped if you like. You may perfume the cream with maraschino or vanilla.

Variations: First half fill a bowl with cream. Whip it lightly, then drop in as many strawberries as it will hold, stirring gently. Leave to stand and chill for an hour. The cream will be a delicate pale pink. Dredge with sugar before serving.

An attractive alternative is to serve them sprinkled with sugar and covered with a raspberry pureé. Put fresh raspberries through a blender with a syrup of wine and sugar, or just mash the raspberries with sugar and a little cream, moistening if you like with a sprinkling of wine.

If the flavour of the strawberries is not of the finest, let them soak up a liqueur or spirit or orange juice with sugar to taste. For a kilo (2 lb) of fruit, add 3 tablespoons each of rum and Cointreau or a little kirsch or Grand Marnier. With orange juice, use as much as you like, flavour with the grated rind of an orange and add a few tablespoons of port. Chill, covered, for at least an hour. Not too long before serving whip up 300 ml (½ pint) double cream until stiff, add 2 tablespoons of castor sugar, or more to taste, and flavour with 3 tablespoons of the liqueur which has been used in the marinade. Mix with the strawberries, folding gently until every fruit is well coated.

A TABLE IN THE GARDEN

Herodotus tells in his *Book III* of an expedition, planned by Cambyses, the son of Cyrus, and King of the Persians, to see a reputed table in the open air which had been mentioned by Homer. In the *Odyssey* the god Poseidon had gone to Ethiopia, 'in the hope of burnt offerings, bulls and rams, by hundreds: and there he sat feasting merrily'. In the *Iliad*, it was Zeus who 'went yesterday to Oceanus, to the blameless Ethiopians for a feast, and all the gods followed with him'.

The expedition was a failure because of the stark natural conditions in that part of Africa. This is how Herodotus tells the story:

Cambyses planned an expedition . . . to send spies first of all into the land of the Ethiopians, in the first place to see the so-called table of the sun that was said to be established amongst these Ethiopians, to find out whether there really was such a thing; besides this they were to look into other matters, carrying for appearance's sake presents to the King. Now the table of the sun was said to be something like this: There is a meadow in the outskirts of the town filled with the cooked flesh of all kinds of quadrupeds; the various magistrates of the city make a practice of placing the meat here every night; in the daytime anyone who chooses is at liberty to go thither and feast. The natives say that the ground itself, from time to time produces all these things. This is the account of the so-called table of the sun.

A table in the sun has always been an object of fascination. When it is in the garden or on the terrace, one has easy access to the kitchen, and if there is any likelihood of rain one can usually transfer the party indoors. It is nice to bring everything out at once and to allow guests to help themselves and to take part in the cooking. Of course all the recipes for food prepared in advance or cooked on the spot are suitable for the garden table.

🍂 Boiled meats and vegetables

In *The Raw and the Cooked* the French anthropologist Claude Lévi-Strauss finds that societies have generally placed boiled meats lower than roast ones in the hierarchy of foods. However, opinion on the gastronomic value of boiled foods has varied over the years. An eighteenth-century encyclopaedia noted that boiled meat was 'one of the most succulent and nourishing foods available to man'. Brillat-Savarin, of a later generation, prejudiced against 'le bouilli', wrote that the truth was beginning to penetrate about the 'meat without its juice'. 'Bouilli is no longer served by the self respecting host,' he said, 'it has been replaced by a roast fillet, a turbot or a matelote.' It was to be used for making broth, then left to the servants' hall.

Others have been lyrical in its praise. The epicurean hero, Dodin-Bouffant, in Marcel Rouff's *The Passionate Epicure* dared to serve it to the Prince of Eurasia and a group of gastronomes. That 'fearsome boiled beef, scorned, reviled, insulting to the Prince and to all gastronomy', placed imposingly on an immensely long dish, produced a magical and total change of heart. This is how Marcel Rouff describes the dish:

> The rather thick slices, their velvety quality guessed at by every lip, rested languidly upon a pillow made of a wide slice of sausage, coarsely chopped, in which the finest veal escorted pork, chopped herbs, thyme, chervil. This delicate triumph of pork-butchery was itself supported by ample cuts from the breast and wing fillets of farm chickens, boiled in their own juice with a shin of veal, rubbed with mint and wild thyme. And, to prop up this triple and magnificent accumulation, behind the white flesh of the fowls (fed exclusively upon bread and milk), was the stout, robust support of a generous layer of fresh goose liver simply cooked in Chambertin.

These days as a result of inverted snobbery and the fashion for peasant and working class foods, boiled meats are justly appreciated. They certainly deserve the overworked cliché of culinary literature, the word succulent. I have often enjoyed the Latin American version at the house of my friend Elisabeth Lambert Ortiz, author of *The Complete Book of Mexican Cooking* and *The Book of Latin American Cooking*. Here is her recipe and account of a Mexican 'indoor-outdoor' picnic as she wrote it for me.

Elisabeth Lambert Ortiz's Fiambre Potosino (cold meats in the style of San Luis Potosí)

'So many houses in Mexico still have large gardens, the weather is totally predictable and Sunday is the day when the family gathers for comida, the large midday meal. It is a perfect occasion for a picnic, but not for us. My mother-in-law hated picnics of any kind. I never found out why. She would simply purse her lips and decline to discuss the matter. And on the day we would have had the picnic it invariably rained, great gouts of water streaming out of an angry sky, and though she would look meaningfully upward she never said 'I told you so'. I was therefore particularly gratified when relatives on the other side of the family invited us to stay, and we had a lovely Northern picnic, Fiambre Potosino, cold meats in the style of San Luis Potosí, a State in the north of Mexico. No one present was actually from San Luis and our picnic took place in the grounds of a small rancho (farm) in Querétaro, also in Mexico's north, that a cousin was running. On another occasion there we had a barbacoa, a whole lamb cooked in an earth oven lined with agave leaves, the plant from which tequila is made. Barbacoa can't be reproduced everywhere, but Fiambre Potosino can.

'Elizabeth Borton de Treviño, the American writer who lives in Mexico, told me that years ago as a young woman she attended a great Fiambre given by the Governor of the State. Behind each two guests at the long tables, set in the open air, sat a young girl in the local costume, full skirt, peasant blouse, rebozo (coloured woollen stole) with dark hair in ribboned plaits, patting out tortillas and cooking them on a little charcoal brazier at her side. The tortillas were put into little napkin-lined woven straw baskets and ensured that guests got them fresh and hot in a never ending supply. It was a very grand affair.

'Traditionally guests sit at a long table covered with a white cloth, with the whole Fiambre in great platters on the table, so little extra service is needed. One helps oneself. Of course the meal can be served as an outdoor buffet, or at small tables set in the garden, or anywhere one chooses. It is a most flexible feast and is very jolly. Since everything can be prepared ahead of time it is practical as well.

The meats:

1 kilo (2 lb) boneless pork loin or shoulder, 2 veal tongues, about ³/₄ kg (1¹/₂ lb) each, OR, 1 ox tongue, about 1¹/₂ kg (3 lb), 1 plump chicken, 3 pig's feet, halved, salt.

Marinade:

1¹/₂ cups olive oil, ¹/₂ cup wine vinegar, preferably white, salt, freshly ground pepper, 2 teaspoons Dijon mustard, ¹/₄ cup finely chopped parsley, 1 clove garlic, crushed, 1 tablespoon drained, chopped capers.

The garnish:

1 small head cos lettuce, shredded, 3 large tomatoes, sliced, 3 large avocados, peeled and sliced, 5 canned chipotle chillies, stuffed with cottage cheese, or pickled jalapeno or serrano or large chillies, radishes, black olives, 1 white onion, finely chopped.

'Cook each of the meats separately, covered, in simmering salted water. Allow about 2 hours for the pork and the veal tongue, 1 hour for the chicken, and 3 hours or longer for the pig's feet. Cool each of the meats in its own stock. When cool enough to handle lift out the tongues, peel and remove any bones or gristle. Slice. Slice the pork. Bone the chicken and cut into pieces. Bone and cut up the pig's feet. Place all the meats in a large bowl.

'Mix all the ingredients of the marinade together. Pour half the marinade over the meat, mixing lightly but well. Allow to stand at room temperature for 2 hours, or longer. Reserve the remaining vinaigrette.

'To serve, make a bed of lettuce on one or more platters. Arrange the meats on top. Garnish the edge of the platter with the tomatoes, avocados, chillies, radishes, black olives and sprinkle the tomatoes with the chopped onion. Serve the remaining vinaigrette in a sauceboat.

'Serve with hot tortillas in napkin-lined, covered, small straw baskets, or with quartered crisp-fried tortillas, or tortillas del norte (flour tortillas) or with tamales blancos (unfilled tamales) or with crisp rolls and butter.'

🍃 Fondue bourguignonne

This convivial dish, where guests dip cubes of tender meat into boiling oil, is not really practical for more than six. You need long-handled forks and the special deep metal pot which narrows at the top to prevent the oil from spattering. Use a table heater or a small barbecue.

Cut fillet of beef into 2¹/₂ cm (1 in) cubes, allowing 150-225 g (¹/₃-¹/₂ lb) of meat per person. Have ready an assortment of condiments – salt, pepper, lemon wedges and three or four sauces – horseradish (see p.50), curried, green or garlicky mayonnaise (see pp.46-7) a fruity chutney (see pp.239-40), a peppery relish (see p.53) will all do very well.

Everyone must look after his own piece of meat: impale it on the end of the fork, put it in the very hot oil and leave it in until it is done to his liking, then dip it into one of the sauces arranged on each plate.

Serve with a basket of sliced French bread, and a good salad.

❧ A Japanese style fondue

Have chicken livers or oysters wrapped in bacon and vegetables such as small mushrooms, pieces of green pepper and onion with the meat. Let everyone sauté the food in a mixture of oil and butter rather than deep fry. Give each person a small bowl of soya sauce for dipping. Add a little vinegar or lemon juice (1 tablespoon for 3-4 tablespoons of soya), a touch of sugar and a squeeze of ginger obtained by pressing a fresh raw piece in a garlic press – all to taste.

❧ Cheese fondue

Very simple for a small party of 4-6 people is the Swiss dish of cheese melted in wine into which everyone dips cubes of bread. If you do not have the traditional dish use a small casserole or heavy-bottomed pan over a table stove or alcohol burner, or any sort of small flame or hot plate. Rub the inside of the pot with a cut clove of garlic. Pour in 450 ml ($3/4$ pint) dry white wine and put over medium heat. When it is warm add about 700 g ($1^1/2$ lb) cheese, grated or cut into small pieces. Use Gruyère, Emmenthal or Vacherin or a mixture of these. You can also combine them with Cheddar for a cheaper meal. Stir gently with a wooden spoon until the cheese melts into a light creamy sauce. Add freshly ground black pepper, a pinch of grated nutmeg and 3-4 tablespoons of kirsch (or whisky, gin or vodka). Bring the pan to the table and let it bubble slowly over very low heat.

Cut up some French bread into squarish pieces, leaving the crust on. Everyone must spear the cubes with forks (long-handled ones if possible) and dip them into the mixture, stirring right down to the bottom of the cheese until it is all finished. Serve with a plate of raw vegetables or a good salad.

❧ Cappon magro – a Genoese fish salad

Though the name implies a fasting dish, it is as grand as the type of fish you use and as colourful and gaudy as you wish to make it.

Boil until just tender a variety of vegetables: salsify, cauliflower, runner beans, carrots, courgettes, artichoke hearts. Toss them in a vinaigrette and arrange on a large serving dish on a bed of hard dry biscuits (galette); or use slices of bread dried out in the oven. Rub them if you like with a clove of garlic, and moisten with vinaigrette or a little vinegar diluted with water.

Surround with an assortment of fish and shellfish. The success of the dish depends on the choice of fish and vegetables. For a grand party use prawns, even lobster, and scallops or mussels with a large firm fish. For a modest affair use cheaper fish and place in the centre instead of around the vegetables. The secret is to almost undercook the fish (poach or bake in foil) so that it is firm and flakes well. Remove all skin and bones and dress generously with a vinaigrette made with lemon juice rather than vinegar.

Pour over the following green sauce. In a blender, put a very large bunch of parsley, finely chopped, 2 cloves of garlic, crushed, half an onion, 1 large boiled potato, 4-5 chopped gherkins and 6 anchovy fillets. Add 6 tablespoons of wine vinegar and about 150 ml ($1/4$ pint) olive oil gradually. Blend to a smooth light cream, adding more oil if necessary. Season to taste with salt and pepper. You may add 1 or 2 tablespoons of capers, a hard-boiled egg yolk, or a few pitted green olives.

Garnish the dish further with any of these: radishes, olives, anchovies, quartered tomatoes, hard-boiled eggs, small lettuce leaves, gherkins and pickles.

?❧ A feast of vegetables, boiled and raw

An assortment of vegetables of the season is a perfect and simple solution for a summer day. Italians like to serve what they can raw; the French prefer them just slightly cooked. Make the selection a feast for the eye and choose from the following: celery separated into sticks, carrots peeled and cut into quarters, cauliflower separated into large flowerets and blanched for 2 minutes in salted water if you must, young lettuce leaves, radishes, green and red peppers cut into strips, spring onions, fennel cut into thick slices, little turnips, courgettes, mushrooms, endives – all must be very young and tender. Trim and wash them before cutting them up.

There are two sauces which will make a feast out of these vegetables.

Bagna Cauda ('hot bath' in the Italian Piedmont). It is a hot anchovy and garlic sauce for the whole company to dip into. Heat some butter and oil very gently – the proportions are variable but it can be 225 g (^{1}/$_{2}$ lb) butter with 3 tablespoons of oil – in a shallow earthenware or heavy-bottomed pan with 6 crushed cloves of garlic. When the butter is sizzling and the garlic has not yet turned brown, take the pan off the heat and add 8 anchovies which have been pounded in a mortar. (You may use anchovy paste instead.) Stir with a wooden spoon. Return the pan to a low heat and continue cooking, stirring until the anchovies have dissolved into a paste. Add black pepper.

Bring the pan to the table and keep hot over a small spirit stove or a candle or in the ashes of a burnt out fire. Let everyone pick vegetables with a fork and dip them in. Thick cream may be used, about 150 ml (^{1}/$_{4}$ pint), instead of butter. Have some good bread cut in thick slices and some young red wine for this cheerful ceremony.

A garlicky aïoli (see pp.47-8) brings the flavour of Provence to the table. In the South of France they would also have some boiled green beans, waxy new potatoes, asparagus and artichoke hearts. Serve any of these with hard-boiled eggs, cut in half, and some good pieces of poached fish, if you want to make a complete meal of it.

Eat with your eyes closed, and a deep blue sky and a sundrenched wall will appear!

?? Crêpes

The happiest moments of my boarding school days in Paris were those spent in the Latin Quarter, with my brothers and Egyptian contemporaries. We were regular clients at a crêperie where we would have a complete meal of crêpes, usually starting with a ham and cheese or a chicken filling and ending with a sweet one with honey or cointreau, all washed down with good strong cider.

Crêpes have remained a favourite food for me, and my children love to be offered a variety of fillings to be rolled up on demand.

The batter recipe I use came from my first cookery book, a 1955 edition of *Tante Marie's French Kitchen*.

275 g (10 oz) flour, 1 teaspoon salt, ¹/₂ litre (1 pint) milk, 1 tablespoon salad oil, 300 ml (¹/₂ pint) water, 2 eggs, optional for sweet crêpes: 1 tablespoon brandy.

Add the milk and water to the flour gradually, beating constantly so that the batter becomes very smooth. Add eggs, salt, oil and brandy. Beat the batter until smooth and set aside to rest for an hour or two. Heat a large frying pan and grease very slightly. Pour a serving spoonful of the batter into the frying pan and move around until its entire surface is covered. Both the batter and the resulting crêpe should be thin. When it is brown, turn with a large spatula and cook a moment on the other side. Continue this process until all the batter is used. Pile the crêpes on to a large piece of foil and wrap them up to keep them warm in the oven until ready to serve. You may make them in advance and keep them in the refrigerator or freezer, but let them thaw slowly for 2-3 hours.

At the table have a frying pan over a small burner of any kind. Keep it well oiled. Put each pancake in, cover with a few tablespoons of filling and cook for 2 minutes, long enough for the ingredients to become really hot. Roll up and serve.

Serving crêpes in this manner is only justified if you have a variety of fillings to offer. Here are some suggestions:

Ham and cheese. Grate 225 g (¹/₂ lb) cheese (Mozzarella, Gruyère, Cheddar – anything that melts well) and cut 4 slices of ham into small pieces. Sprinkle all over the pancake. (This is how we had it in France.) For a grander version, beat ¹/₄ litre (¹/₂ pint) double cream with 2 egg yolks, add cayenne pepper and nutmeg and stir in the ham and cheese.

A Neapolitan filling of tomatoes and cheese. Peel and chop 500 g (1 lb) tomatoes. Soften in 2 tablespoons of olive oil with very little salt, black pepper and a few basil leaves, finely chopped. Mash with a fork and stir in 75 g (3 oz) thickly grated Parmesan. You may like to add 2 anchovy fillets, finely chopped, or a tablespoon of anchovy paste.

Spinach and cheese. This is an Italian filling for pancakes called crespolini. Mix 225 g (1/2 lb) chopped and cooked spinach (you may use frozen), 225 g (1/2 lb) cottage or curd cheese, 2 eggs, 2 tablespoons of grated Parmesan, and 125 g (1/4 lb) chicken livers, lightly cooked in butter and finely chopped. Season with black pepper and a very little salt.

Chicken filling. This will serve a whole party. Boil a chicken until it is very tender (see pp.22-3). Skin and bone it and cut the meat into small pieces. You may add 225 g (1/2 lb) mushrooms sliced and lightly cooked in butter.

Prepare a béchamel sauce. Melt 3 tablespoons of butter in a pan and add 3 tablespoons flour. Pour in 1/4 litre (1/2 pint) of the chicken stock, stirring constantly until the sauce thickens. Add salt and pepper and a touch of nutmeg. Stir in 1/4 litre (1/2 pint) cream and 3 egg yolks, and heat, stirring until the sauce thickens – it must not boil. Add a squeeze of lemon juice or 2 tablespoons of cognac. Stir in the chicken pieces.

Bring hot to the table and roll up a few tablespoonsful in a hot pancake.

Seafood. Use freshly cooked crab, mussels or prawns moistened with whipped double cream, seasoned with salt and pepper and sprinkled with finely chopped parsley.

Seafood in a sauce from Provence. Cook a chopped onion in 2 tablespoons of olive oil until it is golden. Add a clove of garlic, crushed, and when it colours add a medium tin 400 g (14 oz) of peeled tomatoes. Mash them with a fork, season with salt and pepper and fresh or dry herbs such as basil, parsley or thyme. Simmer for 10 minutes, add the seafood and cook through.

A Russian filling. Caviare, chopped herring or smoked salmon mixed with sour cream and finely chopped onion is a typical filling for Russian blinis and is excellent cold, spread on a hot pancake.

❧ Sweet crêpes

For a dessert, heated pancakes may be served with lemon and sugar or spread with jam such as raspberry, apricot or strawberry, or with honey.

Or you may like to try one of these fillings.

Sugar and liqueur. Sprinkle generously over the pancakes. Use cointreau, kümmel, kirsch, Curaçao or cognac. You may even heat a little alcohol in a tablespoon and set it alight and pour it over the rolled up pancakes in the pan. Another way is to beat the flavouring or alcohol into some softened butter with the sugar and spread it all over the pancakes.

Crêpes du couvent are filled with a purée of cooked and sweetened pears.

Crêpes normandes are made with apples, peeled, cored, cut up and sautéed in unsalted butter with sugar to taste and a squeeze of lemon juice. Fold in some whipped double cream and, if you like, a touch of calvados. You may also add some apricot jam and some slivered almonds.

Cheese with orange or lemon. A good filling which is popular in Israel for blintzes is cream or curd cheese flavoured with grated orange or lemon rind and the juice of these fruits. Stir in sugar to taste.

Two family favourites. Into stiffly beaten double cream stir a good quantity of strawberries, chopped and sprinkled with sugar and kirsch, or chestnuts in syrup, also chopped with some of their syrup. Both are truly regal.

A WEDDING PARTY

There is something unforgettable about a wedding celebrated in the open, even if it is under the shelter of a marquee. Emma Rouault's wedding to Charles in *Madame Bovary* was celebrated in a cart shed. Here is Gustave Flaubert's description:

The table had been laid under the wagon shed. It was laden with four sirloins, six fricassées of chicken, veal in the casserole, three legs of mutton, and, as a centre-piece, a handsome roast sucking-pig flanked with meat balls cooked in sorrel. Decanters of brandy stood at each corner, and bottles of sweet cider were frothing round their corks. The glasses had all been filled to the brim with wine in advance. Great dishes of yellow cream, which quivered whenever the table was shaken, bore on their smooth surfaces the initials of the newly-married couple picked out in hundreds and thousands. A pastry cook from Yvetot had been employed to provide the tarts and sweet stuffs. Being new to the district, he had excelled himself, and appeared in person when the sweet stage was reached, bearing aloft an elaborate confection which drew cries of admiration. The base was formed of a cube of blue paste-board representing a temple with a portico, colonnades and statuettes of white plaster with stars of gold paper. Above this was a castle made of Savoy cake, surrounded by tiny battlements of angelica, almonds, raisins and oranges cut into quarters. Finally, at the very top which depicted a green meadow complete with rocks, lakes composed of jam and little boats made of nut shells, was a small Cupid balancing himself on a chocolate swing, the two uprights of which were topped with natural rosebuds by way of finials.

Eating went on until evening. When guests were tired of sitting, they wandered about in the yards or played a shove ha'penny in the barn, after which they returned to the table. When the feast was nearing its end, some of them fell asleep and snored, though they woke up again when coffee appeared.

With relatively little money, some organization and a good shopping list, a few extra borrowed pans and a little help from children and friends, one person can easily cater for a wedding party of 40-50 people in two days. And the result can be far more interesting, delicious and elegant than any caterer can provide.

A cold buffet is the most practical way of entertaining, with everything put on the table for people to serve themselves and return to their own tables set around the garden. Presentation and colour are important for it must be a feast for the eye as well.

As people arrive serve champagne but also have on hand an alternative for those who would prefer a longer more refreshing drink.

Champagne Cup. Just before serving, mix 3 bottles of chilled champagne, 1½ bottles of chilled soda water or white grape juice, 150 ml (¼ pint) orange liqueur and 700 g (1½ lb) or more ripe raspberries or wild strawberries from the garden.

Citrus Cup. To 3 bottles of chilled champagne and 1½ bottles of soda water, add 3 oranges and a pineapple cut into small pieces, 2 lemons, thinly sliced, 125 g (¼ lb) sugar and 3 sprigs of fresh mint. You may add 150 ml (¼ pint) fresh orange juice.

ぶ Appetizers to serve with champagne

Canapés may be served on rounds of shortcrust, puff or flaky pastry, baked till golden, or on crackers or Captain's biscuits or slices of brioche. Bread, fresh or toasted, makes the simplest base. Use any very good bread. Slice it thin and cut it into bite-sized pieces. To toast them, dry them out thoroughly on a rack in the lowest oven until they are a delicate brown. Brush with melted butter as they come out, let them cool and spread the filling just before serving in order to keep them crisp.

All the sandwich fillings given in the chapter *Tea on the Lawn* (see pp.2-5) will make suitable canapés. However, I am especially fond of spreading them thickly with olivade and tapenade, two cream dips offered in Provence with pastis.

Olivade. The restaurant in the Vaucluse which puts this speciality of Marseilles on every table while you read the menu would not give me the recipe. This improvisation is from memory.

Chop and pound or put in a blender or processor 500 g (1 lb) pitted fleshy black olives. Add 350 g (³/₄ lb) cottage cheese – more if the olives are very salty and about 4 tablespoons of brandy. Mash and blend to a smooth paste.

Tapenade. Everyone has their own way of making this cream which derives its name from the capers which go into it. They are called tapéno in Provençal.

Blend 500 g (1 lb) pitted black olives with a 100 g (¹/₄ lb) tin of anchovy fillets and a 200 g (7 oz) tin of tuna and their oil, 100 g (¹/₄ lb) capers and 4 crushed cloves of garlic. Add pepper, 125 ml (4 fl oz) cognac and enough olive oil to achieve a smooth paste.

This mixture goes well with hard-boiled eggs. Chop two finely and sprinkle over the paste.

Smoked salmon cigarettes. This little delicacy was conceived by my friend Clint Greyn when he wanted to spoil himself at camp. Cut thin slices of smoked salmon into 4 cm (¹/₄ in) strips. Season some curd cheese or a bland cream cheese, such as Philadelphia or the one made by Sainsbury, with a good squeeze of lemon juice and a little pepper. Put a tablespoonful along one edge of the strip and wrap the smoked salmon round it. Lightly dip the ends of the rolls in black lumpfish roe (use Limfjord) so that it picks some up.

Stuffed mushrooms. Wash and remove caps and dip them in lemon juice. Stuff them with cream cheese beaten with a little crushed garlic, finely chopped fresh herbs such as parsley, chives or tarragon and salt and pepper.

Little stuffed tomatoes. Cut the tops off 24 small cherry tomatoes. Hollow out, keeping the centres for something else. Sprinkle inside with vinaigrette and stuff with the following mixture: 75 g (3 oz) tuna (or more depending on the size of the tomatoes), 2 hard-boiled eggs, a handful of capers, a few tablespoons of finely chopped fresh herbs (parsley, chives, spring onions) and salt and pepper. Moisten the mixture with 2 tablespoons of mayonnaise flavoured with anchovy essence.

ð Fish mousse

A fish mousse is far cheaper and to my taste more delicious than the classic cold salmon, and you can also decorate it, if you like, with all the trimmings beloved by Escoffier – small pieces of cucumber, anchovy fillets, capers, tomato slices. For me tarragon leaves plastered simply around it are enough. Chervil or flat parsley will also do.

Formerly an arduous task for the ordinary cook, the making of a mousse is now as easy as anything for one who possesses a food processor. Tomato gives this one a pale salmon colour. The quantities should fill three ring moulds and serve 25 people.

1½ kg (3 lb) fish (I use a mixture of haddock, halibut and cod), 8 egg whites, 150 g (5 oz) tin of tomato purée, salt and pepper to taste, a good pinch of nutmeg or a teaspoon of allspice, a pinch of cayenne pepper, 3 cloves of garlic (crushed), a good bunch of fresh herbs (parsley, tarragon, chervil, chives, watercress), juice of 1 lemon or 4 tablespoons cognac; 450 ml (¾ pint) single and double cream mixed, 500 g (1 lb) prawns or fillets of fish (sole, salmon or salmon trout) cut into strips.

Remove the skin and bones and put the raw fish (not the prawns or fillets) in an electric blender or processor with the egg whites, or chop and pound it and beat in the whites, until it is a smooth mixture. Add the tomato purée, salt, pepper, nutmeg, cayenne, garlic and lemon juice. Mix well. Leave in the refrigerator for 1-2 hours. Beat the cream till stiff and add to the fish mixture, stirring it in till well blended. Pour a little into 3 ring moulds lined with well-oiled or buttered foil, alternating with layers of fillets of fish or prawns, and starting and finishing with the fish mixture. Cover with foil. Put in a tray of water in a pre-heated oven 200 °C/400 °F/Gas 6 for 30-50 minutes until the mousse has shrunk slightly away from the sides and the top feels springy.

If you want to keep the mousses for more than a day in the refrigerator, pour some aspic jelly (see p.51) mixed with chopped herbs over them after they have cooled. Turn out when you are ready to serve and peel off the foil carefully.

Serve with a green mayonnaise (see pp.46-7) or another light sauce for fish.

❧ Circassian chicken

My friend Belinda Bather finds that this is one of the most popular dishes at the parties she caters for. She brought back the recipe from Turkey where she lived for 10 years. For about 40 people multiply it by five and prepare it the day before.

Gently boil a chicken in water with an onion, some parsley stalks, celery leaves, a sprig of tarragon and salt and pepper, for almost an hour until it is tender but not yet falling apart.

The sauce. Put 225 g (8 oz) walnuts (make sure that they do not taste rancid as they sometimes do) through a blender and grind them very fine. Put separately in the blender 2 or 3 slices of bread, white or wholemeal, which have been dried out in the oven. Mix together in a saucepan and moisten with enough stock to make a porridge-like consistency. Belinda sometimes adds 4 crushed cloves of garlic at this stage.) Add salt and $1/2$-1 tablespoon of paprika and simmer over gentle heat for a few minutes until the mixture thickens.

Skin and bone the chicken, cut it into thin strips or pull it into shreds with your fingers. Mix two-thirds of the sauce with the shredded chicken, arrange on a large serving dish and pour the rest of the sauce over it. Dribble a few tablespoons of light oil (walnut is best) in which you have stirred a tablespoon of paprika. An attractive way of presenting this is spooned in portions in young cos lettuce leaves.

❧ Vitello tonnato

This Italian picnic favourite may be cooked a day or two before but the sauce is best prepared on the day. To serve 40 multiply the quantities by five.

Cover a 1-1$1/4$ kg (2-$1/2$ lb) boned leg of veal with water and, if you like, half a bottle of white wine. Add a carrot, sliced, a stick of celery, sliced, an onion, chopped, a bay leaf and a sprig of parsley; season lightly with salt and pepper. Simmer gently for about 2 hours until the meat is very tender. Leave it to cool in its broth, and keep covered in the refrigerator.

The sauce. Make a mayonnaise (see p.46) with 2 egg yolks, $1/4$ litre ($1/2$ pint) olive oil and the juice of 1 or 2 lemons. Blend 200 g (7 oz) flaked tuna fish, 5 chopped anchovy fillets, and a little veal stock – just enough for a creamy consistency. Fold this into the mayonnaise and season to taste with salt and pepper.

Cut the meat into thin slices, spoon over the sauce and garnish with a few capers or thin slices of pickled cucumber and little bits of parsley.

❧ Courgettes with raisins and pine nuts

From Sicily, a taste of the Arab world. Make four or five times this quantity for 40 people.

1 large onion, olive oil, 2 cloves of garlic (crushed), 1 kg (2 lb) courgettes (sliced thin), 3 tablespoons wine vinegar, salt and pepper to taste, 3 tablespoons raisins or sultanas, 3 tablespoons pine nuts or 125 g (¹/₄ lb) slivered almonds.

Fry the onion in 100 ml (4 fl oz) olive oil until it is golden. Add the garlic and stir. Add the courgettes and lightly fry, stirring occasionally. Add raisins, vinegar and salt and pepper to taste, and cook gently for 10 minutes. Fry the pine nuts in a separate pan until coloured. Add to the courgettes a few minutes before the end of cooking. Almonds are a cheaper but a good alternative.

🍃 Peperonata

Make it with red peppers to give colour to the table.

3 large onions (sliced), 100 ml (4 fl oz) olive oil, 4 cloves of garlic (crushed), 10 large red peppers (seeded and cut into thin strips), 1 kg (2 lb) tomatoes (skinned and chopped), salt and pepper, a bunch of parsley finely chopped).

Fry the onions in oil in a very large pan until just golden. Add the garlic and peppers and cook very gently, stirring all the time until they soften. Add the tomatoes, salt and pepper and the parsley. Cover and cook until the vegetables are soft.

🍃 A green salad

Prepare several bowls of lettuce with sprigs of cress and a sprinkling of fresh herbs – parsley, chives or chervil, finely chopped – ready to be dressed with a vinaigrette at the last minute.

🍃 A spectacular fruit salad

An elegant way of presenting a salad of the fruits in season is in the half shells of small melons and pineapples. For 40 people have at least 20 of either or 10 of each. Cut in half to serve as cups. Scoop out the whole of the inside, discarding seeds and hard inner cores. Chop up melon and pineapple and mix with strawberries and raspberries and, if you like, sliced bananas, mangoes or fresh figs cut into pieces. You can also have grapes or cherries. Add sugar to taste and flavour with a liqueur. Pile the fruit mixture into the shells.

੨ Peaches and cream

This way of serving peaches is a delightful alternative to the fruit salad. Peel and halve 6 peaches. Make a syrup by boiling 600 ml (1 pint) red wine with 500 g (1 lb) sugar and poach the peaches until just tender. (You can use equal quantities of port and water or flavour with a vanilla pod.) Drain and cool before filling with 300 ml (1/2 pint) sweetened whipped cream and 225 g (1/2 lb) chopped strawberries, and pour over a raspberry purée made by blending 225 g (1/2 lb) raspberries with a little of the reduced syrup.

੨ Croquembouche

This remarkable pièce montée is one of the few pastries which merit a wedding, for there is as much pleasure in its monumental beauty as there is in cracking the caramelized puffs in the mouth. Barbara Maher has given me this recipe from her book *Cakes*.

The shortcrust pastry base on which the choux pyramid rests is often set on a large nut-brittle stand, but you can use a bought, silver paper covered one. The pyramid is built over an oiled conical mould which slides out when the shape has set. Make one with card or heavy foil.

For the base. Bake a flat shortcrust pastry base, at least 30 cm (12 in) in diameter, with 225 g (8 oz) plain flour, 150 g (5 oz) butter, 40 g (1½ oz) castor sugar and 2 egg yolks (see pp.66-7).

For the buns. Prepare about 60 small choux buns with the following ingredients: ½ litre (18 fl oz) milk or water, 300 g (11 oz) plain strong flour, 300 g (11 oz) salted butter, 8 whole eggs, 2 teaspoons sugar, the zest of 1 lemon.

Sift flour with sugar on to a sheet of greaseproof paper. Drop butter, cut in pieces, into a largish pan with the water or milk. Heat gently until the butter has melted, then raise the heat to bring the liquid to a rolling boil. Draw pan aside, shoot in the flour at once and beat the paste vigorously over a low heat until it is smooth and the flour has cooked. It should roll cleanly off the bottom and sides of the pan into a ball (a floury film is left over the base). Leave the mixture to cool for 5 minutes then beat in the lightly forked eggs very thoroughly one at a time (you may prefer to use an electric mixer at this stage as it can be heavy work). Take particular care adding the last egg, as not all may be needed. The mixture should be quite firm but elastic – otherwise it spreads and fails to rise. Add the lemon zest and beat well until the mixture has a glossy sheen.

The paste can be covered with a warm damp cloth and used later. If your oven is inclined to overheat use a layer of aluminium foil or a second baking sheet as added protection, to prevent the bottoms of the pastries from burning. Chill the tray under running water for a few moments; leave damp. Lay spoonsful of the mixture at well-spaced intervals or use a piping bag; remember they expand to about three times their size. Lightly brush the surface with beaten egg to give a glaze. Bake in the middle of a pre-heated oven, 200 °C/400 °F/Gas 6, for about 20 minutes.

Transfer to a wire rack to cool; pierce each pastry with a knife or skewer to release steam and retain crispness. Use within 2 to 3 hours or store when cold in an airtight tin for the following day. They will crisp again, if heated for about 10 minutes at 150 °C/300 °F/Gas 2, and taste almost as good as when completely fresh.

Choux pastry also freezes well. Pipe or spoon *unbaked paste* on to silicone paper and freeze uncovered before packing. Add 5 minutes to the normal cooking time for frozen choux. Freeze baked unfilled pastries in airtight containers. Thaw empty shells in a cool oven for 15 minutes.

For the caramel. Make a sugar and water syrup by boiling together 700 g (1½ lb) sugar and 350 ml (12 fl oz) water with a squeeze of lemon. Cook to the hard crack stage 138 °C (280 °F) and cool slightly by lowering the pan into a bowl of cold water.

Dip each bun into the caramel and build up around the oiled cone (a little smaller in diameter than the pastry base) by sticking one to another. One side of each can be dusted while still sticky with chopped pistachio nuts. When cold remove the mould and fill the cavity with a cream – sweetened whipped cream or crème pastissière (see p.113).

Set this on to the prepared pastry base and bring out into the garden at the last minute.

❧ Almond fingers to serve with coffee

You will find the paper-thin dough called phylo (filo) in Greek grocers or bakers. A 500 g (1 lb) packet of 24 sheets will give you 96 little pastries if the sheets are all good. It keeps for 3 days in the refrigerator.

The filling. Mix 225 g (¹/₂ lb) ground almonds with 125 g (¹/₄ lb) granulated sugar and moisten with 2 or 3 tablespoons of rose or orange blossom water (also found in Greek or Middle Eastern shops). Melt 200 g (7 oz) unsalted butter, cut the sheets of phylo into 4 rectangles and pile them together so they do not dry up, as soon as you have opened the packet.

Brush each rectangle with melted butter and put a heaped teaspoonful of filling at one end. Roll up into a cigar shape, folding the longer sides slightly over the filling when you have rolled it half way.

Place on a buttered baking tray and brush very lightly with melted butter (at this stage you can put the pastries, covered, in the freezer for several weeks). Bake in a pre-heated 180°C/350°F/Gas 4, oven for about 20 minutes or until lightly golden. When they are cold sprinkle with castor sugar. They will keep for several days in a tin.

FOOD TO TAKE OUT

ENGLISH PICNICS

In England picnics for their own sake came into fashion late, at the same time as the mountains, the lakes and the wilderness. Georgina Battiscombe has collected what she calls a gallimaufrey of these in her book *English Picnics*. Influenced by Jean Jacques Rousseau's cult of nature and by the Romantic poets, singing the virtues of the simple life and extolling the beauties of nature, the English, like the French of the early nineteenth century, responded to the Romantic Movement with a newfound passion for their native land, especially its wild and picturesque scenery, and with a sudden taste for alfresco meals.

Before that, the prevailing distaste for nature in her wilder aspects was one reason for the paucity of English picnics. Mountains and moors had been places of interest and not of beauty. Walkers and travellers to remote areas never seemed impressed by the scenery when they wrote of their adventures and even less about the food they ate, unless it was in the warm safety of an inn and the usual roast beef, potatoes and potted trout. They ate where they could, preferably indoors and when outdoors it was usually with disgruntled horror and remembered as cold soggy food endured in the rain in such terms as 'My bread being as wet as my feet.'

In the first decade of the nineteenth century the curious sounding name 'picnic', spelt Pic Nic or Pick Nick was given to a meal out of doors. Its origins are still not clear but the oddly matched syllables had first been used for a variety of things, all different, but all equally fashionable. In 1802 the name was given to a hat and to a collection of poems and stories. A Picnic Club was formed for the private performing of theatricals, charades and music. Though described by one of its members as a 'harmless and inoffensive society of persons of fashion', its activities were generally regarded as slightly despicable and faintly improper. From a hotchpotch of anything, a picnic came to mean a party to which all the guests contributed a share of the provisions.

In *The Times* of 18th March 1802 a contributor wrote that a picnic supper 'consists of a variety of dishes. The subscribers to the entertainment have the bill of fare presented to them with a number against each dish. The lot which he draws obliges him to furnish the dish marked against it, which he either takes with him in his carriage or sends by a servant.'

By then, outdoor parties were all the rage and everyone had their version of the ideal picnic. Surtees described it in *Plain and Ringlets* (1860) as 'one of those good, useful, indefinite sort of entertainments that may be turned to account in a variety of ways', and he went on to say 'We hold that a picnic is not a picnic where there are well arranged tables and footmen to wait. It is merely an uncomfortable out of doors dinner. A picnic should entail a little of the trouble and enterprise of life, gathering sticks, lighting the fire, boiling the pot, buying or stealing potatoes.'

Trollope thought otherwise. In *Can You Forgive Her* (1864) he says 'There are servants to wait, there is champagne, there is dancing, and instead of a ruined priory, an old upturned boat to be converted into a dining room.'

An anonymous writer devoted more than a page of Chambers's *Journal* of 6th June 1857 to picnicking:

A picnic should be composed principally of young men and young women; but two or three old male folks may be admitted, if very good-humoured; a few pleasant children; and one – only one, dear old lady: to her let the whole commissariat department be intrusted by the entire assembly beforehand; and give her the utmost powers of a dictatress, for so shall nothing we want be left at home. It is not 'fun' to find one's self without mint-sauce to his cold lamb; no one who is properly constituted, enjoys lobster without fresh butter, and when you are fond of salad, it is not cheerful to find the bottle of dressing, which was intrusted to young Master Brown, has broken in his filthy pocket: these things all occur, unless we have our (one) dear old lady. Who else would have seen to that hamper of glass being packed with such consummate judgement? Who else would have brought the plate – I confess I dislike steel forks – in her own private bag? Who else could have so piled tart upon tart without a crack or cranny for the rich red juice to well through? Who else has the art of preserving Devonshire cream in a can? Observe her little bottle of cayenne pepper! Mark each individual cruet as it gleams forth from its separate receptacle! Look at the salt box! Look at the corkscrew! Bless her dear old heart! She has forgotten nothing. However humble the meal, let it be complete: and it can't be complete without its (one) dear old lady.

He records his experiences and his views:

> I have sat at rich men's feasts, which were partaken of in the open air, whereat powdered footmen have waited upon us decorously, and a bishop said grace; where everyone had a cushion to sit upon, and a napkin folded upon his plate: but I scarcely call that picnicking. And I have taken my repast brown bread, and eggs and onions, with a flask of the most ordinary wine – outside Disentis, in the valley of the Grisons, and ate it upon the hillside by myself, because the town, and the inn, and the people, all smelt so execrably; but I don't consider that a picnic either. I have been one of a party of three hundred, whose various contributions to the common stock have been decided three weeks before the day of meeting, at a lottery, wherein mustard, and bread and pepper were the prizes. Where there were two military bands to dance to, under a thousand Chinese lanterns; where champagne corks went off like platoon-firing; and where it took half an American lake to ice the wine. And I have joined mighty pleasure-companies of the people, where everybody kept his food in his pocket-handkerchief; and having cut it up with clasp-knives, and devoured it, seized everybody else's hands, and ran down grassy hills at speed; but these things, too, I consider foreign to the picnic, which seems, somehow, to signify something snug and well-selected, and quite at variance with monster-meetings of any sort.

Picnics became so fashionable in the nineteenth century that they were satirized in fiction. Surtees described the usual 'picnic march': '. . . the promoters with their newly caught conquests first, the half-caught couples second, the mere nibblers third and then what the racing reporters call "the ruck"'.

In Jane Austen's *Emma*, Mrs Elton describes the party she is hoping to organize at Mr Knightley's:

> . . . quite a simple thing. I shall wear a large bonnet, and bring one of my little baskets hanging on my arm. Here, probably this basket with pink riband. Nothing can be more simple you see. : . . There is to be no form or parade – a sort of gipsy party. We are to walk about your gardens, and gather the strawberries ourselves, and sit under trees; and whatever else you may like to provide, it is to be all out of doors,

a table spread in the shade, you know. Everything as natural and simple as possible. Is not that your idea?

But Mr Knightley would not allow his guests to be subjected to the 'lurking horrors' of an outdoor meal:

My idea of the simple and the natural will be to have the table spread in the dining room. The nature and the simplicity of the gentlemen and ladies, with their servants and furniture, I think is best observed by meals within doors. When you are tired of eating strawberries in the garden, there shall be cold meat in the house.

While the English became the most passionate picnickers in the world, instructions for preparing food to take out and for equipping picnic baskets proliferated. The following comes from a *Girl's Own Paper* of 1880 quoted in Dorothy Hartley's *Food in England*.

Fitted baskets are only suitable for a small party, of three or four persons, for whom one pie and one sweet would be sufficient. For a picnic party, it is better to divide the loads, and if enough guests attend, there would be plenty for all without anyone being unduly overloaded.

A few hints on packing the hampers.

Put the tablecloth and knives and forks on the TOP of the first basket to be unpacked. Cabbage leaves pack well around cool dishes, and contrast well with the pure white of the table napkins. Cold meat dishes should be carried in the tins, in which they are set. Butter should be moulded, into balls and parsley taken to garnish it after being set out.

A cold shoulder of lamb is an excellent joint for a picnic, accompanied by a bottle of mint sauce.

It is perhaps better to take the ham ready sliced. Meat pies, and pigeon, and veal and ham pies are standard for a picnic.

In all pies, the gravy within should be strong enough to form a jelly when cold.

Lobster; the meat picked out and carried in the shell, with mayonnaise and salad packed separately, (it is thought expensively perhaps?) but fish dishes, such as eel moulded in jelly, are cool.

Cold roast ducks are sure to be popular, and cold dressed green peas not to be despised with them. We have known people take cold new potatoes, but did not consider them a success.

A well made salad every one will enjoy, and a cucumber is indispensable! The picnic would not be a picnic if it were absent.

SOUPS

Gwen Raverat gives an account of a disastrous picnic in her *Period Piece* – about a Cambridge childhood in the late nineteenth century. Hot soup alone could have saved such an occasion.

Once, after we were grown-up, my mother insisted on having rather a large picnic: 'Because you really ought to get to know the young people of your own age.' We sulkily pointed out that we didn't get to know them at picnics; but it was no good, it had to be; and as it was to be a specially grand affair, we were to drive to the Ouse in a private motor-bus, instead of going on the Cam as usual. The open-topped motor-bus was the best part of the business to our minds, for we had seldom been in a motor-bus then, and going bowling along the Huntingdon Road on the roof was rather splendid.

It was at this picnic that I first beheld true heroism. Probably everyone concerned will remember the story in a different way; that is human nature; but I can only tell the story as I remember it myself.

Well, it all went off with the usual kind of grisly brightness, and the picnic part and all its dreary sports were over: the sham cricket with a bun for a ball, the fighting with paddles, the airy badinage about catching crabs: it had all at last drawn to its longed-for close, and everyone was packing up the baskets to go home. I must observe that we liked a Free Picnic, with spontaneous sports and lots of cousins, well enough; it was only the forced labour of a Compulsory picnic which made everything seem so dismal. I hope the guests did not feel it too much; we did try to be agreeable, but I am afraid we were not very good at concealing our feelings.

Now among our guests were two sisters, whom I shall call Cordelia and Jane. The boats were moored in very deep water, beneath a steep bank, perhaps four or five feet high, and Cordelia and I had scrambled into one of them to receive the baskets, when Jane appeared at the top of the bank. A man, standing in my boat, held out his hand and said brightly: 'Jump in.' So Jane simply jumped! From that height! She hit the edge of the boat, which would certainly have upset if I had not instinctively thrown all my weight over on the other side. After wobbling wildly for a moment both she and the man, who tried to hold her, fell with a terrific splash into the deep water. Then, by my side, Cordelia rose grandly to her feet, and with a ringing cry of, 'Oh, Jane!' simply *stepped* into the river, no doubt preferring a watery grave to living on alone; and thus illustrating the verse:

Decisive action in the hour of need
Denotes the hero, but does not succeed.

Then might have been seen the glorious spectacle of English Manhood at its best; one gentleman was already swimming about in the flood; another dived splendidly into the stream, and then found that he had chosen a place which was not really deep enough for diving; and Charles, who had been at some distance away, arriving on the bank when the rescue was already well in hand, obviously felt that, as a host, he must not be behindhand in getting wet. So he waded in, at a shallow place, till the water came just below his watch-chain – (I saw his hand on his watch) – and thus honour was satisfied. There were hardly enough drowning young ladies to go round, and 'one poor Tiger didn't get a Christian', especially as Cordelia managed to climb back into the boat by herself; but for a minute the Ouse was rather like Alice's Pool of Tears, when all the animals were swimming about. But at last everyone was saved. Even the people who had not jumped – or walked – into the water, were nearly as wet as the heroes and heroines, from helping them to climb into the boats; and when at last a friendly house was found – and it was not very near – there were only enough dry clothes for Jane, and they belonged to a very old lady; the rest of us had to drive home as we were. All this made us very late, but finally the two girls, Jane muffled in her borrowed dress, were smuggled in at the kitchen door of their house; and though their mother was told all about it, the adventure, with her connivance, was forever concealed from their father, who was very ill at the time.

But we felt that anyhow *that* picnic had been worth while.

A good way to begin an outdoor meal is with soup, chilled on a hot day, steaming hot and heartwarming on a cold one, especially if the rest of the food tends to be dry. A wide-necked vacuum flask, with a screw top, is ideal for carrying it in.

Remember that after a soup is chilled, its seasoning usually needs adjusting. Heat or cool your flask by rinsing it with boiling or cold water before pouring in the soup either as hot or as cold as possible. Slip in a few pieces of ice with a cold one. The soups will remain hot or cold for up to 6 hours.

ک Minestrone

This soup provides a sustaining meal in itself for cold and windy occasions.

Every region of Italy and indeed every cook has his own version of this vegetable soup. Make it with the vegetables available. The following ingredients make a rather large quantity, enough for 12 servings.

1 onion, 2 carrots, 3 celery stalks 3 potatoes, 2 fennel stems, 3 courgettes, a few green beans, a few shelled green peas, 2 cabbage leaves, 2 cloves of garlic (crushed), 4 tablespoons oil, 1 medium 400 g (14 oz) tin of peeled tomatoes, 3 litres (5 pints) chicken or meat stock, salt and pepper, a few sprigs (finely chopped) of thyme, parsley, basil, marjoram and mint (use all or only 2 or 3 of these), 250 g (9 oz) white haricot beans, chick peas or large brown lentils cooked beforehand without any salt (canned ones may be used), 500 g (1 lb) of a coarse boiling sausage, skin removed and cut in thick slices, or 250 g (9 oz) bacon cut in thin strips, the juice of half a lemon, 50 g (2 oz) grated Parmesan.

Peel or wash and trim the vegetables and chop them small. Warm the oil in a large saucepan and throw the vegetables in, in the order they are listed, allowing 2 minutes between each addition and stirring so they do not stick to the bottom. Now add the peeled tomatoes, the stock and salt and pepper. Cook gently for at least 2 hours, adding the herbs towards the end. Add the sausage or bacon and the beans, chick peas or lentils. Add the lemon juice, adjust the seasoning and cook until everything is soft and tender.

This quantity will fill several vacuum flasks so you may find it simpler to carry it in a large container in a hot box. Pack the grated Parmesan in a small screw-top jar to pass round when serving.

ک Lentil soup with bacon

Another heartwarming and sustaining soup.

1 large onion finely chopped, 2 tablespoons oil, 3-4 rashers of bacon cut into very small strips, 500 g (1 lb) red lentils, 2 litres (3½ pints) water or stock, salt and pepper; 1 teaspoon ground cumin (optional), 1 teaspoon ground coriander.

Fry the onion gently in the oil in a large saucepan until well coloured, stirring occasionally. Add the bacon and fry. Add the lentils and cover with water or stock. Bring to the boil and cook for an hour or until the lentils have disintegrated. Add salt and pepper and the cumin and coriander. Mash with a fork or with a potato masher. These lentils do not generally need to be pressed through a sieve. Add water or stock if too thick.

ൠ Cauliflower and leek soup with cheese

1 medium cauliflower, 3 leeks, 3 medium potatoes, 1½ litres (2½ pints) chicken stock or water, salt and pepper, a few sprigs of parsley (finely chopped), 100 g (¼ lb) grated Cheddar, a grating of nutmeg.

Wash the cauliflower, remove the leaves and cut into flowerets. Trim the leeks and wash them very well to remove all grit. Cut into pieces. Peel the potatoes and chop coarsely. Put the vegetables into a saucepan, cover with stock, and season with salt and pepper. Bring to the boil, then simmer for 20-30 minutes until the vegetables are tender. Put through a sieve or a liquidizer and return the cream to the pan. Add the parsley, the grated cheese and nutmeg and heat up until the cheese has melted. (Milk may be used instead of the stock for a creamier version.)
    Pour into a warmed vacuum flask.

ൠ Yoghurt soup

In the Middle East and India people love drinking yoghurt diluted with iced water. With the addition of chopped cucumber, the drink becomes a soup.

1 litre (1¾ pints) natural/plain yoghurt, 450 ml (¾ pint) water, salt and pepper to taste, 1 cucumber (peeled and chopped), 6 fat spring onions finely chopped), a sprig of mint and a sprig of parsley (finely chopped).

Sprinkle the cucumber with salt and let the juices drain away in a sieve for an hour. Beat the yoghurt and water together with a fork. Season to taste with salt and pepper and add the rest of the ingredients. Chill, then pour into a cold vacuum flask, adding a few cubes of ice.

A less common alternative, which is a favourite of mine, is to make a mixture of 1 part sour cream and 3 parts yoghurt. You may like to add, as they do in Iran, a handful of raisins or sultanas.

❧ Gazpacho

One of the most delightful and best-known iced soups, it is as popular in Portugal as it is in Spain.

¹/₂ kg (1 lb) tomatoes, 1 small onion or a small bunch of spring onions, 2 green peppers, 1 cucumber, 2 cloves of garlic (crushed), 4 tablespoons olive oil, 3 tablespoons wine vinegar, 3 slices of wholemeal bread, crusts removed (optional), salt and pepper; 3 tablespoons tomato purée, finely chopped fresh parsley, chives, mint or sweet marjoram.

Peel the tomatoes by pouring boiling water over them in a bowl. Wash the cucumber and the peppers; there is no need to peel them. Chop them up roughly, removing the seeds from the peppers. Bread gives the soup a more filling and peasant-like quality. If you are using it, soak it in water and squeeze dry. Put in the liquidizer with the rest of the ingredients. Add only enough fresh cold water (¹/₄-¹/₂ a litre/¹/₂-1 pint) to blend to a light smooth cream. (3 or 4 tablespoons of ground almonds are a good alternative to the wholemeal bread as a thickening.) Chill. Pour into a cooled vacuum flask, adding a few ice cubes.

The usual garnish of finely chopped tomatoes, onions, cucumbers and peppers may be dispensed with at a picnic, but you can always take them separately in a plastic box or screw-top jar.

❧ Iced cucumber soup

1 litre (1³/₄ pints) jellied chicken stock, 1¹/₂ cucumbers, 1 medium onion or 5 spring onions, 3 tablespoons butter, 3 tablespoons flour, 150 ml (¹/₄ pint) single cream (optional), salt and pepper, 2 tablespoons chives or mint leaves, finely chopped (optional).

Peel and chop the cucumber coarsely, or you may leave the peel on for a greener appearance. Chop the onion or spring onions. Melt the butter in a large saucepan and gently sauté the onions until they are soft but not coloured. Add the flour and stir until well blended. Add the stock, a little at a time, beating vigorously with a wooden spoon. Bring to the boil, stirring constantly and simmer for 15 minutes. Put in the liquidizer with the cucumber and cream and blend to a smooth cream. Season to taste with salt and pepper and stir in the herbs. Chill before putting into a cold vacuum flask with a few ice cubes.

❧ Cream of avocado soup

3 large avocados, juice of 1 or 2 lemons, 3 tablespoons butter, 3 tablespoons flour, 1 litre (1³/₄ pints) jellied chicken stock, ¹/₄ litre (¹/₂ pint) single cream, salt and pepper.

Purée the avocados with the lemon juice in a blender. Melt the butter in a large saucepan. Add the flour and stir until well blended. Add the stock gradually, stirring constantly until thickened and smooth. Remove from the heat and add the avocado purée and the cream, beating well. Chill and pour into a cooled vacuum flask just before you are ready to leave.

SANDWICHES

❧ Sandwiches, a tradition pioneered in England

Bread has always proved a useful foundation for other food. In Tudor times meat was given out on thickly cut pieces, but it was not until 1762 that a filling was first pressed between two thin slices. The occasion was a 24-hour gambling session when John Montagu, fourth Earl of Sandwich, found this was a clean and handy way of eating without soiling the cards. At the beginning of the nineteenth century sandwiches left the card tables for the great outdoors. Easily wrapped and carried, they made the perfect meal in the pocket, so perfect that they soon became the ubiquitous horrors described by Osbert Sitwell as 'slimy layers of paste like something out of the Ancient Mariner'.

The limp and soggy 'sawdust and plastic' variety with factory bread and mean, miserable fillings were my first taste of Britain in the 50s, encountered in cafeterias and glimpsed in packed lunch boxes. Things have changed since then, but there is much room for improvement, with some inspiration from abroad.

Every type of bread may be used, wholewheat, rye, pumpernickel, white crusty rolls, soft egg rolls, toast, baps, sesame buns, long French baguettes, Indian naan and Greek pitta. Although yesterday's bread is usually considered best for cutting thin slices, the one just out of the oven is the best for me, and with plenty of filling.

Many traditional English sandwich fillings have been given in the chapter *Tea on the Lawn* which will do very well on any picnic. I will add here a few more substantial ones.

Roast beef. In the old days they used to pound it. 'What can be more appalling' said Mrs Steel and Mrs Gardiner in *The Complete Indian Housekeeper and Cook*, 'than a bite at the usual sandwich, which either lands you with no meat at all, or leaves two disconsolate pieces of mustard-patched bread to lament the slice of tough beef which you are struggling to conceal from your neighbour.'

In truth there is nothing better, provided that it is very juicy, tender and rare, than a slice of roast beef. Mash some mustard or grated horseradish into the butter and garnish with cress or lettuce.

Salt beef or tongue may be treated in the same way.

Poach a fat kipper in water for 5 minutes. Drain, skin and flake it. Mash it with 2 tablespoons of lemon juice, 2 tablespoons of butter and 3 tablespoons of single cream.

Danish open sandwiches

These are a good idea as you can assemble them on the spot to everyone's individual taste. They should be beautiful to look at with very little bread and plenty of filling. Take a selection of sliced cold meats in a box, fill another with crisp fresh lettuce and raw vegetables, all washed and clean, and another with seafood, salted or pickled fish. You may also want cheeses, hard-boiled eggs, relishes and sauces. Bring salt and pepper, mustard, lemons, bought mayonnaise and pickles. Arrange the components carefully, starting with a thin flat base.

American sandwiches

Double and triple deckers, aptly called 'super sandwiches' by James Beard, have made American gastronomic history. Evolved as 'club specials' these crusty combinations of thinly sliced chicken, turkey, roast beef, bacon, smoked salmon, and cheddar cheese with ham, tomato, onion, lettuce, cucumber and hard-boiled eggs dressed with mayonnaise or vinaigrette defy the imagination and occasionally also good taste.

A brunch special has come to us from across the Atlantic with all that goes to make an English breakfast very special. Tomato slices, sausages, bacon, mushrooms, all lightly fried or grilled with fried eggs, are served between two or three large pieces of toast.

Cheese and apple special is another English combination from America. For two sandwiches, grate a sharp dessert apple and mix it with 100 g (1/4 lb) grated matured Cheddar and 2 teaspoons of Worcestershire sauce. This is good cold but even better hot so wrap it in foil and warm up when you are ready to eat.

James Beard's egg and onion. Sauté a medium onion or 3 spring onions, finely chopped, in 1 tablespoon of butter until soft. Toss in about 50 g (2 oz) diced mushrooms and cook a further 2-3 minutes. Season with salt and pepper. Chop and mash 4 hard-boiled eggs. Add the mushroom and onion mixture when it is cool and bind with a little mayonnaise. Spread on wholewheat or rye bread.

ಶ French bread

The long crisp bread, cut in four then split through lengthways, buttered generously and filled even more generously with pâté, rillettes, saucisson, ham or cheese, has long been popular in pubs.

Here are some alternatives brought from across the Channel.

For a fishy mixture combine the contents of a tin of sardines (bones removed) and a small tin of tuna with half their weight in butter. Add 3 teaspoons of anchovy paste, a good squeeze of lemon or 2 tablespoons of wine vinegar, 2 tablespoons of finely chopped onion and 2 tablespoons of finely chopped parsley. Work it all to a paste. You can also add 2 mashed hard-boiled egg yolks or a few chopped pickled gherkins.

Another fishy mixture is finely shredded crab with a little chopped anchovy and capers, all bound together with a light mayonnaise.

ಶ Pan bagnat

More an hors d'oeuvre stuffed loaf than a salad sandwich, it is from the Provençal coast of the Mediterranean and as common there as the game of boules.

Usually made in a baguette (a long French loaf) it is equally good in a round flat country loaf or in small individual bread rolls. Prepare at least 2 hours before but preferably the day before.

2 baguettes or 6 rolls, 150 ml (¹/₄ pint) olive oil, 4 tablespoons wine vinegar, salt and pepper, 1 clove of garlic; crushed (optional), 500 g (1 lb) tomatoes, 1 large Spanish onion or a small bunch of spring onions, 2 green peppers, 45 g (1³/₄ oz) tin of anchovy fillets, 125 g (¹/₄ lb) black olives (pitted).

Cut the loaves or rolls in half across. Generously sprinkle the inside of each with a vinaigrette of olive oil and vinegar seasoned with salt and pepper and crushed garlic. Cut the tomatoes, the onion and seeded peppers into thin slices. Lay on the bottom halves of the bread. Garnish with olives and anchovy fillets and cover with the top halves of the bread. Press well together and wrap tightly in aluminium foil. Leave in a cool place and with a weight on top long enough for the juices and oils to be well absorbed. To serve, cut into slices (if using a round loaf, cut in wedges like a cake).

?● Pitta

I am bound to have an affection for the flat hollow bread of my childhood which is delivered to London supermarkets by Cypriot and Lebanese bakeries. But now everyone has discovered its versatility – not least the children (for a children's party see p.126).

Cut in half, pitta bread makes the two perfect pockets which are the traditional holders of shish kebab and the now ubiquitous donner: meats grilled on skewers or on a spit, with their toppings of mixed salad. In fact they can and do hold almost anything. In the Middle East, most things which are sold on the street, from meat balls to whole beans, salads and pickles, are dropped in the pouches by vendors.

A friend who gives a picnic on Primrose Hill for at least 50 people every year stacks piles of cut pitta before a dizzy array of salads and beans, cheeses, eggs and tinned and pickled fish. Everyone fills their own pittas and comes back for more.

It is the ideal picnic bread which does away with cutlery and plates. Warm it up, if you can, just before you need it; it is not nearly so good cold. If it is dry moisten with water, wrap in aluminium foil and leave for a moment in the oven or over a gentle fire.

Fill with whatever you like. In Egypt they pour in full medames small brown beans adding a hard-boiled egg cut up into pieces. In Israel with falafel – fried rissoles of mashed chick peas topped with salad and tahina (see p.49) – it is the national meal in the hand.

Indians, Arabs and Italians all make flat pies of bread dough baked together with a variety of traditional stuffings. It is simple enough to make these fillings and to slip them into a ready-made pitta through a slit on the side or by cutting it in half. Bring them filled to the picnic and warm them up on a gentle fire, preferably wrapped in foil.

An Indian mashed potato filling. Fry half a chopped onion in a little butter and mix with 2 boiled mashed potatoes. Add a few chopped coriander leaves or a little parsley, a good squeeze of lemon juice, 1/4 teaspoon of paprika, a pinch of cayenne, another of ground ginger,

1 teaspoon of crushed coriander, fennel or aniseed and $1/2$ teaspoon of garam masala. Add salt to taste and stir well.

An Indian cauliflower filling. Boil a small cauliflower until it is very tender; boil separately a handful of green peas until they are really soft. Drain. Chop the cauliflower finely and lightly crush the peas. Mix together and add your favourite aromatics: some finely chopped herbs, salt and pepper, cayenne or ground chillies if you like it hot, and a teaspoon of cumin, coriander or garam masala.

Lahma bi ajeen, an Arab minced meat filling. Soften 500 g (1 lb) finely chopped onions in a little oil. Add 750 g ($1^{1}/_{2}$ lb) lean minced beef and fry, stirring until it has changed colour. Add a large tin 800 g (1 lb 12 oz) of peeled tomatoes, drained and mashed, 1 small tin of tomato purée, 1 teaspoon of sugar, 1 teaspoon of allspice, the juice of half a lemon, a small bunch of parsley (finely chopped), salt to taste, a pinch of cayenne pepper and Worcestershire sauce.

Aubergine filling. Put a layer of thin, fried aubergine slices over a layer of thin slices of a good melting cheese, such as Gruyère or Cheddar. Sprinkle with black pepper and a touch of grated nutmeg.

COLD SAUCES AND RELISHES

Since moist foods are not generally considered the right kind to carry, serve or eat out, a good sauce or dressing, or tasty relish is doubly appreciated.

Most people become adventurous when it is a matter of enlivening cold meats, and cold saucery is one area where the exotic is acceptable. France may be the land of sauces but Britain has a greater repertoire of cold ones. And though Escoffier immortalized them with names such as Cambridge, Cumberland, Gloucester and Yorkshire, the flavours of vinegar with sugar, fruits and spices bear tribute to early influences from the Far and Near East dating from the Crusades and the spice trade as well as the colonial heritage.

❧ Vinaigrette

The classic French dressing, a mixture of oil, wine vinegar, salt and pepper, to which fresh green herbs and parsley are often added, mustard occasionally, and garlic by those who like it, plays a very important part in the world of cold foods. It is indispensable with salads and vegetables, excellent with fish, chicken and meat, and it merits special attention.

The excellence of the sauce depends on the quality of the ingredients. Good olive oil is the best but peanut oil, sunflower and other vegetable oils will also do. Walnut oil is particularly delicious, especially if you have some chopped walnuts in the salad. The usual proportion of vinegar to oil is 1 to 3 but you may vary it to your own taste. Use the proportion 1 to 4 with a lighter oil such as sunflower oil. Lemon or cider vinegar may be substituted for wine vinegar. Add salt and freshly ground black pepper to taste and beat vigorously until well blended. (There is a purist notion that beating them into the vinegar alone first will allow the salt to dissolve better.) A little mustard, preferably Dijon, stirred into the vinegar before beating in the oil is good for the stronger tasting salads such as endive, chicory and watercress. Stir in fresh chopped herbs – parsley, chives and basil – just before serving.

Some salads, especially fresh green leaves, are best seasoned at the last minute, so carry the vinaigrette in a separate jar with a well-fitting lid and pour over the salad just before serving. Carry the herbs in a little polythene bag. Other salads, such as those made with cooked vegetables, are best when they have been allowed to absorb their dressing and should be mixed some hours in advance.

With capers and gherkins. Excellent with chicken, beef, veal, fish, and vegetables, is a vinaigrette to which have been added capers, pickled cucumbers, spring onions and a variety of green herbs such as parsley, chives, chervil and watercress, finely chopped.

With cream or sour cream. I very often mix equal quantities of cream or sour cream and vinaigrette with most attractive results.

Another unusually good cream sauce for fish, hard-boiled eggs and vegetables such as leeks is made this way: beat an egg yolk with about 4-6 tablespoons of cream in a bowl until well blended, then add about 150 ml (¼ pint) vinaigrette very slowly, beating vigorously as you would a mayonnaise. You may add a little lemon juice to taste, and stir in some fresh green herbs.

With mustard. I was recently served a creamy sauce with the texture of mayonnaise but which contained no eggs, only mustard, oil and seasonings. It was poured over crisp young leeks and slices of barely cooked Jerusalem artichokes. Beat 3 tablespoons of French mustard in a bowl with 3 tablespoons of boiling water. Now add olive oil a little at a time, beating constantly with a whisk. Add from 75 to 150 ml (⅛ to ¼ of a pint) to make a thick sauce. Season to taste with salt and pepper and some lemon juice. Add parsley or fresh chopped green herbs just before serving.

❧ Mint and herb sauces

For the traditional English sauce for lamb, wash, dry and chop very finely, blend or pound, a handful of fresh mint leaves. Bring to the boil 6 tablespoons of wine vinegar with 3 tablespoons of water and 2 tablespoons of castor sugar. Throw in the mint and remove from the heat.

Variations: do the same with minced chervil, chives, marjoram, basil and rosemary, all of which are good with cold meats.

A less orthodox but delicious mint sauce is made with red currant jelly and orange juice added to taste.

All of these keep well in bottles.

ᶔ Mayonnaise

Until the reign of Henry IV this sauce had no name in France. It was simply called 'cold sauce'. According to Pierre Lacam, the duke of Mayenne was eating a cold chicken dressed with it while Henry's troops were advancing. He refused to leave the table until he had finished and lost the battle of Arques. The sauce was mockingly named 'mayennaise as a result of this episode. Carême transformed it to 'maynonaise' and later the French Academy accepted it as mayonnaise.

A hot day will do it no good. So unless it can be kept cool it is best not to have it at all or to have a good commercial variety instead.

The mystique which surrounded the making of mayonnaise in the days when only a wooden spoon and a bowl were used still clings. Now that it takes only minutes with an electric beater or blender. It still often separates in the making but it can be easily saved.

3 egg yolks, 1 tablespoon wine vinegar or 2 tablespoons lemon juice, 1/2-1 teaspoon salt, a pinch of white pepper, 1/4 litre (1/2 pint) olive oil.

Beat the egg yolks by themselves for at least a minute until they become thick and sticky. Add the vinegar or lemon juice and the salt and pepper and beat for half a minute longer. Pour the oil from a measuring jug drop by drop, beating all the time until the sauce thickens (which it begins to do by the time a third of the oil has been used). Continue to beat, adding the oil in a thin trickle and making sure that it is being absorbed, until the mayonnaise is a very heavy cream. If it separates it can be saved by starting again with a new yolk and beating the spoilt sauce into it by the spoonful at first, then very slowly. If the sauce is to be kept for a few days, 1-2 tablespoons of boiling water beaten in at the end will prevent curdling.

A stiff mayonnaise is obtained by mixing with about half the quantity of melted aspic jelly (see p.51). For a fluffy texture whip the mixture as it begins to set.

For a light mayonnaise, whip in a little fresh cream or sour cream.

For a green version, add as much as you like of finely chopped fresh herbs: chives, chervil, parsley, tarragon, watercress – coriander leaves too. Blanch the herbs if you mean to keep the sauce for several days.

For a red one, add tomato purée.

For an anchovy flavour which goes well with cold fish, mousses and terrines, wash 3-4 anchovy fillets. Chop and pound them to a purée. Add 1 tablespoon of capers, 2 tablespoons of pickled gherkins and 2 tablespoons of parsley, all finely chopped. Beat the mixture into the mayonnaise. These quantities are for $1/4$ litre ($1/2$ pint) of sauce. You may use anchovy paste instead of fillets. Other fishy flavours are obtained by beating in prawn or lobster eggs or any type of caviare which you happen to have.

For a thick Greek version, add a few tablespoons of ground almonds and a mashed boiled potato or slices of bread, crusts removed, soaked in water and squeezed dry.

For a curry mayonnaise, good with chicken and shellfish, add curry powder to taste, about 1 teaspoon for $1/4$ litre ($1/2$ pint) and if you like a pinch of powdered ginger. Stir in 1 tablespoon of raisins which have been allowed to swell in water and 1 tablespoon of slivered almonds or a little fruity chutney.

For all of these you may prefer to use a mixture of olive oil with a lighter one such as sunflower.

ࣷ Aïoli

A garlicky mayonnaise from Provence is an excellent accompaniment for fish and vegetables.

6 cloves of garlic; 2 egg yolks, the juice of $1/2$ or 1 lemon, $1/4$ litre ($1/2$ pint) olive oil, salt and pepper.

Crush the garlic in a mortar or a press. Beat it with the egg yolks. Add the lemon juice and the oil very slowly, beating all the time. Add a few drops of water if it gets too thick to prevent the cream from curdling. If it does curdle, start all over again with a new egg yolk and pour the curdled sauce in a thin stream on to the yolk, beating all the time. Season to taste with salt and pepper.

For a thicker, firmer sauce you may add 1 boiled mashed potato or a slice of white bread, crusts removed, soaked in water or milk and squeezed dry, before you beat in the oil.

❧ Skorthalia

This garlicky sauce from Greece made with bread and no eggs keeps better than mayonnaise. Make it in a blender or use a mortar. Pour it over fish and vegetables.

Cut the crust off 6-7 slices of good white bread. Soak in water and squeeze. Put in the blender with as much crushed garlic as you like (3 fat cloves is usual), the juice of 1/2 a lemon or 2 tablespoons of white wine vinegar. Gradually add enough olive oil to achieve a smooth thick cream – about 150 ml (1/4 pint) – then stir in about 150 ml (1/4 pint) water to thin the sauce. Add salt and pepper to taste and blend well.

❧ Other sauces for fish

A type of mayonnaise based on hard-boiled rather than raw egg yolks which keeps better on a hot day.

Put 2 hard-boiled yolks in a blender with 150 ml (1/4 pint) olive oil, the juice of half a lemon or a tablespoon or two of vinegar. Add salt and pepper to taste. The sauce should be the consistency of mayonnaise. A crushed clove of garlic, 2-4 pounded anchovy fillets and a good bunch of finely chopped parsley will give you a traditional *Italian salsa verde*.

You may alternatively add a teaspoon of mustard and a pinch of cayenne pepper for what Escoffier called a '*Sauce Cambridge*'.

Half an onion, finely chopped, or 2 finely minced spring onions and a few finely chopped pickled cucumbers or capers, turn it into a *sauce tartare*.

A small but strong fresh pimento, well pounded, will make it fiery.

❧ Nut sauces

A whole range of sauces based on a variety of nuts, ground to a paste and highly seasoned, originate in the Middle East. Usually named tarator, they are equally good for meats, chicken, fish and boiled or raw vegetables. They are simple – a matter of mixing and tasting, and cannot fail.

Each country makes use of its indigenous nuts so versions depend on local trees.

Tarator with pine nuts. The favourite accompaniment to fish in Lebanon is the most exquisite as well as the most expensive, for nowhere are pine nuts cheap. However, people cheat and put in more bread and less nuts. It can be made in a blender. Otherwise pound it to a paste in a mortar. Soak 2 slices of white bread, crusts removed, in water and squeeze dry. Add 350 g (12 oz) pine nuts, 2 cloves of garlic, salt and white pepper to taste and the juice of one or more lemons added to enough water to make up $1/4$ litre ($1/2$ pint) liquid. Blend to a very smooth cream.

Turkish Khiyàr Tèrèturu. Grind 225 g ($1/2$ lb) fresh walnuts or blanched almonds in a blender. Add a slice or two of white bread, crusts removed, soaked in water and squeezed dry, 1 or 2 cloves of garlic, crushed, about 4 tablespoons of wine vinegar or the juice of one or more lemons, salt and pepper to taste, and blend, adding enough water to bring it to the consistency of a light cream.

Present with cucumber, cauliflower or another such salad with a dribbling of olive oil poured over it.

⁊ A light tahina

Nothing brings the Arab flavour to a dish more than the pale sauce based on the oily pulp of mashed sesame seeds which you can buy in a jar in Greek and Middle Eastern shops. To a $1/4$ litre ($1/2$ pint) pot of tahina (or tahini) gradually add 150 ml ($1/4$ pint) or more lemon juice, beating vigorously. Add 2 crushed cloves of garlic, salt and pepper and enough water (about 125 ml/4 fl oz) for a light cream. You may put all this through the blender.

As good with fish as it is with any salad, many people pour it on meat balls and chicken.

⁊ Fresh cream sauce

Fresh double cream makes one of the most delicious sauces for cold fish. Bring $1/4$ litre ($1/2$ pint) double cream to the boil with a good bunch of chopped fresh herbs, mixed if you like, and chosen from tarragon, parsley, chervil, chives, watercress and coriander leaves. Season to taste with salt and pepper and simmer for 7-8 minutes. You may also like to add a crushed clove of garlic and a squeeze of lemon. Chill, then whisk until it is thick and smooth. The French, who like this with watercress, call it a mousseline.

Mustard and cream sauce. Stir one dessertspoon of good French mustard into about 200 ml (7 fl oz) fresh cream with the juice of a medium lemon and salt and pepper to taste.

❧ Horseradish sauces

How you make this old English sauce is purely a matter of taste.

Grate as much fresh horseradish as you like into some whipped double cream. About 2 heaped tablespoons should be enough for 150 ml (¼ pint) cream.

You may also stir in a pinch of castor sugar, a few drops of wine vinegar, a sprinkling of salt and pepper and a touch of mustard.

Variations: Sour cream is a delicious alternative to fresh cream.

Here are Jane Grigson's directions for Escoffier's version (from *Good Things*):

50 g (2 oz) shelled walnuts, 50 g (2 oz) grated horseradish, pinch salt, 1 teaspoon castor sugar, 1 tablespoon white breadcrumbs, 150 ml (¼ pint) double cream, 1 teaspoon wine vinegar or lemon juice.

'Pour boiling water over the walnuts and leave them for a moment or two. You will then be able to remove their fine skins (which can add a bitter taste to this sauce). Chop the nuts finely, then mix with the rest of the ingredients. Add the vinegar or lemon juice gradually – the whole teaspoon may not be to your taste, or you may like to add a little more.'

Good for salmon and trout as well as for cold beef.

❧ Cream cheese

For many years now people have been serving cream cheese dips with drinks. Few realize what an excellent accompanying sauce for cold meats, eggs and fish they are. Use a light full-fat cream cheese such as the French fromage frais. Whip it well adding yoghurt, cream or a little olive oil, if it is too thick. Flavour with fresh chopped herbs such as mint, basil, chives, tarragon. Add crushed garlic or very finely chopped onion. If you cannot find fromage frais, a good alternative is to blend equal quantities of cottage cheese and yoghurt.

Make it sharp with lemon juice or beat in a little tomato paste to give it colour. Grated raw cucumber, salted and drained of its juices for half an hour, finely chopped bits of pickled cucumber, fennel, celery and capers, all or one, are pleasant additions.

My own favourite is simply cream cheese mixed with oil, garlic and basil when it is available.

૨⊕ Aspic

Though aspic plays an important part in cold buffet food, in glazing and holding decorations of bits of cucumber, tomato, egg, truffle and tongue in place with a coating of shining jelly, this function is of no interest in this book; for it does not stand up very well to warm weather, and we are concerned with simple presentation rather than decoration. Moderate use may be made of jellied stock to contain and hold food together in a mould provided that it is carried in a cool container.

Aspic is particularly unpleasant when not properly made. The best is made with jellies obtained from boiling knuckle of veal, calf's feet or pig's trotters, clarifying the stock and reducing it. Much simpler for the limited use we are putting it to is one made with gelatine and a well-flavoured stock in the following way:

Simmer 450 ml (³/₄ pint) water and 150 ml (¹/₄ pint) white wine with half an onion, a carrot, a few celery stalks, (all chopped), a few parsley stalks, a sprig of thyme, a squeeze of lemon and salt and pepper for half an hour until the liquor is well flavoured. Strain and let it cool a little. Add a sherry glass of sherry, Marsala or Madeira and sprinkle in 25 g (1 oz) powdered gelatine. Bring it to boiling point, whisking all the time to dissolve the gelatine. This will set firm on cooling. It may be mixed with mayonnaise for a firm sauce.

૨⊕ Fruit purées

These excellent summer companions to cold meat, chicken and fish, simply cooked with no embellishments, are refreshingly acid in the spring time and sweeter later in the summer. They may otherwise be lightly sweetened and exotically flavoured with wines and spirits, spices and vinegars.

Gooseberry sauce was introduced to me by Jane Grigson. It is not only a May-time companion for mackerel. You can serve the early acid green fruit with roast duck, pork, ham, goose or lamb. As the sauce is to be eaten cold I make it with no butter. Top and tail the gooseberries. Put them in a heavy pan. Moisten with a few tablespoons of water, port or left-over white wine (a Muscat is excellent) and let them soften very slowly until they are easily mashed with a fork. If too acid, add a sprinkling of sugar, if too sweet, add a squeeze of lemon or orange juice. Also try the juice of fresh ginger pressed in a garlic press. A few drops are enough.

For an apricot purée for lamb, chicken and duck, simmer dried apricots with water to cover until they are easily mashed. Put through a blender or mash with a fork. You may add a squeeze of lemon juice if the fruits are not sharp enough (they vary greatly) and a pinch of cinnamon or allspice.

For a prune purée, simmer prunes in red wine or port until they are soft. Remove the stones and put the fruit with the liquor through a blender. This is also good mixed with chopped walnuts. Serve with pork, turkey, chicken or beef and try it also with fish. You may also flavour with cinnamon or nutmeg.

For a cranberry sauce for meat and fowl, simmer 1/2 kg (1 lb) cranberries in 1/4 litre (1/2 pint) orange juice with 225 g (1/2 lb) sugar and lemon juice to taste.

A cherry sauce can be made with tinned or bottled pitted black cherries. Simmer in a pan with 3-4 tablespoons of wine vinegar for 225 g (1/2 lb) of cherries to reduce the liquor and soften the fruit. Mash with a fork.

❧ Cumberland sauce

The best English sauce for cold meats depends on good red currant jelly, which is not always easy to find. It is useful to make a small stock in late summer when jars are plentiful in the shops. The sauce keeps for weeks in a jar in the refrigerator.

Here is Michael Smith's recipe in *Fine English Cookery*:

1/2 kg (1 lb) good red currant jelly, 150 ml (1/4 pint) ruby port, 3 oranges, 3 lemons, 1 level dessertspoon dry mustard, 1 small onion (very finely chopped), a little salt, tip of a teaspoon powdered mace, 1 sherry glass cider vinegar.

'Using a potato peeler, remove the rind from all 6 pieces of fruit. Care must be taken that no white pith is taken off with the rind, as this is the bitter part of the citrus fruits.

'Collect the strips of rind together into manageable piles, and with a very sharp, thin-spined knife shred the rind as finely as you possibly can try to shred it as fine as a pin, for this will ensure that your sauce is good looking and elegant.

'Put the shredded peel into a pan and pour over enough water to cover it. Bring the contents of the pan to the boil and immediately pour into a strainer. Cool the peel under running cold water for a minute or so, then put on one side.

'Squeeze and strain the juice of 2 of the oranges, and 2 of the lemons. Bring this to the boil with all the remaining ingredients and simmer for 15 minutes over a low heat, stirring to ensure that the jelly melts evenly and doesn't catch.

'Add the shredded rind and boil for a further 5 to 10 minutes until the sauce starts to thicken. Cool then refrigerate until the sauce is fully thickened. Serve chilled and do not strain.'

❧ A peppery relish

I shall never forget the spoonful of relish offered by a Yemenite family camping on the banks of the Sea of Galilee. I thought I would never be able to taste anything again, so powerful were the peppers with which it was made. Tears running down my cheeks, and gasping for breath, I heard that the other ingredients were onions, vinegar, spices, raisins and sugar.

Here is a similar recipe which will not make you cry. Made with sweet peppers, it is an adaptation of Escoffier's 'pimento pour viandes froides' by Elizabeth David in *Spices, Salt and Aromatics in the English Kitchen*.

'You need 2 large, fat, fleshy, sweet and ripe red peppers (about 1 lb (½ kg) gross weight), ½ lb (225 g) of mild Spanish onions, 1 lb (½ kg) of ripe tomatoes, 1 clove of garlic, ¼ lb (125 g) of raisins, half a teaspoonful each of salt, powdered ginger (or grated dried root ginger), and mixed spices such as allspice, mace and nutmeg, ½ lb (225 g) white sugar, 4 tablespoons of olive oil and ¼ pint (150 ml) of fine wine vinegar.

'Melt the finely chopped onions in the olive oil, add the chopped peppers (well washed, all core and seeds removed), salt and spices, and after 10 minutes the peeled and chopped tomatoes and the raisins, garlic and sugar; lastly the vinegar. Cook extremely slowly, covered for at least one hour and a quarter.'

Good with cold meats; keeps a few weeks in a jar.

VEGETABLES AND OTHER DIPS

With the advent of the food processor many people have been tempted to mash things to a paste and to convert them into mousses and moulds with the addition of beaten egg whites or gelatine.

A few vegetables that have recently become fashionable as dips at cocktail parties have been puréed for centuries by chopping and pounding because the treatment really suited them. These creams make an admirable first course and are ideal to dip into with pieces of bread or a biscuit while waiting for the rest of the meal to cook on the fire. There are also recipes for tapenade and olivade on pp.20-1.

❧ Aubergine purée

This is the 'poor man's caviare' of the Middle East, an appellation it well deserves.

Grill 3 large aubergines until their skin is black and blisters. As soon as you can handle them, peel off the skins, squeeze out some of the juices and mash the pulp with a fork. Season with plenty of olive oil, the juice of one lemon at least and salt and pepper to taste. Use a liquidizer for a smooth cream. Garnish with a little finely chopped onion and plenty of chopped parsley and fresh mint leaves.

Variations: A good alternative to this basic appetizer is to add plenty of yoghurt and a touch of crushed garlic. You may also add 2 tomatoes, peeled and chopped.

❧ Avocado cream (guacamole)

In Mexico, where the fruit originates, there are innumerable versions of this hors d'oeuvre, which also makes a good sauce for chicken, boiled meats and fish.

Peel and mash 2 large ripe avocados. Add 1 or 2 finely chopped green chillies, the juice of half or 1 whole lime or lemon, salt and freshly ground pepper to taste and a pinch of sugar.

Variation: You may leave it as it is or add a peeled, seeded and chopped tomato, a few finely chopped spring onions, a small grated onion or a clove of garlic, crushed, and a small handful of finely chopped fresh coriander leaves (the Mexicans' favourite herb) and beat in a few drops of olive oil.

For some reason it is widely thought that leaving the stone of the avocado in the cream will prevent it from tarnishing; I believe that the lemon juice does this better.

Cover the bowl if you will not be eating it straight away.

?• Bean purées from the Middle East

Each country of the Islamic world has a favourite bean to make those sharply seasoned creams which are the invariable accompaniment to grilled meats and indeed to most things. Chick peas are the base of hummus which has been adopted as the national dish of Israel. All types of beans and lentils can be used. They must be soaked, drained, simmered in fresh water (salt being added when they are already tender) and cooked until very soft. They are then pounded to a pulp or put through a blender or liquidizer with enough of their cooking water to make a thick cream.

After that the fun begins, for it is one of those foods which is made by repeated tasting and adding. Some ingredients are constant: plenty of olive oil, lemon juice, garlic, salt and pepper, though quantities vary. Spices depend on the region, the usual ones being ground cumin, coriander and cayenne (put in a lot of this pepper if you like it fiery).

Garnish with chopped parsley or coriander leaves and a dribble of olive oil.

Serve with pitta bread.

A very popular combination is a mixture of chick pea purée and tahina (see p.49).

࿊ Chicken liver mousse

This makes an elegant first course served with thin toast.

225 g (8 oz) chicken livers, 125 g (4 oz) butter, pinch of thyme or mixed herbs, salt and pepper, 1 clove garlic, 3 tablespoons brandy or Madeira.

Clean the livers, removing bile bag and filaments. Sauté briefly in 2 tablespoons of sizzling butter until they just turn colour. Add a sprinkling of herbs, salt and pepper, a clove of garlic, crushed, and cook for about 5 minutes longer. While they are still pink inside, remove from the fire. Blend to a smooth paste in a liquidizer or food processor with the rest of the butter and the brandy or Madeira. Put into a pot and seal with a layer of melted butter.

Variations: Make a lovely cream by mixing the liver paste with 150 ml (¼ pint) double cream, stiffly beaten, instead of the remaining butter.

Port is a good alternative to brandy and a faint touch of allspice or nutmeg is also good.

🕭 Taramasalata

Smoked cod's roe in a jar is an excellent substitute for grey mullet's roe, the usual basis of this popular Greek salad dip. The roe is pounded to a paste with lemon juice, plenty of olive oil and white bread soaked in water, to become a pale coral cream the consistency of mayonnaise.

It is easier to use a blender. Soak 4 large slices of white bread (crusts removed) in water and put them in the blender with their water and 125 g (4 oz) smoked cod's roe. Blend until smooth, then, with the blender running very slowly, add the juice of 1 or more lemons and 150 ml (¹/₄ pint) olive oil or enough for the right consistency. Taste for sharpness, and finish if you like with a very small onion, very finely grated.

Keep this cool and serve with thin pieces of toast or pitta bread and black olives.

PÂTÉS, TERRINES AND GALANTINES

Terrines, pâtés, galantines and rillettes are part of our dreams of French parties de plaisir. Monet and Manet, Watteau, Tissot and Renoir, and Fernand Léger have depicted them with good bread and plenty of wine on white table-cloths spread on the grass beneath leafy trees.

Meat mixtures blended to smoothness or chopped to coarseness, delicately spiced and flavoured with wines and spirits, have always been French picnic favourites. They are much easier to make than they seem and there are endless possibilities involving a variety of meats, chicken and game. For those who wish to expand their knowledge of the art of charcuterie there is no better guide than Jane Grigson's *Charcuterie and French Pork Cookery*.

James Beard's pâté

This recipe comes from *Delights and Prejudices*.

Wash and sauté in 4 tablespoons of butter ½ kg (1 lb) chicken livers. Chop livers exceedingly fine or whirl them in a blender with 2 eggs, 6 garlic cloves, 1 medium-sized onion (peeled) and ½ cup of cognac. Place this mixture in a large bowl and add 1 kg (2 lb) ground veal, 1 kg (2 lb) ground pork, 2 tablespoons salt (I use less) and 1 teaspoon of freshly ground black pepper. Blend the ingredients well with the hands and add 150 ml (⅔) cup of cognac, 1 teaspoon of thyme, ½ teaspoon of summer savory, a pinch of nutmeg and a small pinch of clove. Blend everything thoroughly. Cut 1 kg (2 lb) cold boiled tongue into long strips, about 1½ cm (⅜ in) thick, and cut ½ kg (1 lb) fresh pork fat into thin strips, about ½ cm (¼ in) thick.

Line a shallow baking dish with bacon strips, place one-third of the mixture on the strips in an oval shape and add a strip of tongue and fat pork. Add another third of the mixture, more tongue and pork, and finally a top layer of the mixture. Form into a loaf. Top with additional slices of bacon and bake at 170℃/325℉/Gas 3 for 3-3½ hours. Let the pâté cool. Remove it to a carving board or platter. Serve it in thin slices.

This pâté will keep under refrigeration for a week if wrapped in foil to keep it moist.

৯ Jambon persillé

This is best packed in a cold box on a hot day as the jelly might not hold.

A 1½ kg (3 lb) piece of ham or gammon, 1 calf's foot or 2 pig's trotters, a few celery leaves, a few sprigs of herbs (tarragon, thyme, chervil, bay leaf), 8 peppercorns, 4 shallots, 1 bottle dry white wine or 1 bottle of strong dry cider, 1 tablespoon white wine vinegar, bunch of very finely chopped fresh parsley.

Soak the ham in cold water for a few hours to remove some of the excess salt. Blanch and drain it. Clean the calf's foot or pig's trotters and blanch them for a few minutes in a large pan to remove the scum. Pour the water out and put the ham in. Add the wine (or cider) and enough water to cover. Add celery leaves, herbs (not the parsley), peppercorns and shallots; then simmer gently, covered, for 2-3 hours. Remove the ham when it is very tender and flakes easily. Discard the calf's foot or trotters and reduce the stock further if necessary, until it coagulates on a cold surface. Cut the ham into little pieces or flake it, then crush it and put it in a bowl. Strain the gelatinous stock through a fine sieve or muslin. Let it cool and remove the fat, then add the parsley and the wine vinegar and taste to correct the seasoning. Stir well. Pour over the ham in the bowl. Let it set in the refrigerator. Either serve from the bowl or turn it out on to a plate and cut it into slices.

৯ Ham mousse

750 g (1½ lb) ham or smoked gammon (boneless), 1 carrot, 1 onion, celery leaves, parsley stalks, 2 tablespoons butter, 2 tablespoons flour, 500 ml (1 pint) part stock, part cider or white wine, 100 g (¼ lb) Gruyère (grated), pinch of nutmeg, 3 eggs.

Poach the joint of ham or gammon in enough water to cover, with sliced carrot, small onion cut into pieces, some celery leaves, a few parsley stalks and some pepper until it is tender – about one hour. There is usually no need to add salt especially if the gammon is smoked. Lift out from the pan and cut up into pieces. Chop it finely or use a food processor.

In another pan, melt the butter, add the flour and stir it in well. Gradually add the stock and white wine or cider, in equal parts, stirring all the time until the sauce thickens. Add the cheese, ham, egg yolks and a pinch of nutmeg and stir well.

Beat the egg whites until stiff and fold them into the sauce. Butter a bowl deep enough for the mousse to rise and pour the mixture in. Put in a low 150°C/300°F/Gas 2, oven for an hour.

Carry it in its bowl to the picnic.

❧ Chicken mousse

1 plump chicken (poached in a flavoursome stock), 150 ml (¹/₄ pint) double cream (stiffly whipped), a few sprigs of tarragon or parsley (finely chopped), a pinch of cinnamon or nutmeg, salt and pepper, a squeeze of lemon juice and a little grated lemon rind, 3 eggs (separated).

Skin, bone and mince or finely chop the chicken. Put it in a bowl with the cream, herbs and spices, salt and pepper and lemon juice to taste. Add the egg yolks and stir well. You may add a little cognac – about 2 tablespoons – or some port.

Beat the egg whites until stiff and fold in gently. Pour into a well-buttered oven dish or mould with enough room for the mousse to rise. Bake in a gentle 150°C/300°F/Gas 2, oven for an hour.

EGGS AND OMELETTES

🐚 Hard-boiled eggs

At a time when women limited their walks to a stroll round the shrubbery, a little governess strode alone and unprotected up the slopes of Snowdon. Nelly Weeton confessed in her diary in 1809 (published by Edward Hall in 1936) to a 'lovely impulse of delight' and a craving for wild solitary places which drove her to brave the terrors of tramps and drovers.

She sometimes even hid from other walkers and climbers 'purposely that they might not distinguish my dress or features, lest seeing me at any other time, they should know where they had seen me; and I should dread the being pointed at in the road or the street as – "That is the lady I saw ascending Snowdon alone!"' She noted: 'I put my maps, memorandum book, three boiled eggs and a crust of bread into a work bag, and thus equipped, sallied forth.'

This time-honoured food is not to everybody's taste, but there are ways of making hard-boiled eggs most agreeable.

In the Middle East, eggs are sometimes simmered for at least 6 hours or overnight until they become hamine, that is, with a pale creamy yolk. A light brown colour is given to the whites by adding onion skins or coffee grounds to the water. Pour in a little oil so as to have a thin film floating on the surface to prevent the water from evaporating.

For extra joy at a picnic colour your eggs with special dyes and polish the shells with a lightly oiled cloth. Or shell them and simmer them unshelled for a few minutes in water with a pinch of turmeric or Indian food-colouring powders. This too is a Middle Eastern festive habit.

Chinese tea eggs (Cha Yeh Tan) with their delicate cracked-china look give an elegant touch to a picnic. They also have a fine taste. Boil 6 eggs in water for 10 minutes. Remove and very gently crack the shells with the back of a spoon. Return them to the pan. Cover with fresh water, adding 1/2 teaspoon of aniseed, 2 tablespoons of soya sauce, 2 tablespoons of tea (preferably orange pekoe) and 1 tablespoon of salt. Simmer on the lowest possible flame for 1½ hours, adding water so that the eggs remain submerged. Leave to cool and soak in the cooking water for 5-8 hours. Shell carefully.

Hard-boiled eggs need not be eaten with salt and pepper alone. They are delicious sprinkled with spices and herbs. A lemon juice and oil dressing suits them too. Either sprinkle on as you eat or dip into a bowl containing dressings and seasonings. My father has taught me to cut up the egg on the plate and smother it with a mixture of olive oil, lemon juice, a little crushed garlic, a pinch of allspice and cumin. He says it is the way of Aleppo in Syria. An Iraqi way is to mix sliced hard-boiled eggs with mango pickle. They make a meal of these accompanied by fried aubergine slices and a salad of tomatoes and spring onions.

If you have not got far to go eggs are always good with home-made mayonnaise (see pp.46-7) and capers. But if it is likely to spoil in hot weather make the Greek garlic sauce skorthalia (see p.48) or a nut sauce (see pp.48-9).

ࣘ Cold omelettes

One thing that Spaniards, Italians and Arabs have in common are the thick omelettes heavy with meat and vegetables and all kinds of foods. They are the Spanish tortillas, the Italian frittatas and Arab ajjas, and I have traced their ancestry to the Persian kuku. Quite unlike light French omelettes, which are quickly cooked over high heat, these are cooked slowly over low heat in a heavy-bottomed frying pan until firmly set. They must also be cooked on both sides, either turned over with a spatula if small, or turned over on a plate then slipped back into the pan or pushed under the grill to brown the top.

They are as good cold as they are hot.

ࣘ Herb omelettes

Of the vast range of Middle Eastern omelettes here are two made with herbs and one with vegetables. A meat one is on p.139.

An Arab ajja. For 6 eggs, fry 1 large onion, coarsely chopped, with 2 well-washed and finely chopped leeks in a little oil until golden. Beat the eggs until yolks and whites are blended, stir in the onions and leeks, add a large bunch of parsley, finely chopped, and salt and pepper to taste. Melt butter in a large frying pan until it foams, then pour in the egg and vegetable mixture and cook very slowly until set; then cook the other side.

An Iranian kuku. Beat 6 eggs in a large bowl with a fork. Add large bunches each of parsley, fresh coriander and chives, well washed, dried and finely chopped. Add salt and pepper to taste, 1 tablespoon of currants or sultanas and a few walnuts, coarsely chopped. Stir well and pour on to foaming butter in a thick-bottomed frying pan. Cook gently until set. Then turn over to cook or brown under the grill.

Ajja khodar meshakel. (A mixed vegetable Arab omelette.) To 3 tablespoons of hot oil add 1 large chopped onion and stir until soft and transparent. Add 2 crushed cloves of garlic, 2 leeks, washed and finely sliced, 3 courgettes, washed with ends removed and sliced medium thick, 125 g (¼ lb) fresh or frozen broad beans and 2 peeled, seeded and chopped tomatoes. Cook, stirring until soft, adding a little water when too dry. Season to taste with salt and pepper and ¼ teaspoon of nutmeg. Then stir in 2 tablespoons of finely chopped parsley.

In a large bowl beat 7 eggs with a fork until blended. Stir in the cooked vegetables.

Put 1½ tablespoons of butter or oil into a 25 cm (10 in) omelette pan and roll over the bottom and sides of the pan. When it is hot pour in the egg mixture and cook gently until the bottom of the omelette is set and the top is still creamy. Place the omelette pan under a hot grill for a minute or two more until the top of the omelette is dry. Turn out on to a large plate. Allow to cool.

Cut in wedges like a cake.

❧ Tortilla de patatas (Spanish potato omelette)

3 potatoes (peeled and diced), 3 onions (chopped), 5 tablespoons olive oil, 6 eggs, salt and pepper.

Heat the olive oil in a heavy frying pan. Add the potatoes and onions and sauté gently. Add salt and pepper and continue to cook over a low heat until the vegetables are cooked (about 20 minutes), stirring occasionally. Beat the eggs in a bowl. Lift the vegetables out of the pan leaving the oil behind. Add them to the eggs and stir well. Keep the oil hot in the frying pan and pour in the egg and vegetable mixture. Lower the heat and press the potatoes and onions down. Cook until the eggs have set firmly. Now either turn the omelette over on a plate and slip it back into the pan upside down to cook the other side, or put the frying pan under the grill until the top is firm and slightly brown.

This basic omelette can be varied endlessly to suit the taste of every region of Spain. Try adding cooked chicken, bacon, ham, chorizos (spicy sausages), cut into small pieces, and cooked vegetables such as spinach, green beans, asparagus, tomatoes. A little chopped parsley, fresh coriander leaves or mint are sometimes used and a good pinch of chilli or cayenne will give the omelette a Mexican flavour.

ও Frittata

An Italian omelette with the flavour of fresh basil and Parmesan, Pecorino or Mozzarella is spooned by the ladleful into hot oil and cooked gently, pancake-like, on both sides. Make a stack to hand out with a salad as a light main course.

Beat the eggs lightly with a fork until yolks and whites are just blended. Add salt and pepper and a good amount of grated cheese if it is a mild one, less if it is sharp (Gruyère may also be used). If you do not have fresh basil, add another herb.

Melt a little butter or oil in a large, heavy-bottomed frying pan. When it begins to foam but before it becomes coloured, pour in the egg mixture by the ladleful and turn the heat down as low as possible. When the eggs are firmly set turn the omelette over to cook the other side or finish the top under the grill.

A variety of fillings may be added to the egg mixture: thinly sliced cooked artichoke hearts or cooked asparagus cut into small pieces, sautéed onions with peeled and chopped tomatoes, thinly sliced fried or boiled courgettes and chopped ham or diced bacon. My children's favourite frittata is made firm and solid by beating in 2 medium mashed potatoes for 6 eggs.

We sometimes pour all the mixture together into the pan and cook it for 15 minutes on a low flame before putting it under the grill.

TARTS AND PIES

Nearly all societies have made a habit of taking pies on their travels and picnics. With their moist fillings and dry crust they are the ideal transportable food.

A thirteenth century Arab traveller and scholar, Abd al Latif al Baghdadi, describes a singular Egyptian pie 'fit to be put before kings and wealthy persons when they go hunting far from home or take part in pleasures in far off places . . . easy to transport, difficult to break, pleasing to the sight, satisfying to the taste, and keeps hot a very long time' (quoted in Zand and Videan's *The Eastern Key*).

This is how he describes Raghif Alsiniyyeh:

They knead it with 5½ rotles of sesame oil in the same way as they make the bread called khoschcnan. They divide the whole into two parts, spreading one of the two parts in a round shape of a rahgif (cake) in a copper plate made for this purpose of about 4 spans in diameter, and which has strong handles. After that they arrange on the dough three roasted lambs stuffed with chopped meats fried in sesame oil, crushed pistachios, various hot and aromatic spices like pepper, ginger, cloves, lentisk, coriander, caraway, cardamom, nuts and others. They sprinkle rose water, in which they have infused musk, over all. After that they put on the lambs and in the spaces left, a score of fowls, as many pullets, and fifty small birds, some roasted and stuffed with eggs, others stuffed with meat, others fried in the juice of sour grapes or lemon or some other similar liquor. They put above them pastry, and little boxes filled, some with the meat, some with sugar and sweet-meats. If one would add one lamb more, cut into morsels, it would not be out of place, and one could also add fried cheese.

When the whole is arranged in the form of a dome they again sprinkle rose water in which musk has been infused, or wood of aloes. They cover it again with the other part of the dough, to which they begin to give the shape of a broad cake. They are careful to join the two cakes of dough, as one makes pastry, so that no vapour escapes. After that they put the whole near the top of the oven until the pastry is solid and begins a degree of cooking. Then they lower the dish in the oven little by little, holding it by the handles, and leave it until the crust is well cooked and takes on a rose red colour. When it is at this point it is taken out and wiped with a sponge, and again sprinkled with rose and musk water, and then brought out to be eaten.

Although Moroccans still prepare giant pigeon pies (bstila) on special occasions, the Middle East today prefers smaller pies of which there are an enormous variety in all shapes and sizes and diversity of pastry and filling.

The great old English pies which contained a stag or a lamb or a stuffed kid surrounded by dozens of goslings have also fallen into oblivion along with the heavy oat and chestnut tarts, but the smaller ones are still traditional English picnic fare. Lately, easy transport and the trend towards lighter food have made the French-style open-faced tarts and flans the most popular. A good way to carry them is in their own pan or tin, covered with a large foil or other cover held together securely with masking tape. If the pan has a removable bottom, tape it to the sides and wrap in a plastic bag or foil.

The range of tarts is wide with most as good cold as they are hot or warm. The choice alone is difficult.

❧ Shortcrust pastry for tarts and quiches

Everyone has a favourite crust. I use the following as a base for most of my savoury tarts. It fills a 30 cm (12 in) tart tin.

In a large bowl work and rub 125 g (4 oz) unsalted butter into 250 g (½ lb) flour – plain white or a mixture of white and wholemeal sifted with ½ teaspoon of salt. (Strong flour is very good to use; it requires an extra 25 g (1 oz) butter.) Add 1 egg and just enough water by the tablespoonful for the dough to stick together (about 3-4). Do not work it any further and let it rest in a cool place for an hour.

Roll out the dough on a floured board with a floured rolling pin. Lift it gently by wrapping it over the rolling pin and let it drop and settle into a pie pan or tart tin which does not need to be buttered. Trim the edges with a knife.

Partially bake the pastry shell before filling: prick with a fork in several places; put a piece of foil or waxed paper over the dough and weight it down with dry beans to prevent it from puffing up.

Bake in a pre-heated 200 °C/400 °F/Gas 6 oven for 20 minutes. Then remove beans and paper, brush the inside of the shell with egg white to glaze it and prevent it from becoming soggy with the filling, and bake 5 minutes longer.

Use the same pastry as the lid for a pie. Brush with egg yolk for a warm brown glaze.

❧ An aubergine tart

A partially baked shortcrust pastry shell (pp.66-7), ³/₄ kg (1¹/₂ lb) aubergines, salt, a light vegetable oil, pepper, 1 medium tin of peeled tomatoes (400 g/14 oz), a few fresh basil leaves (finely chopped) or 1 tablespoon dried basil, a sprig of parsley (finely chopped), 3 eggs.

Slice the aubergines. Sprinkle with salt and let the juice disgorge for about an hour. Rinse and squeeze dry a few at a time. Fry in hot oil, turning over once until soft and nicely browned. Drain on absorbent paper. Spread over the pie shell.

Mash the tomatoes with a fork. Add herbs and seasoning and beat in the eggs. Pour over the aubergines and bake for 20-30 minutes in a 200°C/400°F/Gas 6 oven.

❧ A ratatouille tart

This is one of my favourites which I make differently every time. Make a ratatouille as described on pp.100-101. Fill a well-browned baked pastry shell (see pp.66-7) with it. Sprinkle generously with grated Gruyère, Mozzarella or matured Cheddar. Put in a hot oven until the cheese has melted.

❧ A courgette tart

A partially baked shortcrust pastry shell (see pp.66-7), ³/₄ kg (1¹/₂ lb) courgettes, 200 ml (7 fl oz) double cream (or a mixture with single cream), 3 eggs, salt and pepper to taste.

Trim, wash and slice the courgettes very thinly. Beat the eggs, add the cream and season with salt and pepper. Cover the pie shell with the courgettes and pour the cream and egg mixture over them. Bake in a 170°C/325°F/Gas 3 oven for 30-40 minutes. The courgettes will still be crisp.

~ Another courgette tart

A partially baked shortcrust pastry shell (see pp.66-7), 1 large onion, 4-5 tablespoons oil, 3/4 kg (1 1/2 lb) courgettes (thinly sliced), pepper, a pinch of nutmeg, 225 g (1/2 lb) matured Cheddar (coarsely grated).

Fry the onion in oil in a large pan until it is golden. Add the courgettes and fry, turning them constantly until they are soft. Season with pepper and nutmeg (no need of salt but you may like some). Spread this all over the pie shell and sprinkle on the cheese. Put it in a 200°C/ 400°F/Gas 6 oven for 20-30 minutes. This is good cold but better hot.

~ Pissaladière

This speciality of Nice owes much to neighbouring Italy. It is like an onion pizza but although it is traditionally made with bread dough, it is equally happy in a pastry shell.

For the filling: 1 kg (2 lb) onions chopped, 100 ml (4 fl oz) olive oil, 12 anchovy fillets, 20 stoned black olives, salt and pepper.

Cook the onions in the olive oil on low heat for about half an hour or longer until soft, but do not let them brown.
  Roll the bread dough into a large thin round and put it into an oiled tin or use a partially baked pastry shell (see pp.66-7). Spread the onions all over. Place the anchovies in a star and in between the rays place slices of tomatoes, black olives and garlic, or make a criss-cross pattern with the anchovies. Sprinkle with salt and pepper and a little oil and put in a 200°C/400°F/Gas 6 oven for 20 minutes. Then turn the heat down to 150°C/300°F/Gas 2 for another 20 minutes if you are using the bread dough.

Variation: Add 3 cloves of garlic, chopped, and 4 skinned and chopped tomatoes to the softened onions and cook further with the seasonings.

~ Quiche

Lorraine. Everyone knows this famous bacon tart with a cream and egg custard, but here it is as a reminder.
  Partially bake a pastry shell (see p.66-7). Arrange on it 6 slices of bacon, lightly cooked and cut into pieces. Beat 6 large eggs and stir in

½ litre (1 pint) double cream. Season with salt and pepper and a pinch of nutmeg and pour over the bacon in the partially baked pastry shell. Cook for 30 minutes in a 170°C/325°F/Gas 3 oven until it sets.

With onions. My own favourite comes from Alsace and is made as the one above with the following filling: soften 1½ kg (2¾ lb) finely chopped onions in 3 tablespoons of butter and a little salt. Beat 2 eggs with 3 egg yolks. Add 200 ml (7 fl oz) double cream, salt and pepper to taste and a pinch of nutmeg. Pour into the baked pie shell and bake in a 170°C/325°F/Gas 3 oven for 30-40 minutes.

A cheese filling. Beat 200 g (7 oz) cream cheese with 150 ml (¼ pint) double cream, one egg and the yolks of 3 others. Season to taste with salt and pepper, fill the pastry shell and bake for about half an hour in a 200°C/400°F/Gas 6 oven.

You may vary this by substituting grated Gruyère or Roquefort for the cream cheese.

❧ Mushroom tart

This creamy French tart makes a lovely first course to serve out in the garden. It is as good cold as it is hot.

To serve 8:

For the shortcrust pastry: 200 g (7 oz) flour, ½ teaspoon salt, 100 g (4 oz) unsalted softened butter, 1 egg, separated, about 1 tablespoon water.

For the creamy flan:

4 eggs, 200 ml (7 fl oz) milk, 200 ml (7 fl oz) double cream, ¼ teaspoon nutmeg, salt and pepper.

For the mushroom filling:

½ small onion, chopped, 3 tablespoons olive oil, 500 g (1 lb) mushrooms, sliced, salt and pepper.

Make the pastry by hand as described on pp.66-7 using only the yolk (keep the white aside) or put all the ingredients together in the food processor and blend briefly, then turn out and work lightly with your hand until the dough sticks together in a ball, adding a little water if necessary. Wrap in cling film and leave in a cool place for 1 hour.

For the flan, lightly beat the eggs in a bowl. Add the milk and cream, stir in the nutmeg, salt and pepper, and mix well.

In a large frying pan, fry the onion in the oil until soft, then add the mushrooms. Cook for about 10 minutes with a lid on, stirring and turning the mushrooms over, until they are tender and have degorged their juices and acquired a rich, intense flavour. Then cook with the lid off until the liquid has evaporated.

Press the pastry into a deep tart mould about 28 cm (11 in) in diameter. Using the palm of your hands, take lumps of dough and press very thinly round the bottom and edges of the mould. Brush the entire surface with egg white (you will need about 1/2 the egg white). Bake the pastry in a pre-heated 180°C/350°F/Gas 4 oven for about 15 minutes.

Let the pastry cool before spreading the mushrooms on top and pour the flan mixture all over. Bake at 180°C/350°F/Gas 4 for 35-40 minutes until the flan has set and is lightly browned.

❧ Jane Grigson's kipper flan

Serve this hot, straight from the oven.

Short pastry made with 175 g (6 oz) flour, 1 fat kipper (250 g/9 oz), 200 ml (8 fl oz) double cream of 100 ml (4 fl oz) each double and single, 3 eggs, 1 tablespoon French or German mustard, lemon juice, salt and pepper.

'Line a 21 cm (8½ in) tart tin with a removable base with the pastry. Prick all over and bake blind for 5 minutes until set but not browned. Meanwhile jug the kipper (pour boiling water over it, allow to soak 5 minutes and drain). Remove bones and skin and arrange pieces on the pastry case. Beat together the cream and eggs, add the mustard gradually to your taste. Season. Pour over the kippers and bake at Gas Mark 4, 180°C/350°F for 30-40 minutes, until the filling is golden brown and puffed up. Now quickly squeeze half a lemon over the flan.'

❧ Leek pie

3/4 kg (1½ lb) leeks, 3 tablespoons butter, 5 rashers of lean bacon, 2 eggs, 300 ml (½ pint) single cream, salt and pepper, a pinch of nutmeg, 1 egg yolk.

Carefully trim and wash the leeks. Chop them small and soften in the butter, stirring until just tender. Lightly fry the bacon in its own fat in another pan and cut it into small pieces.

Beat the eggs, stir in the cream and seasonings and pour over the leeks and bacon.

Pour into a pie pan and cover with a thinly rolled shortcrust (see pp.66-7). Brush the pastry lid with beaten egg yolk and bake at 150°C/300°F/Gas 2, for 30 minutes or until set and the crust brown.

৵ Jane Grigson's raised pie

The most traditional of English picnic fare.

'Make either a hot water dough, or shortcrust pastry, with half a kilo of flour, and other ingredients in proportion. Line a cake tin with a removable base, about 16 cm (6-7 in) in diameter, with three-quarters of the dough. Put the rest aside, for the lid.

'Cube a kilo (2 lb) boned meat – either shoulder of pork, or pie veal, or chicken cut from the bone. Mix it with 250 g (8 oz) cubed gammon or ham or bacon (essential for flavour and a nice pinkish colour). Add a finely chopped onion, salt, pepper, parsley, 1 teaspoon thyme, and 1 teaspoon anchovy essence.

'If you want to embellish the pork filling, prepare 3 peeled, cored, sliced eating apples, preferably Cox's, to layer in with the meat. An extra spicing of cinnamon, nutmeg and allspice is also a good idea.

'If you want to embellish the veal filling, hard-boil 4 eggs and shell them. Make the pie in a large loaf tin rather than a cake tin, and put the eggs in a line down the middle, so that they are completely encased in meat.

'When you fill the pastry, mound up the meat inside to support the lid nicely. Lay on the last of the pastry, pinching the edges together. Decorate the top and make a central hole. Brush over with beaten egg. Bake 30 minutes at mark 6, 200°C/400°F then lower the heat to mark 3, 160°C/325°F, for 1½ hours. Protect the lid if it becomes brown too soon, with a piece of foil or butter paper.

'As the pie cooks, make a jellied stock. For this put all the bones from the pie meat into a large pan, plus a pig's trotter or veal knuckle bone if you want a really firm set for the jelly. Not essential, but desirable. Add an onion, carrot, bouquet and water to cover generously. Boil for 2 hours, strain off and reduce by boiling to half a pint. Cool and chill, to be sure of the set. Gelatine should not be necessary.

'Cool the pie in its tin for an hour, then remove it. When it is cold, melt the jellied stock so that it is runny but not hot, and pour it into the pie through the centre hole, using a funnel. Leave until next day. It can be transported in the tin in which it was cooked. Take plenty of salads, lettuce, tomatoes, watercress, celery.'

⪧ Meat pie with an Arab flavour

This filling usually goes on top of a pizza-type dough rolled very thin. For taking out it is best to cover it with any type of pastry such as shortcrust (see pp.66-7) or puff (the commercial one will do).

500 g (1 lb) onions (finely chopped), oil, 700 g (1½ lb) lean lamb or beef (minced), 500 g (1 lb) fresh tomatoes, skinned and chopped, or a 400 g (14 oz) tin skinned tomatoes, 1 small (60 g/2¼ oz) tin tomato concentrate, 1 teaspoon sugar, ¾ teaspoon ground allspice, 1-2 tablespoons lemon juice, salt and black pepper, 3 tablespoons finely chopped parsley (optional), a pinch of cayenne pepper (optional).

Soften the onions in a little warm oil until they are transparent and have lost their water, taking care not to let them colour. Mix the meat, tomatoes and tomato concentrate in a large bowl. If you are using fresh tomatoes, get rid of as much of their juice and seeds as possible, and crush them to a pulp. If you are using a tin of tomatoes, drain them well. Add sugar, allspice and lemon juice, and season to taste with salt and pepper. Drain the onions of oil and add them to the meat mixture. Knead well by hand. Some people like to add a good bunch of finely chopped parsley and a little cayenne pepper as well.

Flatten into a pie tin or baking tray and cover with pastry. Bake in a 170°C/325°F/Gas 3 oven for about 45 minutes or longer, until the meat is done and the crust brown.

Another minced meat filling from the Middle Fast. Fry a large chopped onion in 2 tablespoons of oil until it is golden. Add 500 g (1 lb) minced beef, crush it with a fork and stir well. Add salt and pepper, ½ teaspoon of cinnamon and ½ teaspoon of allspice and cook until the meat changes colour. Moisten with 2 or 3 tablespoons of water and add a tablespoon of raisins or sultanas and 2 tablespoons of chopped walnuts.

⪧ Chicken pie of Moroccan inspiration

Prepare some shortcrust pastry with about 225 g (8 oz) flour and half this amount of butter (see pp.66-7). Boil a large chicken with 500 g

(1 lb) onions, grated, a good bunch of parsley, finely chopped, $1/2$ teaspoon each of cinnamon, allspice and ginger, salt and pepper to taste. Remove the chicken when the flesh is tender enough to fall off the bone. Reduce the stock to $1/4$ litre ($1/2$ pint). Add 8 eggs, lightly beaten with a fork, and cook on a very low flame, stirring constantly until creamy. Fry 125 g (4 oz) blanched almonds in a little oil or toast them under the grill until just golden. Chop or break them into coarse large pieces with a pestle and mortar.

Bone the chicken and cut into pieces. Stir into the egg mixture. Fill a pie dish or baking tray and cover with the rolled out pastry. Bake in a 170°C/325°F/Gas 3 oven for half an hour or until the pastry is cooked and brown. Sprinkle with cinnamon and castor sugar when it comes out of the oven.

For a filling using cooked chicken, soften a large chopped onion in 2 tablespoons of oil or butter. Add 250 g ($1/2$ lb) sliced mushrooms and cook for a minute or two. Make a stiff béchamel sauce with 5 tablespoons of butter, 5 tablespoons of flour and 300 ml ($1/2$ pint) milk. Season and warm the milk. In another pan melt the butter. Add the flour and stir until well blended. Add the milk gradually removing the pan from the heat each time and beating vigorously until smooth and creamy. Let it cool a little and stir in 2 eggs. Skin and bone the cooked chicken and cut it into small pieces. Mix everything together adding a few sprigs of parsley, finely chopped

Phylo pies with paper-thin pastry

All countries that have been under Ottoman rule make all manner of pies with a flour and water dough worked to a soft elasticity and stretched to paper thinness. It is sold here in Greek and Middle Eastern shops as phylo (filo) in 500 g (1 lb) packets of 24 sheets measuring around 30 x 46 cm (12 x 18 in). It makes a convenient wrapping for any sort of filling. Each country has its favourite traditional shapes, from large round pies and rolls, to triangles, cigars, nests and coils. The least fiddly and simplest to make and the easiest to keep hot on an outing are the long rolls common in Greece. Made in individual portions they are easy to hand out.

The secret of handling phylo is not to leave it exposed to air for long, as it will dry out and break easily. Keep it well covered in its cling film wrap. While you work, have all the cut pieces neatly piled. Cover them with a damp cloth if you have to leave them for more than a few minutes.

The meat and chicken fillings given on pp.72-3 can be used for phylo pies but a Greek one is especially appropriate.

On Easter Sunday and Monday on the islands picnics and family gatherings are held everywhere: in the mountains and by the sea or in yards under the shade of grape vines. Lambs are roasted on the spit and wine flows freely. After Mass the village priest stands holding the Cross at the door for everyone to kiss and people hold hands in a large circle which symbolizes the renewal of friendship. Long wooden trestle tables are set out in the church-yard and spread with crisp white table-cloths. Each family brings its own food and wine and passes some of it round. Pies are popular fare. After lunch seesaws and swings are put out for the children, there is backgammon and dancing, and jokes are exchanged.

Spanakopitta filled with spinach and cheese. Bread dough is sometimes used instead of phylo. Although Fetta cheese is used in Greece, cottage cheese will do very well.

1 kg (2 lb) fresh spinach or 500 g (1 lb) frozen, 3-4 tablespoons olive oil, 1 large onion (chopped), 225 g (½ lb) Fetta or cottage cheese, pepper (salt only with cottage cheese), a grating of nutmeg.

Wash the spinach remove large stems and drain and coarsely chop.

Fry the onion in the olive oil till golden. Add the spinach and cook in its own juice, stirring until it is just tender. Add the cheese and seasonings – hardly any salt is needed if you are using Fetta.

To make rolls, put two sheets of phylo together brushing each with melted butter. Put a good line of filling along one of the longer edges and roll up, folding the two ends into the roll as you go. One roll is usually enough for two people. Lay rolls on a greased baking tray and put in a pre-heated moderate 180°C/350°F/Gas 4 oven for about 45 minutes or until it is crisp and golden.

Cheese filling: Mix together 225 g (½ lb) cottage cheese and the same quantity of mashed Fetta or grated matured Cheddar and 2 eggs. Add pepper and a few sprigs of finely chopped parsley or mint.

To make an individual pie wrap up 2 or 3 tablespoons of filling in one sheet of phylo which has been brushed with melted butter, making sure that the packet is leak proof. A rectangular or square shape is simplest. Put in a moderate 180°C/350°F/Gas 4 oven for 30-45 minutes until nicely coloured.

໕ Sausage rolls

These are a tasty and elegant French version of our sausage rolls – *feuilletés de porc* – as good cold as they are hot. Use a good quality puff pastry – fresh or frozen.

Makes 8 large rolls: ¹/₂ a large onion chopped, a good bunch of flat-leaf parsley (4-5 tablespoons), 80 g (3 oz) parma ham or jambon de bayonne, 500 g (1 lb) minced pork, salt and pepper, 500 g (1 lb) puff pastry (defrosted if frozen), 1 egg yolk

For the filling, chop the onion and the parsley in the food processor. Add the ham, and chop finely. Then add the minced pork, salt and pepper and blend to a soft homogenous paste.

Cut the pastry into 4 rectangles in the width. Roll out the pastry as thinly as you can on a floured surface with a floured rolling pin. Then cut each of the sheets into 2 so as to have 8 rectangles about 20 cm (8 in) by 11 cm (4¹/₂ in).

Divide the pork filling into four large lumps. Take each lump and roll it into a long sausage shape, about 7 cm (6¹/₂ in) long. Place one in the middle of each pastry rectangle and roll up the pastry around it, overlapping a little. Moisten one of the long edges with a drop of water, using your finger, so that the pastry sticks together, sealing the rolls. Press the ends to seal them and trim to have clean, straight ends.

Line a baking sheet with foil and brush with oil. Place the rolls on it side by side, sealed-side down. Brush the top of each roll with the egg yolk mixed with a teaspoon of water and bake in a preheated, 180°C/350°F/Gas 4 oven for 35 minutes until golden.

COLD MEATS

With all the miseries brought by the rigours of the English climate, it is not surprising that indoor picnics have sometimes been the most successful, as this one, described by William Hickey in his *Memoirs* (edited by Peter Quennell, 1960), seems to have been.

> The coronation of His present Majesty [George III] being fixed for the month of September, my father determined that all his family should be present at the ceremony. He therefore engaged one of the nunneries, as they are called, in Westminster Abbey, for which he paid fifty guineas. They are situated at the head of the great columns that support the roof, and command an admirable view of the whole interior of the building. Upon this occasion they were divided off by wooden partitions, each having a separate entrance with lock and key to the door, with ease holding a dozen persons. Provisions, consisting of cold fowls, ham, tongues, different meat pies, wines, and liquors of various sorts were sent to the apartment the day before, and two servants were allowed to attend. Our party consisted of my father, mother, brother Joseph, sister Mary, myself, Mr and Miss Isaacs, Miss Thomas, her brother (all Irish), my uncle and aunt Boulton, and their eldest daughter. . . .
>
> It was past seven in the morning before we reached the Abbey, which having once entered, we proceeded to our box without further impediment, Dr Markham having given us tickets which allowed our passing by a private staircase, and avoiding the immense crowd that was within. We found a hot and comfortable breakfast ready, which I enjoyed, and proved highly refreshing to us all; after which some of our party determined to take a nap in their chairs, whilst I, who was well acquainted with every creek and corner of the Abbey, amused myself running about the long gallery until noon, when notice having been given that the procession had begun to move, I resumed my seat.

Exactly at one they entered the Abbey, and we had a capital view of the whole ceremony. Their Majesties (the King having previously married), being crowned, the Archbishop of Canterbury mounted the pulpit to deliver the sermon; and, as many thousands were out of the possibility of hearing a single syllable, they took that opportunity to eat their meal when the general clattering of knives, forks, plates, and glasses that ensued, produced a most ridiculous effect, and a universal burst of laughter followed. The sermon being concluded, the anthem was sung by a numerous band of the first performers in the kingdom, and certainly was the finest thing I had ever heard.

?& Great roasts

Nothing can be simpler to take out than a roast prepared the day before. Cooked (not overcooked) in a way that retains its flavour and moisture it is as good cold as hot. Let the meat stand and cool down gradually. Either take a very sharp carving knife and a chopping board to slice it on the spot or slice it thinly beforehand and carefully wrap the reassembled joint so that it does not dry out.

Tastefully presented with vegetable garnishes a simple meat platter can look very grand.

Arrange slices round a large serving platter, with cold vegetables or a salad in the centre, or garnish with olives, pickled cucumber and radishes. To accompany a fine-flavoured meat serve a good cold sauce or a fruity chutney (see pp.239-40) and a loaf of bread. If you can heat it up serve a garlic or anchovy one. A variety of sauces good with beef, pork, lamb and veal are given on pp.44-53.

?& Flavouring the roast

You may like to try some embellishments of flavour which become more pronounced when cold.

Beef. A coating of mustard and oil suits it very well. Pieces of anchovy may be pushed into a few incisions made with a sharp pointed knife.

Lamb. Make a few incisions with a sharp knife into a leg or shoulder and press into them slivers from 2 or more cloves of garlic, squeezing a mint leaf in with them. Or you can make a paste with a mixture of crushed garlic and rosemary, thyme or marjoram and press it into the cuts.

Lamb also goes particularly well with sharp fruits. Push some dried apricots which have been previously soaked or some sour cherries into the joint in the same way.

A Moroccan way is to press a mixture of salt, pepper, cinnamon and grated onion under the skin. Sometimes fresh grated ginger and chopped coriander leaves are added. Another is to rub the meat with a mixture of paprika, cumin, crushed cloves of garlic, salt and pepper. The meat is overcooked very slowly until it can be pulled off easily with the fingers.

Pork. Various dried fruits give pork a delicious flavour and texture. Use dried figs, raisins and prunes alone or together. Soak them in water (cognac makes it very special) and press them whole, chopped or mashed into deep incisions, with salt and pepper, crushed or slivered garlic and chopped herbs such as parsley and thyme.

Sami Zubaida, who cooks pork very well, sometimes inserts juniper berries or thin slivers of fresh ginger and star aniseed in his large joints.

Veal should be larded for roasting as it tends to be dry. Press a little dried thyme and grated lemon rind into the flesh through incisions; for a bit of fantasy raisins or sultanas can be pushed in behind them.

All meats are improved by steeping in a wine or cider marinade but for most of us that is an extravagance.

You may like to have a joint boned by the butcher. In that case lay the meat skin side down, remove excess layers of fat and spread with a fruity sauce (see pp.51-2) or a garlic and herb mixture before you roll it up and tie or skewer it for roasting.

For a tasty Italian note insert slices of cheese such as Gruyère or Fetta in the pockets of the roll.

❧ Cold tongue

Buy a salted tongue (it is not usually too salted but if it is, leave it to soak for an hour in two changes of cold water). Wash and put in a large pan. Cover with cold water, bring to the boil and skim well. Add a few vegetables – carrot, celery stalks, onion, turnip, all cut up; parsley stalks, a bay leaf and a few peppercorns. Simmer for about 3 hours until the bones come away easily. Cool in the liquid. It is easier to skin the tongue while still a bit warm. Trim away some of the root, removing the bones. Press into a round dish or tin and cover with its own liquid. Cover well with foil and press it down with a weight. Leave overnight.

Cut it up just before serving and serve with Cumberland sauce (see pp.52-3).

❧ Meat salads

With meat salads you can feed many people relatively cheaply and at the same time produce an admirable party dish. The meat is best slowly boiled until tender (see below), but you may also use a left-over roast.

Cut in small pieces into a bowl. Add chopped spring onions and plenty of parsley, a few capers if you like and thin slices of pickled cucumber. Season generously with a vinaigrette (pp.44-5).

For a meal in itself, toss in some boiled new potatoes, cut into slices, quartered hard-boiled eggs, a few olives, radishes, whatever you like.

❧ Jellied meats

Moist boiled meats served in their own jelly, or one made with a calf's foot or pig's trotter, are a delicious alternative to roasts. Use lean boneless cuts. Cook the day before and slice ready for serving into a box with the jelly poured over it. Keep as cool as possible.

Jellied pork. Cover a joint with wine or water. Put in a pig's trotter, which has been well cleaned and blanched for 10 minutes to get rid of the scum. Add salt and pepper, a sprig of parsley and 2 bay leaves. Simmer until the meat is tender. Discard the skin and bones from the foot and leave the meat to cool in the stock. Then chill. To serve, scrape the fat from the top, slice the meat, chop the jellied stock finely and arrange it around the meat.

Jellied veal. A variety of boneless cuts may be used – leg or fillet, loin or shoulder. Turn in 2 tablespoons of oil in a heavy saucepan until it is lightly coloured. Add a well scrubbed calf's foot which has been cut in half and blanched in boiling water for 10 minutes to remove the scum. Cover with wine (Madeira or a little cognac for a grand occasion) or water. Add salt and pepper, 2 bay leaves, a sprig of parsley, a little thyme, 2 cloves of garlic, finely chopped, 2 fillets of anchovy (optional), a slice of lemon, 2 chopped onions, and 2 chopped carrots. Cook slowly for 3 hours until the meat is very tender, adding water if necessary. Take out the meat, slice and arrange it in a bowl or mould. Remove the skin and bones from the foot, add the bits of meat and the strained jellied stock. Chill in the refrigerator.

In Egypt we used to flavour the meat with lemon (half to a whole one), a teaspoon of turmeric which gave it a golden colour and 2 crushed cloves of garlic. We used no wine.

Jellied beef (boeuf à la mode en gelée). Brown a 1½-2 kg (3-4 lb) joint of beef, with the fat removed, in a little oil in a large saucepan. Add half or a whole bottle of red or dry white wine, and enough water to cover, 2 tablespoons of brandy, a dozen or more small button onions, 4 carrots sliced, 4 celery stalks, also sliced, 2 cloves of garlic, chopped, 2 bay leaves, 1 teaspoon of thyme, a few parsley stalks, 6 cloves, and salt and pepper.

In another pan, bring to the boil 2 well-scrubbed calf's feet and simmer for 10 minutes to remove the scum. Then drain and put near the meat in the saucepan.

Cook at a very slow simmer for 3-4 hours until the meat is very tender, adding water to keep it covered. Remove the calf's feet and parsley stalks. Slice the meat into a plastic box for carrying to the picnic, pour the sauce over it and chill. When it has set scrape off the fat which has formed at the top with a spoon and clean off what is left with a paper towel.

To serve, turn out and garnish with parsley, watercress or young lettuce leaves. The meat is kept tender and moist by the jellied stock.

❧ Meat loaf

Most countries have a version of the meat loaf, an all time picnic favourite, but Italy has the greatest variety. One that came early into my life was an Italian polpetone made by our Yugoslav nanny, Maria. It is nicer cold than hot.

700 g (1½ lb) lean beef or veal (minced), 2 slices of white bread with crusts removed, 1 onion (finely chopped or grated), 1 egg, 1 bunch of parsley (finely chopped), 1 teaspoon ground allspice or a pinch of cinnamon and a pinch of nutmeg, salt and pepper, 3 shelled hard-boiled eggs, flour.

Work the minced meat to a smooth paste with your hands or pound it with a pestle and mortar. Soak the bread in water and squeeze dry; add the onion, the egg, lightly beaten, the parsley, spices and seasoning. Roll the hard-boiled eggs in a little flour so that the meat sticks better to them. Either divide the meat mixture in three and pat some round each egg individually or make one long roll with the eggs embedded in it in a row. Pat into a solid compact loaf or loaves and wrap in well-oiled sheets of foil. Bake for 45-60 minutes in a medium 180°C/350°F/Gas 4 oven. Open the wrapping for the last 10 minutes to let the meat colour.

In the meantime make a tomato sauce: fry an onion in 2 tablespoons of oil. When it is brown, add 2 crushed cloves of garlic, then a small tin of tomato purée, ¼ litre (½ pint) water, a bay leaf, a few celery leaves, salt and pepper. Simmer gently for at least 20 minutes.

Let the meat cool down before cutting it into thick slices or it will break. Use a sharp knife very carefully. Put the slices together again in a box and cover with sauce. This is best done the day before serving.

Variations: Italians like to add grated Parmesan (about 3 tablespoons) and 2 or 3 slices of chopped ham and they may simmer the rolls in wine.

A Middle Eastern version is with a handful of fried pine nuts and a few sultanas worked in with the meat.

❧ A polpetone from Italy

Like the previous one, this loaf may be stuffed with hard-boiled eggs, but it is simpler and just as good without. You can always serve the eggs separately with it.

700 g (1½ lb) minced veal, 1 large onion (finely chopped), 500 g (1 lb) fresh spinach cooked in its own juice, or 225 g (½ lb) frozen (thawed and finely chopped), 75 g (3 oz) Gruyère (grated), salt and pepper, 2 eggs, 2 slices of bread, crusts removed, soaked and squeezed dry.

Mix all the ingredients together working them to a paste with your hands. Press into a buttered terrine and cook in a medium 170°C/325°F/Gas 3 oven for 1 hour.

Variation: Add 2 big handfuls of cooked rice to the mixture (as well as the bread).

❧ Lamb cooked in foil – a Greek idea

To use your hot box (see p.286) for meat, there is no better meal than the Greek lamb cooked with cheese. Season individual portions of lean meat (such as a good thick slice from the leg) with salt and pepper and wrap up with a slice of Fetta or Kefalotiri cheese in oiled aluminium foil, closing the packets tightly. Cook gently in a medium oven for at least an hour, until the meat is very tender. Put the packets as they are, straight into the hot box.

My brother brought back an exquisite version of this dish, made with vine leaves, from a recent visit to Athens. I have tried it with leaves from my neighbour's garden and matured Cheddar. If you do not have access to fresh leaves you may use those in brine which need soaking in many changes of water to remove the excess salt. Simply poach fresh ones for about a minute, until they change colour and become limp. Line the foil with leaves to cover the meat and cheese.

Variation: An alternative flavouring comes with a sprinkling of dried or fresh chopped mint and if you like a touch of crushed garlic.

If you do not have a hot box you can always heat up the packets over a fire at the picnic.

❧ Meat balls with nuts and raisins

However humble the status of meat balls, they are the perfect food to hand out when the company is large. These are rather special and very tasty.

Into a large bowl, put 1 kg (2 lb) lean lamb, beef or veal, or a mixture of these, 1 large onion, grated, 2 lightly beaten eggs, 2 tablespoons of raisins or sultanas moistened in a little water, a handful of walnuts, coarsely chopped, and a small bunch of parsley, finely chopped. Season to taste with salt and pepper and 1 teaspoon each of ground cinnamon and allspice.

Knead well with your hands to achieve a smooth texture which holds well together. Roll into balls the size of a walnut. Fry gently in a little oil, shaking the frying pan and turning them over until they are coloured all over and cooked through. You will need to do them in batches. Drain on absorbent paper. Pack them hot or cold.

❧ French pork fricadelles

Combine and knead to a smooth paste: 1/2 kg (1 lb) minced pork, 1 large potato, boiled and mashed, 2 cloves of garlic, crushed, 2 tablespoons finely chopped parsley, 3 tablespoons grated Parmesan and 2 lightly beaten eggs, seasoning to taste with salt and pepper. Shape into flat round cakes, dip in flour and gently fry in oil till brown, turning over once. Drain on kitchen rolls before packing hot or cold.

❧ Coppiette

Islam may be responsible for the pine nuts and raisins in these Roman style rissoles.

Mix and knead together in a large bowl: 1 kg (2 lb) lean minced beef, 3 slices of ham, finely chopped, 2 cloves of garlic, crushed, a few sprigs of parsley, finely chopped, a sprinkling of marjoram, a grating of nutmeg, 2 eggs, lightly beaten, 2 thin slices of bread, crusts removed, soaked in milk and squeezed dry, 2 tablespoons sultanas, 2 tablespoons pine nuts (they may be lightly fried first), 4 tablespoons grated Parmesan, salt and pepper.

Shape into cakes or balls, roll in fine breadcrumbs and deep fry in oil till crisp and golden brown, turning over once. Drain on absorbent paper. Take hot or cold.

❧ Cold chicken

For chicken to be good cold it is especially important for it to have been cooked in a way that preserves its moistness. Cooking it in foil, in its own juice, is a particularly simple method.

Place the cleaned chicken on a large sheet of aluminium foil. Rub the bird with butter or oil, and wrap it up with the aromatics of your choice into a well-sealed parcel. I put an onion in the cavity and sprinkle the bird liberally with lemon juice, crushed garlic, fresh tarragon when I have it, otherwise parsley or coriander leaves, sometimes rosemary from my garden, and salt and pepper.

Cook the bird at a high temperature, 220°C/425°F/Gas 7, for 1 hour. Open the wrapping for the last 10 minutes if you like it brown. Close it again to take on your picnic.

Variation: Otherwise, braised or boiled chicken is better than chicken roasted without the foil, which is too dry. Simmer gently in water to cover with an onion stuck with cloves, a carrot, 2 bay leaves, a sprig of parsley, celery leaves, salt and pepper, for an hour or until the juices are no longer pink. Let the chicken cool in its own stock.

You will find sauces to go with cold chicken on pp.44-5, 48-9, 51-2, 226-7.

🍂 Chicken salads

Salads will make a chicken go further; here are some suggestions to be made up with a chicken poached in a flavoursome stock.

Remove skin and bones and cut the meat into strips. Toss in a vinaigrette (see pp.44-5) or one which has been mixed with fresh or sour cream.

Or dress with a light mayonnaise (see pp.46-7), to which may be added coarsely ground walnuts, almonds or hazelnuts. Garnish before serving with sliced or quartered hard-boiled eggs and some chopped parsley. You may like to arrange the salad on a bed of young cos lettuce leaves.

Another excellent salad is chicken mixed with a small handful of toasted split almonds and coarsely chopped walnuts, a small bunch of grapes, seeds removed, 2 finely sliced apples, dipped in lemon juice, and a bunch of cress. Dress with fresh cream whipped with salt and pepper to taste, and flavoured if you like with a touch of crushed garlic.

COLD FISH AND SEAFOOD

Salmon and salmon trout are not the only fish which are good eaten cold. Sea bream, sea bass, cod, haddock, halibut, turbot, indeed most seafood make excellent cold dishes.

It is not often practical to take a large fish whole on a picnic; the answer is to skin and cut it into pieces when it is already cooked, for it is best cooked whole.

Poach the fish in a stock made by simmering water (with an equal quantity of dry white wine or cider if you like) for half an hour with a carrot, an onion, 2 sticks of celery, all chopped, a few parsley stalks, 2 bay leaves, a sprinkling of thyme, salt and a few peppercorns and a tablespoon of vinegar or a squeeze of lemon. Let it become warm before you put in your fish, then slowly bring it to a simmer again. The timing depends on the size of the fish; cook until the flesh is translucent and flaky. It is best to undercook for the fish continues to cook in the broth off the fire.

It is better still to bake your fish in foil with a moistening of oil or white wine and seasonings. In this way, flavour and texture are at their very best. Do not overcook. You can tell when it is done when it begins to flake.

All the fish needs is a good sauce, many of which are given in the section on sauces (see pp.44-53).

ᝌ Fish and seafood salads

Not many people realize the pleasure and attractiveness of a salad made from the produce of the sea. It is one of the best and simplest first courses to offer.

Any firm flaking fish can be used alone or together with any of the following: cooked crab, prawns, scallops, mussels. Cook as directed in the preceding recipe and dress generously with a vinaigrette and plenty of finely chopped fresh herbs and spring onion.

Variations: A light mayonnaise with whipped cream or sour cream, or the creams alone with fresh herbs, can be used instead of the vinaigrette.

My favourite salad is a version of this one, mixed with fluffy rice. The combination of fish, white rice and greenery is as pleasing to the eye as to the palate. I like it just as it is but it is also pleasant combined with finely chopped raw vegetables such as tomatoes, olives, peppers, cucumber and celery.

For the rice: Use long-grain rice, basmati or patna, soaked in boiling water and salt first, to remove the starchy dust which may cause it to become sticky, then rinsed in cold running water. Cook in any way you like. My way is to boil the rice in plenty of salted boiling water for only 4 minutes until it is still a little hard. Drain in a sieve and put back into the same pan with a few tablespoons of a light oil. Return it to the heat with the lid on for it to continue to cook in its own steam.

❧ Fish salad with roasted tomatoes and olives

This is good for an outdoor buffet. The tomatoes have an incredible sweet fruity taste. They take hours to cook slowly in the oven, but they can be prepared days in advance and kept in the refrigerator. Use any firm white fish such as monkfish, cod or haddock.

12 tomatoes each weighing about 100g (4 oz), 9 tablespoons olive oil, 2-3 teaspoons sugar, 1 kg (2 lb) fish fillets (skinned), salt, water and white wine (optional), 1½ tablespoons sherry or cider vinegar, 1½ tablespoons balsamic vinegar, pepper, a dozen or more black olives (optional).

Cut the tomatoes in half. Lay a sheet of foil on a baking sheet and brush with olive oil. Arrange the tomatoes on top, side by side, cut side up. Sprinkle them with sugar (use your fingers to drop a pinch over each). Use the brush to sprinkle them with about 2 tablespoons of oil. Bake at 150°C/300°F/Gas 2 for 4½ hours until they are shrivelled and shrunken.

Poach the fish in salted water or in a half and half mixture of dry white wine and water on a slow simmer for 5-10 minutes, until it is only just cooked and when the flesh begins to flake and is just becoming translucent.

For the dressing, mix 6 tablespoons of olive oil with the sherry or cider vinegar and balsamic vinegar. Pour over the fish and mix gently, breaking it up into pieces.

Serve the fish surrounded by the roasted tomatoes and sprinkled, if you like, with olives.

૨ Fish and potato salad

Use a firm white fish such as cod, haddock, halibut or monkfish.

750g (1½ lb) new potatoes (washed), 750 g (1½ lb) fish fillets, olive oil, 12 spring onions, chopped, a bunch of chives, chopped, the juice of 1½ lemons, 6 tablespoons olive oil, 1 garlic clove, crushed, salt and pepper

Boil the potatoes in salted water till tender, then drain and cut them into slices in a bowl. Pan fry the fish in about 2 tablespoons olive oil for 8-10 minutes or until it begins to flake, turning it over once.

Break up the fish into large flakes and add to the potatoes with the spring onions and chives. Make a dressing with about 6 tablespoons olive oil, the lemon juice, garlic, salt and pepper. Pour over the salad and mix gently.

૨ Polynesian raw fish salad with coconut cream

Lemon juice 'cooks' the fish, and coconut cream gives it a very delicate flavour .

For 4, cut a 500g (1 lb) very fresh skinned fish fillet into bite-sized pieces (you can use any fish). Cover with the juice of 2 lemons and leave in the refrigerator for 2 hours. Drain the juices away in a colander and dress the fish with 100-150 ml (3½-5 fl oz) coconut cream and a little salt and pepper. Refrigerate before serving sprinkled with 6 finely sliced spring onions and garnished with ½ a sliced cucumber.

❧ Poached fish with fresh tomato dressing

Use any white firm fish. Accompany with potatoes mashed with olive oil and chopped parsley (see pp.99-100).

To serve 4:

150 ml (5 fl oz) dry white wine, 150 ml (5 fl oz) water, salt and pepper, 4 fish steaks or pieces of fillet.

For the dressing:

3 tomatoes, skinned and finely chopped, 1 small red chillies, very finely chopped, 1 garlic clove, crushed, the juice of a 2½ cm (1 inch) piece of ginger, grated or crushed in a garlic press, ½ a red onion, finely chopped, the juice of ½ a lime or lemon, 4 tablespoons extra-virgin olive oil, salt and pepper, 1 teaspoon sugar

Prepare the dressing first, mixing all the ingredients to taste.
    Put the wine and water in a pan wide enough to contain the fish in one layer. Add salt and pepper, bring to the boil, and lower the heat to a simmer. Put in the fish and simmer gently for 3-8 minutes, depending on the thickness and type of fish, until the flesh flakes when you cut into it with the point of a knife. Lift the fish out carefully and serve, hot or cold, with the cold dressing poured over.

❧ An unusual dressing for prawns

For 225 g (½ lb) prawns, mix the juice of half a lemon, 1 teaspoon of anchovy paste, 2 tablespoons of water, 2 tablespoons of olive oil and ½ teaspoon of English mustard. Toss the prawns in this and serve on a plate with a border of radish and cucumber slices.

❧ Fish terrine

This is another dish like the fish mousse on pp.21-2 which is made easy by the use of a food processor.

You may use salmon for the forcemeat, alternating with layers of fillet of sole or trout; or a cheaper fish such as whiting for the forcemeat between slices of salmon. The fillets remain slightly undercooked very much to my taste, but you may prefer to poach them first.

Here is the basic principle for a forcemeat made with bread and whiting. Chop and pound 500 g (1 lb) fish, skin and bones removed. Add 120 g (1/4 lb) butter, 120 g (1/4 lb) white bread, crusts removed and soaked in milk. Pound or blend in a food processor with 3 whole eggs, salt and pepper and a pinch of spices (mace, nutmeg or allspice) to a smooth paste. Add a small bunch of finely chopped herbs (tarragon, chervil or parsley) the juice of half a lemon and 1 crushed clove of garlic, and blend well.

Remove skin and bones from 1/2 kg (1 lb) salmon, sole or trout, and cut into 1 cm (1/2 in) slices. Spread a layer of forcemeat at the bottom of a buttered terrine. Cover with a layer of salmon slices seasoned with salt and pepper and continue alternating layers, finishing with a layer of forcemeat. Cover with a buttered greaseproof paper and the lid and put in a pan of water in a moderate 200°C/400°F/Gas 6 oven for 3/4-1 hour, until the top feels springy.

To keep a long time, cover when it is done with a layer of melted clarified butter. Otherwise make a jellied broth with fish cuttings and bones. Reduce and flavour if you like with dry white wine. Stiffen if necessary with gelatine (see *aspic* p.51). When it has cooled, pour over the terrine by degrees as much as the contents will absorb. This gives the terrine a fine texture. Cool overnight in the refrigerator.

For an alternative presentation, cover the terrine with a firm pie crust (see pp.66-7). Decorate with pastry leaves and make a hole for the jelly. Serve with a cucumber salad.

❧ A kipper or crab mousse

Poach 4 fat kippers in boiling water for 5 minutes. Keep 200 ml (7 fl oz) of the liquid and dissolve 1 tablespoon of gelatine in it. Bone the kippers and leave them to cool. Put them in an electric blender with the slightly cooled jelly. Add a pinch of cayenne and 200 ml (7 fl oz) double cream and if you like 4-5 tablespoons of sherry or the juice of 1 lemon. Blend until smooth and pour into a wetted mould. Leave to set.

Serve with fresh wholemeal bread or toast.

A good-sized crab may be used instead of the kippers. Remove all the flesh and put it through the blender.

Serve with a cucumber salad.

ࣷ Smoked mackerel pâté

Other smoked fish may be used such as buckling. Smoked trout is expensive but particularly good. Kippers have to be immersed for a few minutes in boiling water.

2 fleshy moist smoked mackerel, 150 ml (¹/₄ pint) sour cream, 150 g (5 oz) cream cheese or cottage cheese, juice of half a large lemon, salt and pepper.

Remove skin and bones and flake into a blender. Add sour cream and cheese (sieved if the cottage variety) and blend until smooth. Season to taste with salt and pepper and lemon juice. You may need to do the blending in batches. Press into a pot. I once covered the pâté with a layer of gooseberry sauce (see pp.51-2) with magnificent results.
Serve with thin toast or brown bread and lemon wedges.

ࣷ Fried fish

Cold fried fish often appears in old continental cookery books named 'à la juive'. This is how it is prepared here with any of the following: haddock, cod, hake, plaice or sole. Depending on the fish it may be filleted or cut into thick steaks. Wash and drain the fish and season with salt and pepper. Dip in beaten egg yolk and then into fine matzo meal. Fry in deep hot oil, turning over once until both sides are a golden brown. Drain on absorbent paper.

My mother-in-law reverses the process. She covers the fish in breadcrumbs first and then dips in lightly beaten egg.
Serve with lemon wedges.

ࣷ Goujons

Little fried strips of fish (mock gudgeon) fried the day before, make a lovely communal dish, piled on to a plate garnished with parsley and with a bowl of sauce such as aïoli (see pp.47-8) to dip into.
It is best to use sole, but plaice and other flat fish are also good. Cut into strips and dry on paper towels. If you are going to serve right away it is enough to dip in flour or in egg and breadcrumbs. If the fish is going to wait for several hours or a day, it will stay firm and crisp if you

dip in a light batter made in the following way. Mix 125 g (4 oz) flour, 1 tablespoon of oil, an egg yolk and 150 ml (¼ pint) water, beating well. Leave for an hour, then fold in the stiffly beaten egg white. Deep fry in very hot oil, keeping each piece of fish separate until crisp and golden. Drain on absorbent paper and keep covered in the refrigerator.

❧ Fish fritters

In the countries around the Mediterranean they like to use salt cod, desalted and freshened, but any kind of fish may be used, fresh or smoked. Fritters take time to shape and to fry, but they are lovely when they are done, and easy to hand out. You can keep them hot in an insulated box but they are also good cold. Where necessary soak or poach the fish first. Skin, bone and flake, then chop, mince or shred as finely as possible.

For the binding: a stiff béchamel sauce or soaked bread are sometimes used but mashed potato gives a much better texture. For ½ kg (1 lb) fish use ½ kg (1 lb) potatoes. Boil in water or milk; mash thoroughly and add to the fish with salt and pepper, 2 lightly beaten eggs, 1 crushed clove of garlic, a little finely chopped parsley and 1 or 2 spring onions, also finely chopped.

Knead well together and shape into small flat round cakes. Roll in flour and fry in hot oil till golden.

For a crisper shell dip in beaten egg then in breadcrumbs before frying.

Variation: Add 2 or 3 tablespoons of grated Parmesan or another sharp cheese.

VEGETABLES AND SALADS

There is no more pleasant way to celebrate the summer months than with the season's fresh vegetables and those from abroad to add variety. Have them raw or lightly cooked and still crisp, to preserve their natural taste and appearance. No picnic should be without vegetables and the more there are the better, especially when they are in the form of a salad. Even Brillat-Savarin who had not much time for vegetables made an exception for salad which: 'freshens without enfeebling and fortifies without irritating'.

❧ Crudités
(raw and cooked vegetables in a vinaigrette dressing)

The French have a most alluring way of serving up all manner of raw and cooked vegetables as an hors d'oeuvre, each vegetable arriving singly in its own dish or in an assortment arranged on a large plate. It makes a regal side dish.

Prepare a selection of these fresh salads with an eye on harmony of taste, colour and texture, with a fruit or two as a pleasant surprise. Dress them in advance and carry each vegetable in a separate polythene bag ready to arrange when it is time to eat.

Radishes. Clean and wash in cold water. Serve alone with bread and butter and salt, or as part of an arrangement.

Cucumbers. Peel and slice very thinly or cut in longish thin sticks. Salt generously and leave in a strainer to allow the juices to drain away for at least an hour before serving. If the cucumber is still salty, rinse with a little cold water. Dress with a vinaigrette. You may replace the vinegar with lemon juice and add a few tablespoons of fresh cream or sour cream. Sprinkle with fresh chopped chives, chervil and tarragon, whichever is available. Or make a cream dressing without oil: beat 3 parts single cream with 1 part lemon juice, adding salt and pepper to taste.

Tomatoes. Wash and cut into slices (do not peel). Toss in a vinaigrette dressing. Sprinkle with finely chopped or grated onion or some chopped spring onion, parsley and when available basil and tarragon. Some people like to add a little crushed garlic.

Marinated mushrooms. Wash well. Trim off a thin slice from the earth-covered ends. Leave them raw or blanch them first for a minute in lemon acidulated salt water. Marinate for at least an hour in a vinaigrette with a few finely chopped spring onions or a little crushed garlic, plenty of finely chopped parsley, a little thyme and a crumbled bay leaf. You may like to use lemon juice instead of vinegar.

Carrots. Old carrots are tastiest. Scrape off the skin and grate. Stir in a vinaigrette made with lemon instead of vinegar and add a little sugar to taste, usually about a teaspoon for 3 medium carrots. Add finely chopped fresh parsley and any fresh herbs available: chives, chervil, tarragon or the feathery fennel leaves. Dried mint crumbled on to the carrots gives them an especially fresh taste.

Red or white cabbage. Slice very thinly or grate and season with a sharp vinaigrette. You may also sprinkle with salt and leave to lose their water and soften in a strainer for up to 4 hours before dressing.

Cauliflower. I like them raw, the flowerets thinly sliced and macerated in a vinaigrette for at least an hour before serving.
   Another way is to break into flowerets and boil them in salted water for a few minutes until only slightly tender but not too soft and dress with a vinaigrette and chopped herbs or with 2 tablespoons of fresh cream, beaten well, 1 tablespoon of French mustard and 1 tablespoon of finely chopped fresh tarragon, chervil or chives. Mayonnaise also makes a good dressing. Sprinkle if you like with slivered or chopped almonds.

Avocado. Peel and cut in half to remove the stone. Slice and dress with a vinaigrette or fresh cream beaten with lemon juice, salt and freshly ground black pepper.

Melon. Remove the rind and cut the melon into cubes. Serve as it is or dress with a vinaigrette or with port.

Grapefruit. Peel the skin with a sharp knife, removing all the pith. Cut into slices then into pieces. Sprinkle with sugar and a few drops of sherry.

Oranges. Peel the skin off with a sharp knife and remove all the pith. Cut the fruits into thin slices and sprinkle with cinnamon just before serving. This is also excellent mixed with a large bunch of watercress and dressed in a vinaigrette sauce.

Beetroot. Boil them in their skins till just tender. Peel while still hot and dress with a vinaigrette made with lemon juice and a generous amount of sugar to taste. You may also add a good squeeze of orange juice. Or dress with fresh cream beaten with a touch of French mustard, a little lemon juice, salt and pepper.

Asparagus. Pour over them a well-flavoured vinaigrette with a little finely chopped gherkin or blanched toasted almonds. Alternatively use 1 tablespoon of vinegar and 4 tablespoons of fresh cream.

Pears. Peel and slice some firm pears – I prefer Conference. Season with sugar, lemon and chopped fresh mint.

Fennel. Remove the outer leaves. Cut into thick slices and dress with oil and lemon, salt and pepper.

Green or red peppers. Turn under the grill or over a flame until the skin becomes blistered and charred. Peel or rub off the skin. Core and seed and slice the soft mellowed flesh into fairly wide ribbons. Dress with a well-flavoured vinaigrette. Sprinkle with chopped parsley and a little crushed garlic if you like.

You may like to serve this pepper salad mixed with tomatoes or with anchovy fillets.

Celeriac. Peel, wash and shred the raw celeriac for 'céleri-rave remoulade'. Cover with water and a little lemon juice to prevent discolouration. Blanch for 2 minutes in well-salted boiling water and drain well. Mix with mayonnaise or fresh cream flavoured with a little lemon juice and French mustard (1 tablespoon for 200 ml/7 fl oz cream).

In Provence the grated celeriac is fried in oil with chopped onions and a little garlic until it is just coloured. It is served cold with a vinegar, salt and pepper dressing, mixed with chopped anchovy, black olives and capers and a sprinkling of chopped parsley.

Celery. Separate the sticks so as to wash off the earth lodged deep between them and serve with salt.

Jerusalem artichokes. Peel and boil in salted water until barely tender. Drain, slice and dress with a mustardy vinaigrette, plenty of chopped parsley and a little crushed garlic.

Aubergine in vinegar. Dice. Salt and leave to stand until they lose their juice. Fry in a pan in half a glass of olive or light vegetable oil with a little crushed garlic. When they are cooked and lightly coloured, add 1 tablespoon of sugar and 2 tablespoons of vinegar. Cook for a further 5 minutes. Allow to cool.

Green runner beans: Peel the beans by breaking the ends off with your fingers and pulling off the tough thread which surrounds them. Wash and plunge into salted boiling water and boil vigorously until just tender. Drain and season while still hot with a vinaigrette sauce and chopped parsley. You may also like to sprinkle with a little finely chopped Spanish onion.

It is good with flaked tuna from a tin or strips of herring.

Lettuce and green leaf salads

Whether you use soft round lettuce, Webb's Wonder or cos, chicory or endive, season it at the last minute, just before serving with a vinaigrette. Add French mustard if you like for the stronger tasting leaves and sprinkle with parsley or fresh chives, chervil or tarragon, all very finely chopped.

Variations: Add cress and walnuts just out of their shells. Diced Gruyère or grated Roquefort may be thrown in, or sliced apples or oranges. Other additions which find favour these days are sliced hard-boiled eggs, raw mushrooms, bits of celery, spring onion, green pepper, pears, chopped anchovy and capers.

My own favourite additions are fried croûtons with garlic and fried bacon pieces.

Salade Niçoise

Some mixed salads are a meal in themselves.

There are not one or two or three versions of salade Niçoise – but dozens, depending on what is available. The constants are tuna, anchovy fillets, hard-boiled eggs, tomatoes and black olives. Suit yourself with the other vegetables, but here is one good version. Add more of one thing if you have less of another.

Basic ingredients:

4-6 tasty ripe tomatoes quartered or 8 small cherry ones, 3 hardboiled eggs, 1 large tin of tuna, 6-10 anchovy fillets, a dozen fat black olives, half a mild red onion sliced into thin rings.

Optional additions:

Up to 500 g (1 lb) French beans cooked briefly, a small handful of cooked dried haricot beans, 1 pepper sliced into rings, 3 sliced artichoke hearts (cooked or tinned), 1 crisp cos lettuce heart, 6 large radishes (sliced), 1 pickled cucumber (sliced).

The salad may be dressed before setting out with a vinaigrette made with plenty of good olive oil, chopped basil or parsley, a little crushed garlic and a few capers.

Present it on a bed of young lettuce leaves.

❧ Greek salad with cheese

My favourite meal on the island of Skopelos was a salad made of crisp cos lettuce cut into pieces, with strips of green pepper, 3 or 4 quartered tomatoes, a few onion rings, 12 black kalamata olives and the white crumbly Fetta cheese, about 120 g (4 oz), cut into cubes. Toss this in a dressing of olive oil and lemon juice with a little salt and some freshly ground black pepper.

I have also eaten this same salad with a sprinkling of chopped dill or fennel leaves, a few capers and chopped gherkin.

A French version is made with very thin slices of Gruyère and some toasted croûtons rubbed with garlic thrown in.

❧ Italian pepper and Fontina cheese salad

Cut 3 peppers into thin strips, removing the core and seeds. Grill until the skins blacken and peel and slice them. Put them in a bowl with

120 g (4 oz) sliced Fontina and toss in 2 tablespoons of olive oil mixed with 1 teaspoon of French mustard, 2-3 tablespoons of cream and salt and pepper to taste.

❧ Couronne marinière

Bread in a salad is not uncommon, usually in the form of croûtons, little toasted or fried cubes. In this simple country dish from the South of France it forms a soft moist bed.

Slice good farmhouse bread and remove the crust. Lay at the bottom of a serving dish. Moisten with a sprinkling of water, or vinaigrette dressing, but not enough to become too soggy. Cover with a layer of tomatoes which have been softened in boiling water, peeled and mashed with a fork and seasoned with a little crushed garlic, chopped basil, oregano, salt and pepper. Lay on top as many anchovy fillets as you like.

Panzanella – Tuscan bread salad

Cut into thick slices and remove the crusts of about 200 g (7 oz) stale coarse bread, then tear into small pieces and put in a bowl. Sprinkle with enough cold water so that it is well moistened but not soggy. Add 6 ripe tomatoes cut into pieces, 1 chopped or thinly sliced red onion, 1/2 diced cucumber, 2 thinly sliced celery sticks, and a good bunch of basil leaves, torn into pieces. Dress with a mixture of 6 tablespoons extra-virgin olive oil, 2 tablespoons red wine vinegar, salt and pepper. Leave for 1/2 hour for the bread to absorb the dressing and juices before serving.

Bean salads and lentils

Beans are nourishing and sustaining picnic fare, but they must be properly cooked, and dressed.

If you can find fresh ones just wash and boil vigorously in salted water until tender, and season.

All types of dried bean can be used: white haricot beans, red kidney beans, black eyed beans, navy beans, flageolets, butter beans, as well as chick peas and large lentils. Soak in water to cover overnight, drain and bring to the boil in fresh unsalted water. Simmer slowly and add salt only when they start to become tender. When you can crush them between your fingers, after 1/2-11/2 hours, depending on the variety, drain and place in a bowl. Season while still warm with a vinaigrette or with an olive oil and lemon juice dressing, adding fresh herbs such as chervil, marjoram, basil and parsley, chopped very fine.

Variations: Peeled and chopped tomatoes and finely chopped Spanish or Italian onions may be added, as well as black olives and quartered hard-boiled eggs. A little crushed garlic and cayenne may be stirred into the dressing. Some people like to sweeten the beans with a little sugar.

Or flavour with crushed garlic and plenty of powdered cumin.

Spring vegetables in white wine

This green medley, a most delicious and exciting combination of spring vegetables, is as good hot as it is cold. I buy the peas and broad beans sold already podded. When they are not so young and tender it is best to use frozen ones. The proportions of vegetables can be varied.

300 g (11 oz) peas, 200 g (7 oz) broad beans, 4 dwarf courgettes each cut in half, 12 asparagus spears, 1 small fennel bulb cut into thin slices longways, 6 tablespoons olive oil, 200 ml (7 fl oz) fruity white wine, 3/4-1 litre (1¼-1¾ pints) chicken stock (you may use a stock cube), salt and pepper,1 baby lettuce, shredded, the leaves of 5-6 sprigs of mint, torn.

Put the peas, broad beans, courgettes, asparagus and fennel in a pan. Add 3 tablespoons of the olive oil, the wine, and chicken stock, so that the vegetables are covered with liquid. Cook for about 15-20 minutes until the vegetables are tender, adding a little salt and pepper (take into account the saltiness of the stock).

Add the lettuce and mint and cook 5 minutes more. Transfer all the vegetables into a serving bowl with a slotted spoon. Reduce the remaining liquid by boiling hard, then beat in the remaining 3 tablespoons of olive oil and pour over the vegetables.

❧ Potato salads

Everyone has a different recipe for the most common salad used to 'fill up' on a hungry picnic.

I like one made with marinated herring fillets and dessert apples. Cook waxy new potatoes in their skins in salted boiling water.

Peel and slice them into a bowl. Dress while still hot with a vinaigrette sauce into which have been stirred some French mustard and a good amount of finely chopped Spanish onion or spring onions, parsley or chervil. Add as many marinated herring fillets as you like and thinly sliced eating apples which have been dipped in a water acidulated with a little lemon to prevent them from darkening.

Other good alternatives are made with one or a few of the following: quartered hard-boiled eggs, sliced artichoke hearts, green beans, fennel and celery, small quartered tomatoes, pickled gherkin slices, watercress, bits of prawn, shellfish, tongue or ham.

You may like to use lemon juice instead of vinegar or a mayonnaise dressing instead of the vinaigrette and garnish with watercress.

The Japanese have an attractive way of sprinkling a potato and prawn salad with blanched and seasoned chrysanthemum petals.

❧ Mashed potatoes with olive oil and parsley

Peel and boil 1 kg (2 lb) floury potatoes in salted water till very tender. Drain, keeping about 130 ml (4½ fl oz) of the cooking water. Mash the

potatoes and beat in 6-8 tablespoons extra-virgin olive oil and enough
of the cooking water to have a soft, slightly moist consistency. Add salt
and pepper and plenty of chopped flat-leaf parsley.

Variation: You can turn these mashed potatoes into a salad by adding
3 tablespoons each of chopped black olives and capers or chopped
anchovy fillets in oil.

❧ Mushrooms à la grecque

The Greek method of cooking vegetables in oil is one of the most
delicious for vegetables that are to be eaten cold. Almost all vegetables,
except perhaps peas, are suitable. They keep very well, for weeks even,
covered and refrigerated.

Mushrooms treated in this manner are the most popular and now
habitually carried by the hors d'oeuvre trolley in hotels and restaurants
throughout the world.

Use small button mushrooms. Wash them and cut off a thin slice
from the end of the stem. Leave them whole if they are small; otherwise
cut them in four.

Bring to the boil the following: 3 tablespoons olive oil, 3 tablespoons
lemon juice, half a teacup white wine or water, 1-2 cloves of garlic,
crushed, 1 bay leaf, a sprig of thyme, a small bunch of parsley, finely
chopped, salt and pepper. Throw in 250 g (1/2 lb) mushrooms and cook,
stirring constantly for 5 minutes. Taste and adjust the seasoning.

Refrigerate and carry in its sauce.

For a different flavour, try a little bit of rosemary, a few celery leaves and
a couple of cloves.

❧ Ratatouille

This Provençal dish, better cold than hot, may be served as an hors
d'oeuvre, a salad, as a filling for an open tart (see p.67).

Cut 2 large aubergines into cubes. Sprinkle liberally with salt and
allow the juices to drain away in a colander. Heat half a glass of olive
oil in a large pan. Fry 2 Spanish onions, thickly sliced, until they are soft
and slightly golden. Add 2 crushed cloves of garlic and stir. Add the
aubergines, their juices squeezed out, and 2 green peppers, seeded and
cut into small strips. Stir, and when they begin to colour, add 5
tomatoes, peeled and cubed, and 5 courgettes, washed and trimmed

and cut into thick slices. Season with salt and pepper. Cover the pan and stew the vegetables in their own juices on a very low flame for 30-45 minutes. Stir in a good amount of finely chopped fresh herbs such as parsley, basil, oregano or marjoram and cook a few minutes longer. Add 2 or 3 tablespoons of lemon or vinegar.

❧ Aubergines in a sweet and sour sauce

My favourite alternative to cold ratatouille comes from Italy. The refreshing sweet and sour taste suits cold dishes so much better than hot ones.

1 kg (2 lb) aubergines (cubed), salt, olive oil, 1 large Spanish onion (coarsely chopped), 3 cloves garlic (crushed), 1 medium 400 g (14 oz) tin peeled tomatoes, 1 good bunch of parsley (finely chopped), 3 tablespoons wine vinegar, 1 tablespoon sugar, pepper.

Wash and cube the aubergines. Sprinkle with salt and leave for about an hour in a colander for the juices to drain away. Rinse and squeeze the water out with your hand, a few at a time. Cover the bottom of a pan with olive oil. Sauté the aubergines until coloured. Do as many as will cover the pan at a time and drain on absorbent paper.

In a large heavy-bottomed saucepan, fry the onion in 2 tablespoons of olive oil, stirring occasionally. When it is lightly coloured add the garlic and when this begins to colour add the peeled tomatoes. Cut them up or mash them with a wooden spoon. Add a good amount of pepper, the sugar and vinegar, and cook for 10 minutes over moderate heat. Add the aubergines and cook for 10 minutes more, adding salt to taste (remember that the aubergines have already been salted). Add parsley a few minutes before the end of cooking time. Serve cold.

❧ Little onions

A la grecque. In a large pan put half a teacup each of olive oil, wine vinegar and dry white wine, a bay leaf, a sprinkling of thyme, tarragon, oregano or basil, 2 cloves of garlic, crushed, and 2 teaspoons of sugar. Add 500 g (1 lb) small pickling onions and water to cover. Bring to the boil and simmer gently until they are tender but still firm (about 10-15 minutes).

Sweet and sour. Sauté 500 g (1 lb) button onions in 5 tablespoons of olive oil, shaking the pan occasionally, until they are golden. Add 2-3 tablespoons of wine vinegar, 2 teaspoons of sugar, salt and pepper, a sprinkling of herbs such as mint, thyme, tarragon, basil or parsley, 2 cloves of garlic, crushed, and cover with white wine or water. Simmer gently until the onions are tender but still firm.

A Moroccan way. Add a handful of sultanas or raisins and 1 or 2 tablespoons of tomato purée to onions as they cook slowly in oil.

❧ Rice salad

Rice makes an excellent salad but it must not be mushy. Cook it so that each grain is separate from the others and still has a little bite (see p.86). Toss while still hot with a dressing heavier in olive oil than vinegar or lemon juice, and salt and pepper to taste. Add plenty of finely chopped fresh herbs: parsley, basil, tarragon, chives, whatever you like.

To this basic salad a variety of finely chopped vegetables may be added – asparagus, cauliflower, runner beans, carrots, all barely cooked, pickled gherkins and juicy black olives. Each region around the Mediterranean seems to have its own special version.

An Andalusian one has tomatoes, peppers and spring onions or mild red onions with parsley.

In the Poitevin they add plenty of mushrooms slightly cooked in salted water with tomatoes and onions.

Dried fruits make a good alternative to vegetables. While still hot add a good amount of moist raisins or sultanas, chopped up, dried and soaked apricots and toasted almonds or pine nuts. To the dressing, add a sprinkling of allspice or a little nutmeg and cinnamon.

Another good way to eat cold rice is with great pourings of yoghurt or sour cream or a mixture of both.

❧ Macaroni, spaghetti and spaghettini estivi

Italians find it hard to spend the day without their own home-made pasta. The answer, when it is too difficult to bring primus and pans away from the kitchen, is the cold 'festive' version. It is as tasty and unusual as it is simple and inexpensive.

Boil until barely tender to the bite. Drain and pass under the cold water tap. Put in a bowl with a vinaigrette dressing. Add some fresh basil, coarsely chopped, or if this is not available, some parsley, and a little crushed garlic.

I like it as it is, but you may prefer to add a few tomatoes cut into thick wedges and a mild sweet onion cut into thin rings or a few chopped spring onions.

CHEESES

Fromage, poésie!
Parfum de nos repas,
Que deviendrait la vie
Si l'on ne t'avait pas?

For Monselet, the writer of these lines, cheese was the poetry and perfume of his meals.

In recent years the Anglo-Saxon world has come to appreciate cheeses almost as much as the French do. Indeed for many who have adopted the habit of serving a well-chosen selection before the dessert, it has become a preoccupation like wine – one of the good things of life. For them the necessity of a well-assorted cheese board is as evident outdoors as it is indoors.

Colette once confided that if her daughter should ever ask her advice as to what to contribute on a picnic her ready answer would be: 'If you provide the dessert they will be content. If you choose the cheeses they will be grateful.' In fact Colette blushed with pride when her daughter brought the cheeses as well as the desserts on such an occasion.

Now that many grocers and specialist shops carry a good and large selection there is much to choose from. Bring three or four, different in flavour and consistency and whenever possible buy local cheeses matured on the spot. Cheeses that do not sweat or become too runny are preferable on a hot day. As they are susceptible to temperature and air, wrap each one separately in polythene bags and remember to wrap up tightly any left-overs as soon as you have finished. The best way to keep hard English cheeses like Cheddar is to wrap them in a tea towel rung out in vinegar.

If you carry them in a cold insulated box or bag, take them out at least half an hour before serving depending on the weather. Bring a simple cheese board or platter to pass round or lay the cheeses on a bed of leaves in a flat basket.

It is worth noting that many people are happier with a piece of cheese followed by fruit than with any sort of pudding and share Brillat-Savarin's feeling that 'a last course at dinner, wanting cheese, is like a pretty woman with only one eye'. It was he too who described a modest picnic in romantic terms. 'Then from his knapsack very calmly and contentedly he takes cold chicken and golden encrusted rolls, packed for him perchance by loving hands, and lays conveniently by the wedge of Gruyère or Roquefort which is to be his whole dessert.'

DESSERTS

❧ Fruits of the season

The young nineteenth century curate Francis Kilvert noted in his diary during one of his many long walking expeditions: 'my luncheon in my pocket, half-a-dozen biscuits, two apples and a small flask of wine'.

Even when it is a banquet there is no doubt that fruit is the happiest conclusion to an outdoor meal. Nothing is more delicious than the fruits of the season when they are at their best. When they are past their prime or have not quite reached it, they can be macerated in fruit juice and spirits, turned into a salad, poached in syrup, or made into fools and purées, jellies and tarts. These are summer desserts which cannot be bettered.

If you take the trouble to peel and cut up the fruit and give each one the treatment that suits it best, be it a sprinkling of sugar, a certain perfume or a touch of spice, your friends will be grateful. If they are to macerate in spirit or fruit juices the longer they do so the better. Leave for a few hours or a whole day in a cool place.

Oranges. Peel with a sharp knife, removing the white pith as well. Cut into thin slices and sprinkle with castor sugar and a little cognac or Cointreau. Dust with powdered cinnamon when serving.

Pears. So that they do not darken, squeeze some lemon juice over freshly peeled and cut slices. Sprinkle with castor sugar and a little kirsch.

Melon. Flavour with a sweet dessert wine, port or sherry. Make a circular incision round the stem, remove the top and take out the seeds. Sprinkle the inside with 1 or 2 tablespoons of sugar and pour in a wine glass full of the wine. Replace the top and chill.

Peaches make one of the most delicious fruit desserts. Skin and cut into eight pieces, removing the stone. Sprinkle with castor sugar and a little lemon juice and cover with a sweet wine, a red bordeaux or a rosé and leave for an hour or longer.

Served on a bed of vanilla ice cream, and covered with fresh raspberry purée, they form the dish made famous by the singer, *Melba*. Alternatively, Jane Grigson suggests using gin and fresh orange juice with peaches. The Italians fill them with chopped candied fruits and peel.

Strawberries, which I have gone into at length on pp.7-8, are good with port.

Raspberries are best flavoured with kirsch or Grand Marnier. Both raspberries and strawberries may or may not need a sprinkling of sugar.

Large dessert gooseberries. Top and tail them, sprinkle with sugar and cover with a white dessert wine – Muscat de Frontignan is the one that suits them best.

Pomegranates. Cut them open and turn out the cluster of seeds, each surrounded by clear sharp pink flesh, into a bowl with a spoon. Sprinkle with sugar and a few drops of rose water or orange blossom and chill.

Blackberries, bilberries, mulberries, loganberries, barberries. Gathered or bought, these must be very ripe. Sprinkle generously with sugar and leave them in the hot sun to give up their juice and soften for as long as possible. Crush them lightly if they require a little help. They need only their own fragrance to enchant, but if you must, no one will stop you from adding a little red wine or cognac, and bilberries like a mint leaf placed here and there amongst them.

Bananas and dates are usually indigenous to the same countries. They also go very well together. Put alternate layers of banana slices and peeled and halved pitted fresh dates (or the semi-dried ones from California) straight into a plastic picnic box. Pour fresh single cream all over and leave for at least an hour – the longer the better. The fruits will acquire a lovely creamy stickiness.

Pineapples. The finest dessert fruit grown in tropical lands can make the most spectacular presentation (see pp.24-5) but for a picnic the best way to offer it is simply sliced. Remove the rind with a sharp or serrated knife. Cut into thick slices, sprinkle with castor sugar only if it requires it and pour a little maraschino over each slice at least an hour before serving.

You may like to cut the slices into pieces, macerate them in a liqueur with a little sugar if necessary and smother with double cream whipped till very thick and flavoured with a little sugar and the same liqueur. This is known as *pineapple Romanoff.*

૨ゐ Mixed fruit salads

There are countless different ways of making a fruit salad using single fruits or combinations depending on what is available. Use any fruits in season, as well as imported ones; for a good combination, contrast flavours, textures and colours: the acidity of citrus with sweet soft peaches, bananas and pears and sometimes with the unexpected hardness of coarsely chopped walnuts or slivered blanched almonds. Prepare straight into the serving bowl or picnic box.

All the fruits must be ripe and unblemished. Peel them, remove the pith from oranges, hull, top and tail or simply wash, drain and dry well. Some, like strawberries, must be washed very quickly without letting them soak in water as this impairs their flavour. Remove stones and slice or cut larger fruit into small pieces. Leave the berries whole. Squeeze a little lemon juice where necessary to prevent the fruits from browning.

Sprinkle generously with sugar, preferably castor. It will draw out the natural juices, softening the fruit and providing extra liquid for the dressing, which is usually made with lemon juice or orange juice or a combination of both. If you like add some sweet liqueur or spirit or wine. Try adding a touch of spice such as cinnamon or ginger or a sprinkling of chopped fresh mint for an unusual flavouring. I often add a tablespoon or two of rose water or orange blossom water instead of alcohol when there are children who do not care for it.

Variations: Most delectable are fruits left to macerate in a glass of cognac or some champagne with a little sugar until they are truly impregnated.

Another good dressing is a syrup made by simmering the juice of 1 lemon and 2 oranges with 200 g (7 oz) sugar and 200 ml (7 fl oz) water until it thickens enough to coat a spoon. Add 3-4 tablespoons of kirsch, rum, maraschino, Benedictine or cointreau.

The salad should be allowed to macerate for at least 2 hours in the refrigerator or cold box, but soft fruits such as strawberries or raspberries are best added only half an hour before or when serving. Carry them separately.

Cream, light or thick, whipped and flavoured if you like with sugar and a little of the spirit used in the salad, may be passed round.

Fresh unsalted cream cheese is a good alternative to cream for fruit salads. Lately my family has become addicted to fruit salad smothered in a light French cream cheese beaten with sugar and folded into stiffly beaten egg whites, which we put in the freezer for an hour. We carry it out in a cold box.

An elegant container for a fruit salad is a melon or water melon shell. Cut a slice off the top and scoop out the flesh without breaking the rind. Fill the empty shell, put the lid on and carry in a sealed polythene bag.

৯. Fruit fools

Sweetened fruit purées combined with double cream are as British and as old-fashioned as jelly. They are easy to make and they are one of the delights of summer. Opinion varies as to the proportion of cream and fruit and the amount of sugar, but that of course is a matter of preference.

All kinds of fruits can be made into fools and they can be put into the freezer to become simple and delicious ice creams.

Gooseberry fool. This is my favourite fool, which I first learnt from Jane Grigson. Cook 500 g (1 lb) gooseberries very slowly in 2 tablespoons of butter until they soften and change colour. Crush them with a fork and add sugar to taste. Whip 300 ml (1/2 pint) fresh double cream and stir it into the cooled purée. Pack and chill it before putting in a refrigerated box or bag.

I like this fool as it is, but you might like it better with a little Muscat wine. Another old flavouring for gooseberry is elderflower. Put a head of flowers in the gooseberry while it is stewing and remove it before mashing the fruit.

Strawberry and raspberry fools. These soft fruits make lovely fools if they are very ripe. You may use slightly battered ones going cheap but be careful to throw away any bad ones. Hull 500 g (1 lb) fruit, wash very briefly and drain. Whip 300 ml (1/2 pint) double cream in a blender until it is very firm. Add the fruits and sugar to taste and blend until they are well mashed.

Although to my taste the fool is perfect with no other flavouring, some people like to add 2 or 3 tablespoons of kirsch, port or Madeira.

A custard may be used instead of the cream. Whisk 3 egg yolks in a bowl placed over a pan of boiling water. Add 300 ml (1/2 pint) cream, a little at a time, beating constantly, and continue to stir until the custard has thickened. Let it cool; then fold it into the fruit purée. Put it in the freezer if you want ice cream.

♨ Fruit mousse

A fool becomes a mousse when it is lightened with a snow of egg white.

Stew 500 g (1 lb) fruit in as little water as possible, until it is soft. Pass through a sieve or put through an electric blender. Sweeten to taste. When cooled, stir in about 150 ml (¼ pint) whipped double cream and fold in 2 stiffly beaten egg whites. Chill to serve very cold.

♨ Fruit jellies

One delicious way of taking fruit cream on an outing is to set it with gelatine.

Fruit shapes, moulds, dillies and tivolies were very popular in the nineteenth century, inspired by the voluptuous shapes produced by the chefs who left during the French Revolution. The new techniques of the Industrial Revolution turned out moulds of extraordinary shapes. Arrowroot and cornflour or calf's foot jelly were used to set them. Today powdered gelatine is easier to use and works very well. It is not necessary to turn out the jelly, but if you must have an elegant sculpture, brush the mould well with almond or another light oil before pouring in the mixture.

All kinds of fruits may be used. Strawberries, raspberries, melon and mangoes are best raw or macerated in spirit; pears, plums, peaches, apricots, apples, are best poached in syrup. Dried fruits should be stewed.

Fruit jellies need not be nursery food. You can flavour them with spirits. Use rum with pineapple and calvados for apple kirsch and maraschino are good with most fruits and you can flavour with spices such as cinnamon and cloves.

Turn to a pulp by passing through a sieve or in a blender or simply mash with a fork.

Dissolve 30 g (1 oz) gelatine in ¼ litre (½ pint) fruit juice such as orange juice or the poaching syrup (see p.114) in a bowl placed in a pan of boiling water. Then blend well into ¾ litre (1½ pints) fruit purée. This makes a quantity enough for 10-12 people.

Pour into a bowl, or into an oiled mould if you want to turn it out. Refrigerate for at least 4 hours until it sets.

Try varying the texture by stirring in some pieces of fruit.

Or you can build alternate layers of jellied purée and sponge fingers or boudoir biscuits soaked in liqueur.

Whipped double cream can also be stirred into the jellied fruit purée when it is cool and has begun to set – 150-300 ml (¼-½ pint) cream for ½ litre (1 pint) purée.

⁊ Cream cheese desserts

So much can be done with ordinary cream cheese with very little trouble. Unsalted curd cheese such as Ricotta and a variety of cream cheeses can be turned into delicious desserts simply by stirring in some castor sugar and flavouring. They must be as fresh as possible without a trace of sourness. Some people like to pass them through a sieve or an electric blender, but for me beating with a fork will do. Stir in a little fresh cream if you like, and let everyone decide how they would like to eat it – with honey, as we used to do in Egypt, with sugar and a dusting of cinnamon, as I learnt in Greece, or stir in a spirit or liqueur such as rum, or kirsch, which is a popular Italian way. Or add a squeeze of lemon or orange juice and a bit of zest.

You may lighten the cream cheese by adding a stiffly beaten egg white for each 225 g (½ lb). Or you can stiffen it with a teaspoonful of powdered gelatine, thoroughly dissolved in 2 tablespoons of very hot water for the same quantity, and leave to set.

For a romantic picnic, make the following mixture: 150 ml (¼ pint) whipped double cream, 225 g (½ lb) cream cheese and about 2 tablespoons of castor sugar; fold in a stiffly beaten egg white. Line a heart-shaped container (a basket or pierced metal or china mould) with fine muslin and press the mixture in. Let it drain overnight in a cool place. Turn it out on the picnic and surround it with strawberries. You will feel like a poet.

Paschka, a Russian Easter dish, is the inspiration for this. Drain 1½ kg (3 lb) curd or cottage cheese in a sieve. Beat in 3 eggs, 200 g (7 oz) unsalted softened butter, 150 ml (¼ pint) double or sour cream and sugar to taste; blend well until smooth.

Stir in 225 g (½ lb) chopped mixed crystallized fruits and the grated rind of an orange or lemon. Find a mould with a hole in it. A good idea is to use a clay flower-pot (soak this in water for at least an hour to remove any taste of clay). Line with muslin. Fill with the cheese mixture, pressing it down well. Lift the sides of the muslin over the cheese and press it down hard with a weight. Place on a rack over a bowl or tray and leave to drain overnight in a cool place. Unmould it on a plate only when you are ready to serve. Decorate with bits of crystallized fruit if you want to be grand.

Mascarpone. This simple Italian country dessert can easily become your family and party favourite.

500 g (1 lb) bland cream cheese, 75 g (3 oz) castor sugar or to taste, a little rum or brandy, 3 large eggs, 2 packets boudoir biscuits (or sponge fingers), 75 g (3 oz) raisins or sultanas.

Let the raisins or sultanas swell in rum or brandy in a bowl. Beat the cream cheese and sugar with the egg yolks. Add rum or brandy by the tablespoon, to taste, and beat until a smooth cream. Stir in the raisins or sultanas.

Arrange the boudoir biscuits side by side at the bottom of a wide shallow bowl. Sprinkle with enough rum or brandy to make them moist but not soggy. Whip the egg whites until stiff and fold gently into the cream cheese mixture. Spread this light fluffy cream over the biscuits. Cover and chill.

Mascarpone can be made into an ice cream. Put it straight from the freezer into a cooled cold box. In Italy when it is to be served at home, it is often put straight into individual wine glasses after it is made.

An excellent variation is made with bitter chocolate shavings, and another with chopped-up crystallized fruit instead of raisins or sultanas. My favourite is with a very fine pulverized coffee. Use 2 tablespoons for $1/2$ kg (1 lb) cream cheese.

🍂 An orange dessert

Boil 2 large oranges whole for about an hour until they are very tender. Cut them open and remove the pips, then reduce to a cream in a blender with 6 eggs, the juice of 2 more oranges, juice of half a lemon, 2 tablespoons of brandy or orange liqueur, and about 10 or more spoonfuls of sugar to taste. Pour into an ovenproof dish and bake in a low 150°C/300°F/Gas 2 oven for about an hour or until firm.

Serve cooled but not chilled.

❧ Fruit tarts

French open tarts are the most welcome hot-weather pastries, especially when the fruits of the season appear in them. Usually, a sweet pastry is baked blind, then filled with a cream or custard on which a variety of fresh or cooked fruits are arranged.

A fruit purée or a jam such as apricot, diluted in water, or even jelly may be poured over the fruit to give it an appetizing glaze. Apples, peaches, apricots, greengages, plums, cherries, grapes and strawberries all make excellent tarts. These pastries must be transported with care in their tin or dish and covered with a foil secured with sticky tape.

A biscuity pastry shell. For a 30 cm (12 in) tart:

250 g (8 oz) flour, 2 tablespoons castor sugar, 125 g (1/4 lb) unsalted butter, 2 egg yolks, 2-4 tablespoons water or milk.

Work and rub the butter into the sifted flour and sugar. Add the egg yolks and just enough water to bind the soft dough, stirring with a knife and then briefly with your hands.

Cover and leave in a cool place for an hour. Then roll out on a floured board with a floured rolling pin. Lay the dough gently into the tart pan or flan mould and pat it snugly into place, pressing it into any fluted sides. Trim the edges, prick with a fork and line with paper weighed down with dried beans. Bake in a pre-heated 200°C/400°F/Gas 6 oven for 15 minutes. Take out of the oven and brush with egg white to seal the crust and prevent it from becoming soggy. Return to the oven for 5-10 minutes longer until it is a light biscuity colour. It will become crusty as it cools.

A bed for the fruit – crème pâtissière (confectioner's custard). Beat 175 g (6 oz) sugar into 5 egg yolks until light and pale, then beat in 75 g (3 oz) flour. Bring to the boil 450 ml (3/4 pint) milk with a vanilla pod (or add a few drops of vanilla extract when it has boiled). Pour on to the egg mixture gradually, beating vigorously until well blended. Pour into a heavy-bottomed saucepan and bring to the boil, stirring constantly. Simmer for 3 minutes longer, stirring occasionally, so that the cream does not burn at the bottom of the pan. You may like to add 75 g (3 oz) ground almonds or pulverized macaroons and 2-3 tablespoons of kirsch, rum or cognac. Let it cool before you spread it on the pastry shell.

The fruit filling. The most appreciated are often those with the shortest season – strawberries, raspberries, cherries and seedless grapes. Rinse them briefly and pack as many as you can over the bed of custard.

Plums, greengages, pears, apples, apricots, gooseberries, cherries, peaches and tangerines all make lovely tarts. They may be left raw, peeled, halved and stoned where necessary. But it is usual to poach them for a few minutes only in a light syrup.

For the syrup, simmer ½ kg (1 lb) sugar with ½ litre (1 pint) water, orange juice or red wine and 2 tablespoons of lemon juice, until the sugar has melted. Poach the fruit for 5-10 minutes depending on the fruit, until just tender. Drain thoroughly and arrange on the custard. You may slice the peaches, apples and pears.

A light glaze gives a tart a professional touch. Simply melt a jam or jelly such as apricot, red currant, raspberry or strawberry with a few tablespoons of water and coat the fruit with this.

A sauce of puréed fresh fruit adds a new dimension of flavour. Purée in a blender very ripe, sweet fruits such as strawberries, raspberries, black currants or the large sweet gooseberries, with a little syrup made by simmering 4-5 tablespoons of sugar with 7 tablespoons of water and the juice of half a lemon (enough for ½ kg/1 lb fruit). Or you can use any stewed fruit. Put it in the blender with a few tablespoons of the syrup they were cooked in – enough to make a light purée.

Pour over the fruit filling.

Or you may dispense with the custard and use a fruit purée as a bed for the fruit.

Take some whipped cream to serve with your tart.

❧ Mixed fruit crumble or pie

This is easy to make and carry. Use any of the following, alone or together: pears, apples, plums, greengages, gooseberries, apricots and cherries.

Wash, peel and stone as required. Cut the fruit in half or slice into a deep oven dish.

Sprinkle with sugar to taste, depending on the sweetness of the fruit. For 1 kg (2 lb) of fruit, 4-6 tablespoons may be right. Dot with shavings of butter, about 50 g (2 oz).

Flavour if you like with a sprinkling of cinnamon and a few cloves or a dusting of powdered ginger, or with a squeeze of lemon juice, or with

2 or 3 tablespoons of a fruit brandy such as calvados, marc or William pear brandy, or with a little grated orange rind.

If it is the season for quinces, peel and chop one up and mix it in – it gives a delightful perfume.

You may also add a handful of split or slivered blanched almonds or some raisins or sultanas.

To make the crumble, mix 225 g (¹/₂ lb) flour with 75 g (3 oz) sugar. Rub in 175 g (6 oz) unsalted butter to make a crumbly effect and spread it evenly over the fruit.

A short cut is a crumb crust. Simply crush or grind or put in a blender, digestive biscuits, or dry cake. Work in a little butter, just enough to make the crumbs hold together.

To make a pie, use the pastry given on p.113 instead of the crumble over the fruit. Roll it out and lay over the top of the dish to make a lid. Press down round the edge and make a little hole in the centre for the steam to escape. Brush with egg yolk and sprinkle with suagar.

Bake crumble or pie in a moderate 180°C/350°F/Gas 4 oven for at least 45 minutes until nicely browned.

DRINKS

One tries to simplify things outdoors and I am quite happy to wash down pies and cold meats, vegetables and desserts with one wine only. But for the dedicated drinkers who believe like Brillat-Savarin that 'the palate becomes cloyed and after three or four glasses, it is but a deadened sensation that even the best wine provokes', it is right to offer two. Have a light refreshing white, commended by Savarin as 'less affected by movement and heat and more pleasantly exhilarating', which you can carry chilled in a refrigerated box or keep cool in the river, and a hearty stout red wine which cannot be unduly harmed by the journey, or a rosé, which is said to be particularly delicious by the sea.

Serve straight-forward and relatively inexpensive wines. They will taste better on a picnic, while the fine aged ones are too delicate for rough outdoor handling and will be overpowered by all the competing perfumes of nature.

If you are not having wine, it is well known that Englishmen are happy with good beer and women with good cider and that beer mixed with Stone's ginger wine makes Shandy Gaff. And, of course, there is nothing as grand as a champagne picnic.

Provide all the non-alcoholic drinks that you can in hot weather. You cannot beat freshly pressed citrus fruit and home-made lemonade for their sharp clarity. It is fun to serve them with bits of fruit and plenty of ice.

My own summer favourites are fruit cups and punches, which quench the thirst, provide a little stimulant and are most agreeable without being expensive. Mix them up beforehand and pour them in chilled flasks or bottles, leaving the soda to add just before serving. Keep them in a cold box along with lots of ice cubes.

And don't forget the coffee and tea.

৯৯ Kir

This makes a cool and elegant aperitif to welcome guests as they arrive for a party on the terrace. Mix it individually in the glass. Stir 1 tablespoon of cassis, the black currant liqueur, or black currant or raspberry syrup into a glass of chilled white wine.

Pimm's

A refreshing and deceptively strong drink. In a large jug pour 1 part of Pimm's to 2 or 3 parts of lemonade. Add a few sprigs of fresh mint, borage if you have it, and slices of cucumber, lemon and orange.

Sangria

There are endless recipes for this hispanic citrus drink which conjures up for me orgies of grilled sardines and roast pork, windswept beaches and Portuguese voices – children love it too.

Pour 2 bottles of red wine into a large jug. Add an orange and a lemon, thinly sliced and 1-2 tablespoons of sugar. Leave to macerate, chilled, in a refrigerator for 2 hours. When ready to serve, put in a handful of ice cubes and as much or as little soda water as you like.

A Yoghurt drink

This is an everyday drink in India and the Middle East. Beat equal quantities of yoghurt and water with a good sprinkling of crushed dried mint, and season to taste with salt and pepper. Chill and pour into a cold vacuum flask.

Smetana or sour cream may be used instead of yoghurt.

Instant borsht with beetroot or tomato juice

I discovered these two drinks in Israel at my aunt Germaine's.

Beat together equal quantities of bottled beetroot juice and sour cream and season to taste with salt and pepper and a squeeze of lemon.

Tomato juice and yoghurt are just as happily coupled. Season to taste. Both are best chilled.

Sweet and sour syrup

A most refreshing drink which comes from Iran. Boil 1/2 litre (1 pint) water with 1 kg (2 lb) sugar and 1/4 litre (1/2 pint) red wine vinegar until the syrup is thick enough to lightly coat a spoon. Drop a small bunch of mint in and let it cool. Dilute in ice-cold water in a vacuum flask, or better still do so on the spot directly into the glasses.

🌿 Tea

Many an English picnic has been saved by a good hot cup of tea. The following one described in Gwen Raverat's *Period Piece* was a calamity.

> Not long after this we ourselves organized a picnic, which no one could call a success. It was just before Frances' wedding; Uncle Frank was very gloomy at the idea of losing her, and Frances thought that something ought to be done to cheer him up, and to entertain the uncles and aunts assembled in Cambridge for the occasion. So a river picnic was arranged, entirely for their sakes; a family party, given by the young for the old.
>
> It was a grey, cold, gusty day in June. The aunts sat huddled in furs in the boats, their heavy hats flapping in the wind. The uncles, in coats and cloaks and mufflers, were wretchedly uncomfortable on the hard, cramped seats, and they hardly even tried to pretend that they were not catching their deaths of cold. But it was still worse when they had to sit down to have tea on the damp, thistly grass near Grantchester Mill. There were so many miseries which we young ones had never noticed at all: nettles, ants, cow-pats . . . besides that all-penetrating wind. The tea had been put into bottles wrapped in flannels (there were no Thermos flasks then); and the climax came when it was found that it had all been sugared beforehand. This was an inexpressible calamity. They all hated sugar in their tea. Besides it was Immoral. Uncle Frank said, with extreme bitterness: 'It's not the sugar I mind, but the Folly of it'. This was half a joke; but at his words the hopelessness and the hollowness of a world where everything goes wrong, came flooding over us; and we cut our losses and made all possible haste to get them home to a good fire.

Strain tea into a warmed flask as soon as it is made and please carry milk and sugar in separate pots!

Iced tea is as refreshing on a hot day as hot tea is heartwarming on a cold one. Strain and chill before pouring into a cooled vacuum flask.

Apart from lemon there are many flavourings that marry well the tangy taste of tea when it is cold. Mint is a traditional one. Add a few dried leaves of spearmint when you brew. Vanilla also goes particularly well – a discovery I made in the Seychelles where both leaves and pod grow and where the vanilla is ground and packed together with the tea. Put a pod in the pot. It can serve again and again.

You may like to try spices such as a stick of cinnamon or a few cloves, to be strained off when the tea goes into the flask, and allow people to sweeten with honey in the glass as you serve.

Rose petals give tea a special fragrance; otherwise add a drop of rose water or orange blossom essence. This is what we were given to drink as children in Egypt to make us sleep. It was very soothing.

If you are going to drop some ice cubes into the flask make the tea a little stronger than you would normally, to allow for the dilution.

ૐ Coffee, hot or iced

Make good coffee and strain into a warmed vacuum flask. It keeps very well this way. For an iced drink make it extra strong, not too long in advance. Strain into a jug, cover to preserve as much of the aroma as possible and chill before pouring into a cooled flask. Add a few ice cubes.

You may add sugar and cream or milk. Or you may like to try a few spices such as cinnamon, nutmeg or a few cloves or a cardamom pod. Sweeten with honey and add a strip or two of pared lemon peel if you like.

Best of all, especially in cold weather, is to lace with spirit: cognac, rum, whisky, all are excellent.

A CHAMPAGNE MENU FOR GLYNDEBOURNE

Part of the charm of the Glyndebourne Festival Opera is the picnic. This unique summer institution, founded by John and Audrey Christie in 1934 in their country estate, is as remarkable for the beautiful gardens and downland setting as for the excellence of the singing and acting, the orchestra, the scenery and costumes.

Indeed there can be few delights to compare with the pleasures of an elegantly chosen meal taken by one of the lakes, while watching the sun go down with the second half of Mozart still to come.

People travel in evening dress (Mr Christie's original recommendation that the audience should 'take trouble' as a compliment to the artists) in a special train or by car and even by helicopter. They leave their hampers in a favourite spot in the gardens, sometimes with the champagne bottle left to cool in the lake, tethered to a tree, until the interval. And they have 75 minutes to enjoy their picnic before the bell rings to warn them that the time is up. Now, a large marquee with pine tables and candles has removed any worries over grim weather conditions.

Although it is the traditional time to order smoked salmon and strawberry hampers, many people now find that it is also the best place for their own culinary zeal. It is here if anywhere that the grand dishes of picnic repertoire should be produced.

The Argentinian pianist Alberto Portugheis, who is well known for his gastronomic talents, has given me one of his many enchanting menus for Glyndebourne. It should be taken in a cold box. Quantities are for four.

❧ Mousse de Caviare

120 g (4 oz) Red Caviare (lumpfish roe will do), a 142 ml (5 fl oz) pot sour cream, 2 dessertspoons lemon juice, 40 g (114 oz) unsalted butter, 2 egg whites, black pepper, salt.

Melt the butter over a double boiler and blend it with the caviare, soured cream, lemon juice and black pepper. Put in refrigerator for an hour. Salt the egg whites and beat them until very stiff. Add lightly to the caviare mixture and put back in the refrigerator.

Variations: Instead of 2 dessertspoons of lemon juice, use 1 dessertspoon each of lemon juice and vodka; or 1½ dessertspoons of lemon juice and 14 dessertspoon of Aquavit; or use some white bread soaked in milk instead of the egg whites (or nothing at all, if you are happy with the volume as it is) and keep these to make miniature meringues to serve with the dessert.

❧ Chaudfroid de canard

1 duck (about 3 kg/6 lb when complete), 1 small stalk celery, 1 small leek or parsnip, 2 carrots, 1 onion, 2 cloves garlic, 1 sprig parsley, white pepper, salt, 1 teaspoon nutmeg.

Sauce:

3 tablespoons butter, 3 tablespoons flour, a 142 ml (5 fl oz) pot cream, 1 tablespoon powdered gelatine, 2 egg yolks, black truffles to decorate, but you can use black olives.

In a large saucepan put the duck giblets (except the liver, which the cook reserves for his own selfish snack!), all the vegetables, coarsely chopped, salt, pepper and nutmeg. Cover with water (about 1 litre/ 2 pints), bring to the boil, then simmer for half an hour.

Now add the duck, cut in four, bring to the boil and simmer until the duck is cooked – about 75 minutes.

Remove duck and leave to cool. Strain stock and boil fiercely, uncovered, until the liquid has reduced to about 450 ml (¾ pint).

Put in refrigerator. When cold, remove all the fat from the top. Skin and bone the duck. You will have four nice pieces and several small bits which can be put together.

To make the chaudfroid sauce: melt the butter in saucepan, add the flour and blend over low heat for 3-5 minutes. Slowly add the reheated stock, stirring vigorously to avoid lumps, and cook slowly, stirring constantly until the sauce is thick and smooth.

Blend the gelatine into the egg yolks, then beat into the sauce as you take it off the heat.

Pour the sauce over the duck pieces in the serving bowl, turning them so as to coat them entirely. Leave to set. Then decorate with truffles or olives.

🐾 Tomates Farcies

4 large tomatoes (ripe but firm), 225 g (¹/₂ lb) asparagus, 15 g (¹/₂ oz) butter, 1 dessertspoon ground pine nuts (optional), 4 tablespoons olive oil, 1 tablespoon lemon juice, 1 coffee spoon dried thyme (or 2 spoons fresh), 1 coffee spoon Dijon mustard, salt and pepper.

Poach the tomatoes for a few seconds in hot water and skin. Leave to cool. Remove centres. Marinate for several hours in a vinaigrette made with the oil, lemon juice, thyme, mustard, salt and pepper.

Meanwhile, cook the asparagus, strain them and put them through the mincer, with the tomato centres, drained of their liquid. Add butter, nuts, salt and pepper. Remove any excess vinaigrette from the hollowed tomatoes and fill with the asparagus mixture.

🐾 Pêches aux fraises

2 very large peaches (these are particularly recommended if you are dextrous enough to peel them and cut them in perfect halves), or 3 or 4 medium-sized peaches (peeled, cored, and sliced), 125 g (¹/₄ lb) ripe strawberries, 200 ml (7 fl oz) fruity white wine, 2 tablespoons red wine, 5 tablespoons sugar, 25 g (1 oz) gelatine.

Prepare peaches and soak in white wine for a couple of hours. Remove peaches. Bring wine to the boil with 2 tablespoons of sugar. Boil for 2 minutes, remove from heat and add gelatine. Put the strawberries, red wine and remaining sugar in a blender, then through a sieve. Line the bottom of a dish (or individual dishes) with the purée. Place the peaches on top and cover with the white wine glaze.

If you do not feel like opening a bottle of red wine for this recipe, you can replace it with ¹/₂ tablespoon of red wine vinegar and 1¹/₂ tablespoons of water.

A CHILDREN'S TREAT

Picnics are a seasonal highlight of the nursery and picnic episodes have always been a characteristic feature of children's books in England. Stories abound of secret picnics in secret gardens, of parties coming to a sad ending, of fires which cannot light because too many sticks have been crammed on top of each other, of clouds of thick smoke and roaring flames and fetching water and washing up and packing away. Groups of happy faces on the eagerly awaited day assemble at the breakfast table 'triumphing in the gay morning which gives promise of a fine clear day'. Tea is the usual repast, with bread and butter and a surfeit of sweet and sticky things which children's fantasies are made of, apple and mulberry tarts, plum cake, sponge cake, biscuits and shortbread. The Mad Hatter's tea party in *Alice in Wonderland* is the most famous of all the picnics, but it was so mad that there was nothing to eat. The plates were bare and the teapot empty.

The most successful picnic is the one beautifully told by Kenneth Grahame in *The Wind in the Willows*. Water Rat is taking Mole for his first trip down the river in a boat. Mole waggles his toes from sheer happiness, spreads his chest with a sigh of full contentment, and leans back blissfully into the soft cushions.

'What a day I'm having!' he said. 'Let us start at once!'

'Hold hard a minute, then!' said the Rat. He looped the painter through a ring in his landing-stage, climbed up into his hold above, and after a short interval reappeared staggering under a fat, wicker luncheon-basket.

'Shove that under your feet,' he observed to the Mole, as he passed it down into the boat. Then he untied the painter and took the sculls again.

'What's inside it?' asked the Mole, wriggling with curiosity.

'There's cold chicken inside it', replied the Rat briefly, 'coldtonguecoldhamcoldbeefpickledgherkinssaladfrenchrollscresssandwichespottedmeatgingerbeerlemonadesodawater –'

'O stop, stop,' cried the Mole in ecstasies: 'This is too much!'

'Do you really think so?' inquired the Rat seriously. 'It's only what I always take on these little excursions; and the other animals are always telling me that I'm a mean beast and cut it very fine!'

The Mole never heard a word he was saying. Absorbed in the new life he was entering upon, intoxicated with the sparkle, the ripple, the scents and the sounds and the sunlight, he trailed a paw in the water and dreamed long waking dreams.

I recently offered to prepare some food for a picnic on Hampstead Heath which reunited my daughter's friends from her old primary school. She said firmly that all that was wanted was crisps, chiplets and sweets and 'nothing foreign'. Children's outdoor gastronomic culture may be conservative, but my experience of what is actually appreciated belies the official limitations.

Here are some special versions of their traditional fare which they can make themselves.

ᘰ Cheese and watercress sandwiches

Mix together grated Cheddar, half the quantity of butter and moisten with sour cream. Stir in some watercress, washed and cut small with scissors.

You will find other ideas for sandwich fillings using the much loved fish, ham, chicken and eggs in the section on sandwiches (pp.2-5, 38-43).

ᘰ Pitta sandwiches

One type of sandwich which never fails to please is stuffed pitta bread (see pp.42-3). My children fill them with tuna and olives and slices of tomato, cucumber and onion sprinkled with a dressing.

They also have a whole repertoire of pizza type fillings: press into the pouch of bread combinations of tomatoes (sliced fresh ones or mashed tinned ones), slices of Mozzarella or other good melting cheeses, pitted olives, anchovy fillets, thin salami slices, seafood or strips of cooked ham.

The result is close to the stuffed pizzas from the region of Calabria which contain the filling inside a covered bread dough pie. They are good cold, but even better hot. You can wrap each in foil, heat in a moderate oven until the cheese melts and pack in a hot box. Otherwise make a fire on the spot and warm them up in the foil.

❧ Barbecued foods

If you are having a barbecue, let the children help in the preparation. Apart from the usual sausages (see p.162) and hamburgers (see p.186) they love little morsels on skewers such as the kebabs (see pp.189-195).

Bread and cheese skewers. In France these brochettes are likely to be made with Port Salut. In Italy, Provatura is used for crostini. Saint Paulin, Gruyère and Emmenthal may also be used.

Cut good bread into thick slices. Remove crusts and cut into squares. Cut the cheese into slices and then into squares the same size as the bread. Sprinkle with pepper if you like. Thread alternately on to skewers, beginning and ending with bread. Place over dying embers for a few minutes, turning from time to time until the bread is crisp and brown and the cheese has melted.

You may also put small pieces of ham between the cheese and the bread.

Desserts. When the fire is dying down you may put marshmallows for a minute on the grill.

For those who like bananas, cook them in their skins, split them open and press inside a tablespoon of jam or honey.

❧ Ice cream cones

An enterprising group will not find it too cumbersome to carry between them a cold bag or box with a large home-made ice cream pack.

The simplest ice cream which children can make for themselves is a fresh fruit ice cream made in the same way as a fool (see pp.109-110).

Use strawberries, raspberries, pineapple, gooseberries, apricots, peaches – sweet and ripe. Blend to a purée, add sugar to taste, a squeeze of lemon juice and plenty of stiffly whipped double cream ($1/2$ litre/ 1 pint of cream for $1/2$ kg/1 lb of fruit pulp is about right). Pour into a plastic box and freeze until stiff before putting in a cold box. Also try mascarpone ice cream on p.112.

Accompany with a box of cones and a scoop for serving.

HUNTING FEASTS, STALKING AND SHOOTING PARTIES

The earliest picnic meals in England were the medieval hunting feasts at the hunting lodges, the luxurious encampments which accompanied the great hunts.

When the conventions of the hunt became ritualised in the fourteenth century, the feast took on a special importance at the gathering or meet before the chase. The rules and regulations were borrowed, like all the niceties of savoir vivre of the time, from France. One source of these directions 'after the guise of beyond the sea' was Gaston de Foix whose famous book *Le Livre de chasse*, written in 1387, was translated into English by Edward, Duke of York, grandson of Edward III, while imprisoned for treachery in Pevensey Castle in 1413. In the English translation, *Master of the Game*, he gives a detailed account of the procedure of the feast.

The place where the gathering shall be made shall be in a fair mead, well green, where fair trees grow all about, the one far from the other, or beside some running brook. And it is called gathering because all the men and the hounds for hunting gather thither, for all they that go to the quest shall all come again in a certain place that I have spoken of. And also they that come from home, and all the officers that come from home shall bring thither all they need, every one in his office, well and plenteously, and should lay the tables and board cloths all about upon the green grass and set diverse meats upon a great platter after the lord's power. And some should eat sitting and some standing, and some leaning upon their elbows, some should drink, some joke, some play, in short, do all manner of disport and gladness.

He does not describe the dishes, but they too, like the manners and social habits of fourteenth century England, were the same as those of medieval France: pastries, hams and baked meats flavoured with wine, honey and spices, mixtures of sweet and savoury and combinations of fruits with bone marrow.

A century and a half later George Tubervile recorded the Elizabethan hunt in *The Noble Arte of Venerie* published in 1575. He too borrowed his directions from Gaston de Foix. Here they are in verse as quoted by Georgina Battiscombe in *English Picnics* following a lyrical description of the perfect spot which echoes *The Master of the Game*.

The place should first be pight, on pleasant, gladsome green
Yet under shade of stately trees, where little sun is seen:
And near some fountain spring, whose crystal running streams
May help to cool the parching heat, ycaught by Phoebus' beams.
The place appointed thus, it neither shall be clad

With arras nor with tapestry, such paltry were too bad:
Nor yet those hot perfumes whereof proud courts do smell,
May once presume in such a place, a Paradise, to dwell. [. . .]
Then such a place once found, the butler first appears,
He shall be foremost Doctor there, and stand before his peers:
And with him shall he bring (if company be great)
Some wagons, carts, some mules or jades, yladen till they sweat,
With many a medicine made for common, quaint diseases
As thirsty throats, and tippling tongues, which Bacchus' pipe
    appeases;
These little pinching pots, which pothecaries use,
Are all too fine, fie, fie on such, they make men but to muse.
My doctor brings his drugs, to counterpoise all quarrels,
In kilderkins and firkins full, in bottles and in barrels.
And yet therein he brings (I would you wist it well)
No rotten drams, but noble wine, which makes men's hearts to swell,
And down he doth dismount, his things for to address,
His flagons in the fountains fair are placed more or less,
Or if such fountains fail, my doctor has the skill
With sand and camphor for to cool his potions at his will.
That done, he spreads his cloth upon the grassy bank,
And sets to show his dainty drinks, to win his Prince's thanks.
Then comes the Captain Cook, with many a warlike wight
Which armour bring, and weapons both, with hunger for to fight,
Yea, some also set forth upon a manly mind
To make some means to quarrel with my doctor for to find,
For whiles cold loins of veal, cold Capon, Beef, and Goose
With pigeon pies, and mutton cold, are set on hunger loose,
And make the forlorn hope, in doubt to scape full hard,
Then come and give a charge in flank, else all the rest were marred,
First neats' tongues powdered well, then gambones of the hog,
Then sausages and savoury knacks, to set mens' minds on gog
Then King and comely Queen, then Lord and Lady look
To see which side will bear the bell, the Butler or the Cook.
At last the Cook takes flight, but Butlers still abide,
And sound their drums, and make retreat, with bottles by their side.

The Elizabethan hunt, unlike the medieval one ended as well as started
with a picnic, for the hart was killed, skinned, cut up and cooked there
and then as Tubervile directed:

> You shall also present before the Prince or chief personage in the field,
> some fine sauce made with wine and spices in a fair dish upon a

chafing-dish and coals, to the end that as he or she doth behold the huntsman breaking up the deer they may take their pleasure of the sweet dainty morsels, and dress some of them on the coals, making them carbonadies, and eating them with their sauce, rejoicing and recreating their noble minds with rehearsal which hound hunted best, and which huntsman hunted most like a woodman, calling their best favoured hounds and huntsmen before them, and rewarding them favourably as hath been the custom of all noble personages to do.

In Victorian times elegant hunting lodges called gazebos and pavilions were constructed in the great parks of the gentry to protect hunters from the treachery of the elements. Some were open to the winds, others were miniature houses. People gladly escaped to these pastoral fantasies in idyllic settings of cultivated wilderness which maintained the character and illusions of an outdoor picnic.

The food provided was that of the sophisticated French cold buffet table, if one is to go by Mrs Beeton's luncheon menus for a shooting party:

Filets de Soles à la mayonnaise.
Mousse de Homard frappée.
Boeuf braisé à la gelée.
Langue a l'écarlate.
Filets de Caneton à la Lorraine.
Cailles poelées à Ia Parisienne.
Faisan en Robe de Chambre.
Salade à la Japonaise.
Bordure de Riz aux Prunes.
Gâteaux à l'Africaine.
Batons Gruyère.
Fromage.
Dessert.

Fillets of Sole in Mayonnaise.
Iced Lobster Soufflé.
Braised Beef with Savoury Jelly.
Dressed Ox-Tongue.
Fillets of Duckling with Goose Liver Farce.
Braised Stuffed Quails. Roast Pheasant in Crust.
Japanese Salad.
Border of Rice with Stewed Prunes.
African Cakes.
Savoury Cheese Fingers.
Cheese.   Dessert.

These days the picnic feasts advocated by Gaston de Foix, originator of all hunting lore, survive in the handing round of port at lawn meets and in the hunt breakfasts and picnic luncheons at shooting parties in Scotland. The traditional fare for these affairs varies according to the season, for shooting starts on 12th August (the 'glorious 12th') for grouse and continues until 10th December, while for pheasant the shooting season lasts from 1st October till 1st February. Sir Ian Mactaggart, from whom my information comes, says 'A popular lunch when stalking deer is one or two fried egg and bacon sandwiches. The bacon should be fatty so that the mouth does not become dry (much drinking of water is bad for climbing hills). The sandwich should be made with thick toast for structural strength, as otherwise a bag of greasy crumbs may be all that is left after a lengthy crawl – a poor reward after a hopefully successful stalk.'

Catering arrangements for a shoot of eight guns must include wives and friends who sometimes turn up at lunch. This usually takes place in a shepherd's hut or a cottage let for the shooting or on the open hillside. If the food has not arrived in the boot of the car it is sometimes brought up by pony. The pattern of wives coming up with the picnic basket was set by Prince Albert, who loved shooting in the hills around Balmoral. Queen Victoria revealed their routine in her *Leaves from the Journal of our Life in the Highlands*; she would arrive with her carriage and the food at a spot where ponies waited to take her to Albert's encampment. When the weather was bad she lunched with him in a little hut she called 'housie' while their people ate in a second hut.

Popular summer fare for the grouse moor is cold meat, pies and salads with biscuits and fruitcake, a vacuum flask of clear soup laced with sherry, another of hot coffee and plenty of lager to wash down the food. On the hills, through the winter, nothing is more appreciated than a heartwarming soup or a good stew (see pp.34-7 and 271-273). The day starts with soup for breakfast with porridge, haddock or kippers, sausage and bacon (see pp.257-9) at the lodge or house, and the same soup or a stew is taken out with sandwiches for lunch.

A German cookery book of the early part of this century, quoted by Lady Harriet St Clair in her *Dainty Dishes*, suggests the drinks for a shooting breakfast or luncheon: 'both red and light white wine, as well as port or Madeira should be served, and particularly in cold weather, punch and mulled wine, which ought to be sent in jugs with a wooden cover over them, that they may be kept as hot as possible; not less than half a bottle is to be allowed for each gentleman'.

LAMPRIES IN CEYLON

A letter from Malkanthi Scott

Dear Claudia,

A typical Ceylon picnic even today would be Lampries, that is rice cooked in a rich chicken stock fried in ghee with onions, accompanied always with forcemeat balls (Dutch style) dry chicken curry aubergine curry, plantain curry Ceylon style pickles and sambols. About 2 tablespoons of the ghee rice is placed on the plantain leaf which has been steamed to make it flexible, the forcemeat balls, curries and sambols are placed on top of the rice, you then add about 2 tablespoons of coconut milk, (poured over the arrangement) make a neat parcel with the banana leaf, fasten with bamboo skewers and bake in a moderate oven for 10-15 minutes. This is eaten cold and when the parcel is opened the fragrance is most appetizing. We always take along bottles of iced water and aerated water which is fizzy and drunk in vast quantities by the women and children.

As most people take their servants along, the rush mats are spread on the ground and then a table-cloth spread over this; one usually eats with fingers on the banana leaf which serves as a plate – the servants have ready bowls of water with soap and towels for washing one's fingers. Fruit which is in abundance always end the meal.

Sometimes instead of Lampries, we take along pots of our favourite curries which have been cooked the day before and if there is wood available (which is always) we make a fire and cook the rice on the spot, delicious piping hot plain rice and cold accompaniments.

No Ceylonese would consider it an enjoyable occasion if you gave them a bread roll, sandwich or Pizza. Picnics are elaborate affairs which don't make any concessions for being eaten out of doors.

The peasants or working people, if they have to eat at all, for example when they go to the temple or to a festival or even awaiting admission to be seen at a hospital, take their entire family with them and cook their meal in a shady spot by the road. They do not eat for pleasure in public, eating is a very private activity, it is not a social occasion.

Basically a picnic is a Western concept and the Ceylonese, that is the educated Westernized person just takes along his servants and expects to eat more or less the kind of food he would eat in his home on a festive occasion. There are also other hazards which don't make picnicking very enjoyable, as the ants that swarm round as soon as one sits on the ground or the danger from snakes and lizards is very real.

There is so much more to say but it will take a whole day to say it!

A MIDDLE EASTERN AFFAIR

Some of my happiest childhood memories are of picnics in Egypt. My favourite was on the dunes of Agami in Alexandria. It was timed to coincide with the arrival of migrating quails on the beaches. The birds fell exhausted, to be caught in large nets and collected in baskets. They were cleaned and marinated in a rich cumin and coriander sauce and grilled on the beach over small fires. Fresh Arab bread was bought from the vendors who sang their wares on the beaches and played odds and even for a handful of pistachios or peanuts. The hollow rounds of bread were cut in half, opened out and placed under the birds to catch their flavoursome juices; then the quails were gathered in them to be eaten as a sandwich, soft bones and all. Water-melons and pieces of coconut and sweet nutty pastries, bought from the vendors, ended the meal.

Another popular picnic spot was near a small dam we called simply le barrage. We would bring large quantities of ful medames (Egyptian brown beans) in giant saucepans, on top of which were embedded shelled eggs which had been boiled gently for many hours with onion skins until they became light brown and their yolks creamy. A large box lined with foil held a salad of coarsely chopped tomatoes, cucumbers, cos lettuce, spring onions with parsley and fresh coriander leaves.

The beans were warmed up over a primus stove while we unrolled our rugs and settled down in expectation of the 'gala-gala', a magician who invariably produced baby chicks out of metal cups and eggs out of noses. We filled pouches of bread with the beans and sprinkled them with olive oil and a squeeze of lemon. Some people liked to add a crushed clove of garlic. We placed an egg cut in four in each portion, pressed down the beans and topped them with salad. A basket of fruit was followed by a variety of pastries filled with pistachio nuts, almonds, walnuts and dates, scented lightly with rose water and orange blossom water.

In an area which harbours many of nomadic ancestry and over which the sun shines constantly, eating out is a way of life. There are even official occasions for picnics.

Among these are the 'mulids' when people flock to the principal scenes of religious festivals, public gardens, shrines, tombs of saints and burial grounds. Thousands gather sometimes for days and nights, sleeping under tents. Dervishes perform and itinerant entertainers recite ancient romances of unrequited love and 'crime passionnel'. Conjurers no longer astonish with their age old tricks but people watch enthralled. They laugh at the buffoons and admire the acrobat's skill with the same pleasure that children have in listening to the same bed-time stories for years, noticing every little addition and new twist to the plot. Stick dancers, white robes flowing and turbans swaying, simulate a fight. Food is prepared for the whole period of the festival. It can be supplemented from the numerous stalls, erected with the swings and whirligigs, which sell falafels, kebabs, pastries and sweetmeats and stay open all night, lit up by lanterns. When the festival is over and the tents and stalls are taken down, cracked egg shells, dyed red or yellow to bring joy and happiness, limp lettuce leaves and discarded empty melon seeds carpet the areas of activity.

The most important of the national picnics in Egypt is not a religious occasion. It is Shem en Nesseem, which celebrates the arrival of spring. Town dwellers go out in the country or in boats, generally northwards, eating out in the fields or on the river bank, smelling the air which is thought to be particularly beneficial on that day. The main traditional food of the occasion is fessikh, a salted cured fish.

But no one waits for an official occasion.

In the Levant a picnic is not for the silent enjoyment of nature. You are too busy and too merry to notice the sea, the mountain or the river bank. The rule is the larger the group the better the picnic. The more for backgammon and cards. The more there are to tell jokes, the wealthier the gossip. The more there are that will sing and dance and the more dishes to choose from.

Few occasions can satisfy at the same time the convivial Arab spirit, the pleasure of being entertained and the legendary hospitality, as a picnic does. You are generous host and joyous guest at the same time, and the ultimate aim, to please, is developed to the point of an art in the contents of the picnic basket.

What one eats, as an enthusiast put it, is 'anything without a sauce, that is easily transportable, that can be eaten cold, or that is not too difficult to heat up'. And that does not leave very much out, for the open air gourmets will stop at nothing, armed with giant pans and primus stoves, to bring their food for a picnic.

Relatives, friends and neighbours are invited to join a party. Each family announces what it will contribute – usually its own favourite, one that it is hoped will be appreciated above all others, supplemented by a last minute surprise dish. There must be enough to serve at least one portion to each person present. Generosity must be boundless: honour is at stake. Even those who live frugally will surpass themselves in preparing a variety of delicacies.

When I was a child in Egypt, there were the traditional specialities more fondly taken on certain outings; seaside favourites and desert favourites, those taken on festivals, and very simple foods for casual, spontaneous affairs.

More often, and especially in a large party, the variety of dishes is absolutely stunning. Set out on a table-cloth or the traditional specially woven for outdoor revelling, rug, plates jostled for space. Numerous pies were invariably represented: sanbusak, half-moon shaped shortcrust filled with spicy meat or sharp cheese; fila (the Greek phylo), the paper-thin dough wrapped into little packets around fillings of spinach or cheese or fried minced meat with pine nuts; and the Sephardi speciality pasteles, the small pot-shaped pies filled with khandrajo, similar to a ratatouille. Kibbeh was always a favourite, its outer shell of soft lamb worked with cracked wheat holding the traditional fried minced meat with onions and pine nuts delicately

seasoned with cinnamon. Regional versions such as one with raisins or an easier one of layers smoothed flat in a tray sometimes replaced it. Rice-stuffed vine leaves were almost always offered. Other vegetables commonly stuffed were tomatoes, courgettes, small aubergines, onions and peppers. For eating cold, minced meat was not included in the stuffing, but the rice was generously partnered with chopped tomatoes, onion, crushed garlic, a great deal of parsley and occasionally other herbs such as fresh coriander leaves and mint. Much appreciated, though common, was a meat loaf – blehat lahma – holding a variety of surprises such as hard-boiled eggs and apricots, differing according to the family that produced it. Cold chicken was juicy from being cooked sofrito in a pan with oil and a little water, sharply lemony with a taste of garlic and cardamom and beautifully yellow with turmeric. Otherwise cooked chicken was minced, mixed with veal and pistachio nuts, and patted into balls or shaped as a loaf and cooked again. Fish usually made an appearance as blehat samak, finger-shaped rissoles of minced fish flavoured with cumin and coriander. Occasionally it was elaborately stuffed.

Salads, a variety of them, simple and unpretentious or rich and exotic, were always present. Vegetables either raw or cooked, cracked wheat and pulses and even cheese were usually dressed with olive oil and lemon juice rich in chopped onions.

Another dish always encountered was ajja – an omelette in the style of the Spanish ones, thick with vegetables or minced meat and excellent cold, accompanied by a bowl of yoghurt.

And for the sweet-toothed as most of us were, there were always pastries to follow the fruit. Baklava, layers of crisp fila filled with chopped pistachios; konafa with the appearance of shredded wheat also filled with a choice of nuts; basbousa of semolina with coconut, all soused with a slightly lemony sugar syrup perfumed with orange blossom water. For those who did not like sticky fingers, afters were ma'amoul, tartlets filled with date paste, or assabih bi loz, almond fingers, or the numerous petits fours made with almond paste or caramelized nuts, dried apricots and dates.

Everything was carefully prepared and well set out in a manner pleasing to the eye. Parsley was sprinkled over or laid in a bunch next to a dish. Colourful pickles, some pink from beetroot, and olives were placed in small plates and spread out evenly amongst the bigger ones. Portions were cut diagonally, cayenne pepper was mixed with oil and dribbled on tahina, the popular sesame meal dip, in a criss-cross pattern.

'The more one loves, the more one offers and the more one eats'; an Arab proverb assured us that food equals the affection.

The recipes mentioned above and others suitable for picnics are given in my *A Book of Middle Eastern Food*. I have included here a few different versions of special outdoor favourites.

Share the preparation if you are going with a crowd; otherwise choose one or two of the main dishes to serve with a bowl of yoghurt or tahina (see p.49) and a large salad made of lettuce, cucumber, and tomatoes all chopped up (not too small). Pack it in a plastic bag, ready to be dressed just before you eat. Follow with fruit.

Blehat samak (fried fish balls)

Poach for 5 minutes, drain and flake 1 kg (2 lb) cod and haddock or a mixture of any other fish.

Soak 5 medium thick 10 cm (4 in) slices of brown or wholemeal bread, crusts removed, in water. Squeeze dry and crumble.

In a large bowl combine the flaked fish, bread, and 4 medium eggs. Add 2 cloves of garlic, crushed, and 2 teaspoons of cumin, and season to taste with salt and pepper. Mix well and knead until a smooth paste. Shape the mixture into $2^1/_2$ cm (1 in) balls.

Sauté in hot oil until brown, then drain on absorbent paper.

Meat ajja – an omelette

This is an Iraqi recipe from Sami Zubaida's family.

Chop a large onion and a large potato finely. Fry 125 g ($^1/_4$ lb) lean minced beef in a little oil and stir well until it has changed colour. Add a small bunch of parsley, finely chopped, and remove from the heat. Lightly beat 6 eggs and stir in the meat, potato and onion. Add salt and pepper to taste and a teaspoon each of cumin and coriander and stir until well blended.

Pour a spoonful at a time into hot oil in a frying pan. Turn as soon as the bottom has set firmly and cook the other side. These are easily stacked in a plastic box.

Tabbouleh (cracked wheat salad)

This Lebanese salad, which now has an international reputation, is refreshing on a summer's day with its abundance of chopped parsley and its lemon and minty flavour. It is the traditional accompaniment to kibbeh naye. In the mountain villages of Lebanon freshly picked sharp vine leaves are passed around to scoop up the salad. In towns the pale crisp leaves from the heart of the cos lettuce are provided.

150 g (5 oz) burghul (cracked wheat or bulgur), 150 g (5 oz) spring onions or mild Spanish onions (finely chopped), 3 tomatoes (chopped), 100 g (4 oz) parsley (finely chopped), a few sprigs of fresh mint (finely chopped) or 2 tablespoons dried mint, 6-8 tablespoons olive oil, juice of 1 1/2 lemons or more to taste, salt and pepper to taste.

For serving: *Vine leaves, lightly poached, or fresh cos lettuce leaves.*

Soak the burghul in cold water for 10 minutes. (There is much controversy about this time.) Drain well and put in a large bowl with all the other ingredients. Prepare at least an hour before serving to allow the wheat to absorb the dressing and become plump and tender.

Serve in individual plates lined with vine leaves or lettuce leaves. Place a bowl of firm young lettuce leaves to use as scoops for the salad on the table.

⁊ Stuffed vegetables

A tray of mixed stuffed vegetables, cooked in oil is ordinarily brought on outings, as well as rolled vine leaves prepared with the season's new crop. Firmer and less fragile vegetables are best for obvious reasons. A sweet and sour flavour is particularly good for these vegetables when they are to be eaten cold the day after they have been cooked.

Stuffed onions. Peel 2 large Spanish onions. With a sharp knife, make a cut from top to bottom through to the centre on one side of each onion. Throw into boiling water and cook until the onions are soft and start to open so that the layers can be detached. Drain and cool slightly before separating the layers carefully.

For the filling: mix 175 g (6 oz) rice, washed and drained, 175 g (6 oz) tomatoes, skinned, seeded and finely chopped, a small bunch of parsely, finely chopped, 2 tablespoons of raisins or sultanas and 2 tablespoons of pine nuts (optional). Season to taste with salt and pepper, 1/2 teaspoon of cinnamon, 1/4 teaspoon of allspice, and an optional 2 teaspoons of fresh mint (or 1 of dry). Put a tablespoon in each hollow onion layer and roll up tightly.

Put a little oil in a large heavy-bottomed pan, then a layer of lettuce leaves or discarded onion pieces, so that the vegetables do not get burnt and pack them closely in layers over this. Cover with water mixed with 2-3 tablespoons of wine vinegar, 1 tablespoon of sugar and 5 tablespoons of olive oil. You may substitute 1 tablespoon of tamarind paste (obtained from Indian shops) for the vinegar.

Cover the pan and simmer gently for about 45 minutes until onion and filling are done.

Stuffed courgettes. In *A Book of Middle Eastern Food* I gave a recipe for stuffed courgettes cooked in apricot sauce. Here I have put the apricots in with the filling so that they are less messy to hold in the hand.

Choose 1 kg (2 lb) medium-sized courgettes. Slice off the stem. Using a narrow apple corer, make a hole at the stem end and scoop out the pulp by twisting it round, being careful not to break the skin. The other end must remain closed.

Do not throw away the pulp which comes out in thin long fingers. Boil and dress with a vinaigrette to serve like mock asparagus.

For the filling: mix 175 g (6 oz) rice, washed and drained, 1 large onion, finely chopped, 175 g (6 oz) tomatoes, skinned, seeded and finely chopped, a small bunch of parsely, finely chopped, and 225 g (1/2 lb) sharp dried apricots, finely chopped. Season with salt and pepper, a teaspoon of cinnamon and a pinch of allspice. Mix well.

Fill each courgette three-quarters full only to allow the rice to swell.

Lay a few thin slices of tomatoes or lettuce leaves at the bottom of a wide heavy pan so that the vegetables do not stick or burn. Pack them side by side tightly in layers over this. Cover with water mixed with the juice of 1 lemon, 2-3 cloves of garlic, crushed, and 1 teaspoon of dried crushed mint. Simmer very gently, covered, for about an hour or until the courgettes are tender and the filling cooked, adding a little water if necessary.

❧ Lemon chicken

In a large heavy saucepan, heat 3 tablespoons of oil with 1 teaspoon of turmeric, 2 crushed cloves of garlic, 1 cracked cardamom pod, the juice of 1 whole lemon and half a glass of water. Put the chicken in the pan, add salt and pepper, and cook very slowly over low heat. Turn the chicken often, adding a little water to keep it moist and to have enough sauce at the end of the cooking when the chicken is tender (about an hour). Cut into pieces and remove the skin and some of the larger bones. Arrange in a box and pour the sauce over it.

❧ Lahma bil karaz (meat balls with cherries)

1 kg (2 lb) lean lamb or veal (minced), salt and black pepper, ½ teaspoon grated nutmeg, ½ teaspoon ground cloves, ½ teaspoon ground cinnamon, oil, ½ kg (1 lb) sour or morello cherries (pitted), sugar and/or lemon juice, rounds of Arab bread or slices of white bread.

Knead the meat with your hand to achieve a smooth, pasty texture. Season with the salt, pepper and spices, and knead again. Form marble-sized balls with the mixture and fry them gently in oil, shaking the pan to colour them all over.

Fresh, pitted black cherries should be used for this dish if possible. If these are not available, use tinned cherries or black cherry jam. Stew the fresh cherries in a large pan with very little water, adding sugar and/or lemon juice to taste according to the sweetness or acidity of the fruit. If using tinned fruit or jam, add only lemon as they will be sweet enough already. Add the sautéed meat balls, and simmer gently until cooked through crushing the cherries with a fork when they become soft enough. Let the sugar in the sauce become caramelized a little, but add more water if this happens before the meat balls are cooked and the fruit is soft.

Serve on pitta bread, soft side up. If this is not available, cut thinnish slices of white bread, remove the crusts and arrange the slices on a large serving dish. Cover each slice with several meat balls and some cherry sauce. This traditional way of serving makes it an easy food to pick up at a picnic.

A JAPANESE PICNIC

For centuries, no pastime has been considered more pleasurable and more elegant in Japan than an excursion into the countryside with food and wine and a few companions, where verses are composed, inspired by the ever changing faces of nature. Sensitive to the seasons and the weather and to the products of land and sea, the Japanese people celebrate their deep and ancient love for their hills and waters and the progress of the year from spring to winter with poems and food. They have even made a ritual of gazing at the moon, and celebrate the blooming of chrysanthemums and cherry blossom. In a booklet written in 1936 for the understanding by the West of Japanese food and ways, Professor Kaneko Tezuka describes 'flower-viewing' and 'moon-viewing' foods which the Japanese take on large party outings with their families and company colleagues, fellow workers and employees. The cherry blossom is the national flower, and it is customary to rejoice under the trees when they are in full bloom, and to share the 'flower-viewing' food.

'Chrysanthemum-viewing food' is also prepared for an ancient autumnal festival on the ninth day of the ninth month of the lunar calendar. Each family carries a varied and traditional feast in stacks of three or four vermilion or pale green lacquered wooden boxes together with small wooden plates to serve on. Those who treasure ancient refinements carry their sake in gourds slung in heavy red cords with tassels. With a mixture of hedonism and an ingrained love of beauty, days are spent enjoying food and extolling the virtues of the evanescent cherry blossoms, which will fall tomorrow like snow, and the first grasses of spring or the chrysanthemum, which will close up for the night but whose roots will never die.

No one in Japan can remain unmoved in the presence of the moon, which is loved in all its shapes and moods; in the spring, shining hazily on the blossoms, in the summer, cool beside the water, and in the winter clear and cold on frosty nights. They may gaze for hours at it, retiring only when at last it sinks toward the hills, and recite with emotion:

> Must the moon disappear
> In such haste,
> Leaving us still unsatisfied?
> Would that the mountain rim might flee
> And refuse to receive her
>
> ORIWARA NARIHIRA

But most loved of all is the full moon of the autumn harvest called meigetsu, which the nobles of ancient times used to woo at Waka-no-wra and Suma, now famous places for 'viewing'. On the evening of the fifteenth of the eighth month, families sit out on the verandah, enjoying its autumn calm, praising it effusively and eating the traditional offerings: the fruits of the season, persimmons and grapes, and vegetables such as taros, green soy beans and little dumplings made of rice flour symbolizing the round silver moon. For the last day of the year there is also ritual outdoor food. Hot soups and stews are served, cod and buri are grilled, and boiled radish is eaten with sweetened miso and buckwheat.

The delights of the packed lunch box are not only reserved for moments of inspiration and ritual, they are very much part of everyday life. Among the attractions of travelling by train, as Kimiko Magasawa and Camy Condon write in *Eating Cheap in Japan*, are the special lunches for travellers which are sold on platforms and trains and in shops near the main stations. This fashion started 90 years ago and spread throughout the country. Different lines have their own specialities and many stations are known for a particular kind of food – Yokohama Station for Chinese meat balls, Chiba Station for clams and rice. These lunches, called eki-ben, are sold in wooden boxes of various shapes, wrapped in beautiful paper and tied with string. Etiquette requires that the packaging is kept intact for rewrapping in exactly the same way after eating. The contents are usually cold seasoned rice with bits of cooked fish and vegetables. Similar boxes called o-bento are sold on motorways, grilled eel being the most popular meal.

A favourite picnic food for children is onigiri, balls of rice containing a pickled plum and a small piece of salted salmon or pink cod fish in the centre. One special picnic lunch, maku no uchi, originated as a meal to be eaten between the acts of the long kabuki plays and came in a half-moon shaped lacquered box. Four sections contain small rice rolls sprinkled with black sesame seeds, a piece of grilled fish or shrimp, a slice of egg, a few vegetables and pickles. As always in Japan the arrangement is particularly beautiful to stimulate the appetite.

ॐ Sushi

Everywhere in Japan are the sushi shops serving snacks to take away in little boxes. They contain combinations of fish and seafood, cooked, marinated or simply raw on a bed of fragrant rice. Although in Japan these picnic favourites are prepared by skilled professionals, they are an easy and delicious way to start an acquaintance with that simple and elegant cuisine which is so different from that of the rest of the world, having evolved in long periods of isolation. Many Japanese shops have now opened in London, selling the necessary ingredients, and very fresh fish is obtainable for sashimi, the sliced raw fish which is the best part of sushi.

Prepare everything in advance, ready to assemble at the last minute. The fish must be kept covered and refrigerated in a cold box, but the rice need not. Take sake or a dry white wine to serve with the food.

The rice: Learn how to make rice with vinegar dressing and the rest is easy. Use short grain rice which holds together. This recipe is from *The Complete Book of Japanese Cooking* by Elisabeth Lambert Ortiz with Mitsuko Endo.

500 g (1 lb) rice, 8 cm (3 in) square kombu (kelp), 600 ml (1 pint) water, 4 tablespoons rice vinegar, 1 tablespoon sugar, 2 teaspoons salt.

'Thoroughly wash the rice in several changes of water until the water runs clear, and drain in a sieve for at least 1 hour. Put into a heavy saucepan with a tightly fitting lid. Clean the seaweed with a damp cloth and cut with kitchen shears into a ($1/2$-inch) fringe. Bury the seaweed in the rice. Add the water, cover and bring to a boil over high heat, removing the seaweed just before the water boils. Otherwise it will flavour the rice too strongly. Reduce the heat to moderate and cook for 5 to 6 minutes, then reduce the heat to very low and cook for 15 minutes. Raise the heat to high for 10 seconds, then let the rice stand off the heat for 10 minutes.

'In a small saucepan combine the rice vinegar, sugar and salt. Heat through, stirring to mix. Turn the rice out into a large, shallow dish, preferably wooden. In Japan a bandai (sushioke), a large round wooden dish, would be used. Pour the vinegar mixture little by little over the rice, mixing it with a shamoji (wooden spatula) or a fork, and fanning it vigorously to make it glisten. It is a good idea to have a helper do the fanning, though it can be managed alone. The fanning cools the rice quickly and this is what makes it glisten.

'Cover the rice with a cloth until ready to use. It can be left standing at room temperature for several hours before using if necessary.'

The fish. Have a selection of very fresh raw fish or shellfish which may include salmon, tuna, bass, bream, red snapper, mackerel, sardines, sole, scallops, flounder, squid, clams, sea urchins – any that can be eaten raw. Prawns must be cooked for 1/2 minutes, conger eel for a little longer, and octopus must be tenderized by bashing and boiling. It is possible to settle for one kind of fish only but a selection is an opportunity for sampling fish at its very best in its natural state. 500 g (1 lb) of fish will serve 4 people as a main course.

The art lies in filleting, skinning and cutting the fish in 1/2 cm (1/4 in) thick diagonal slices about 2 1/2 cm by 5 cm (1 in by 2 in) and arranging it with style on a flat dish or wooden platter with a decorative array of raw vegetables, cut in very thin slices or strips. Carrots, white and red radish, cucumber, onions, spring onions, turnips and pickled ginger are mostly used as garnish.

The dip. Have small bowls of soya sauce and of wasabi (green horseradish powder which is very powerful and can be obtained from Japanese and Chinese stores) mixed to a paste with a little water. You only need the slightest amount of horseradish for a slice of fish.

For a special soya sauce mix in to taste a little vinegar preferably rice vinegar) and a pinch of sugar.

To serve. In sushi restaurants, Japanese cooks wet their hands with vinegared water to shape the rice into oblong patties about 2 1/2-5 cm (1-2 in) long without it sticking to their fingers. But it is just as good to spread and press the rice on to a large platter and arrange the fish and garnish on top for everyone to pick up morsels and dip them in the horseradish and soya sauce.

COOKING IN THE OPEN

COOKING OVER EMBERS

Barbecuing has become a fashionable way of entertaining in the summer months, opening a whole new tradition of cookery in England. Although enthusiasm for the activity has come from America, people have begun to look to the Old World for their culinary inspiration. Amongst the many theories about the origin of the word barbecue, a plausible one is the Spanish barbacoa, the frame on which the Spaniards saw the Mexican Indians smoke-dry their fish and cook their meats.

Cooking over a wood or charcoal fire is of course the most ancient form of cooking. It imparts a unique appetizing smoky flavour to food which no other method can capture, and which has caused it to remain a matter of pleasure throughout the world rather than mere necessity. An old Italian saying claims that 'Even an old shoe tastes good if it is cooked over charcoal', and the smell, as anyone who has passed a kebab vendor knows, is most alluring and plays a great part in sharpening the appetite.

Although perfectly simple, there is an art in good grilling and roasting which can be acquired with practice. The secret lies in making a good fire, controlling the heat and distributing it evenly. The food is so good that all one needs to accompany it is a salad, and fruit to follow.

An open wood fire

If you are building a fire choose a spot sheltered from strong winds. Dig or scrape a small trench around the spot to stop roots catching fire and smouldering underground.

Build it between large stones, bricks or logs, lifted by small stones so as to let the breeze circulate underneath and fan the flames. They will act as a windbreak, prevent the fire from spreading, and also hold the grill. A more easily lit and maintained alternative is to dig a shallow pit 20-50 cm (8-20 in) deep (its depth depends on the size of foods to be cooked) and build the fire in it. Dig it in the direction of the wind so as to allow it to fan the flames. Line it with thin stones if the earth is wet.

Wood takes a long time to burn to a bed of embers especially if it is large or a little damp, so you must start preparations well over an hour before you would like to eat.

Build your fire gradually, beginning with crumpled paper, dry leaves or bark, pine needles or acorns in a loose pile. Cover with dry twigs – use dead wood and breakable small wood, then sticks converging at the top to let the air circulate.

Thrust a burning match in the centre, then add larger pieces of wood, crossing them so as to let air circulate. Split the wood if it seems wet; the inside will be drier. If the logs are too thick, they will take too long to produce a bed of embers. Cut them into relatively small pieces of uniform size so that they burn down to embers at the same rate. Keep your fire small. It is easier to handle and as effective as a larger one.

Do not leave the fire unattended while it burns and watch for sparks that might catch a nearby branch or grasses. Start cooking only when the wood is reduced to embers. This usually takes about 30-45 minutes.

Small pieces of wood or a large pile of dry twigs which die down to embers in 10-15 minutes suffice for steaks and foods which cook so quickly that there is no need for embers that will hold their heat for long.

The choice of wood. Alcide Bontou in *Traité de la cuisine bourgeoise bordelaise* describes the old way of cooking entrecôte in Bordeaux: 'In times gone by gourmets did not disdain an invitation to go down into the wine cellars and eat an entrecôte with the cellar master and the tonnelier who had a reputation for preparing it well. They made their fire with hoops of chestnut wood from old barrels and claimed that this gave a particularly good flavour to the meat.

The choice of wood is important. It should of course not be rotten, crumbly or damp. For a good fire use dry slow-burning hard woods that give long-lasting coals such as oak, ash, beech (which burns green), hickory, walnut and maple. Chestnut, lime and sycamore also make good fuel. Use soft woods which burn quickly and are only good for kindling to start a fire. Avoid resinous woods such as pine, which gives a turpentine taste to your food. Elder and elm wood are not much good for burning. Spruce, cedar and birch are soft but add a distinctive biting flavour. Aromatic woods such as fruit woods, especially vines, and branches of juniper or bay tree can be added to perfume the fire and give a delicious taste to the food being cooked. Hazel-nut is good too, and its thin green branches may be used as a spit or as skewers. For some reason, superstition has branded poplar and aspen as 'unlucky' woods.

The first Mogul Emperor Babur (1483-1530) had some advice regarding the firewood to be found around Kabul in his diary.

This selection is from Arette Susannah Beveridge's translation (1921):

The snow fall being so heavy in Kabul, it is fortunate that excellent fire-wood is had near by. Given one day to fetch it, wood can be had of the khanjak (mastic), bilut (holm-oak), badamcha (small almond) and gargand. Of these khanjak wood is the best; it burns with flame and nice smell, makes plenty of hot ashes and does well even if sappy. Holm-oak is also first rate fire-wood, blazing less than mastic but, like it, making a hot fire with plenty of hot ashes, and nice smell. It has the peculiarity in burning that when its leafy branches are set alight, they fire up with amazing sound, blazing and crackling from bottom to top. It is good fun to burn it. The wood of the small-almond is the most beautiful and commonly-used, but it does not make a lasting fire. The gargand is quite a slow shrub, thorny, and burning sappy or dry; it is the fuel of the Ghazni people.

❧ Charcoal fires

Though it is perfectly sensible to burn wood in a commercial barbecue, charcoal, the fuel commonly used for it, is more manageable and burns quickly and well. Most ironmongers supply it in lumps or briquettes.

Briquettes give a more uniform heat, are longer lasting and do not spark.

❧ Buying the barbecue

The barbecue trade has blossomed in recent years, and department stores are ready at the first song of the cuckoo with an evergrowing selection at prices to meet every budget and with a vast array of equipment and tools.

If you are ready to invest in a good portable or permanent barbecue there is a wide variety to choose from. New models come out every year, and it is therefore most advisable to visit a store with a large selection before you make your choice. Buy a barbecue that is large enough to accommodate your family, larger still if you entertain.

Our first barbecue, a wedding present, was a very light fire-bowl on wheels which we could easily take out on day excursions. It lasted 10 years until rust eventually ended its days. For almost as many years now we have had a hibachi (the Japanese word for fire box). It is the 'triple' version which can provide for a large number of people. Although heavy, the sturdy and simple cast-iron bowl is easily transportable in the boot of a car and has accompanied us on a boating holiday on the Norfolk Broads. We do not mind its ground level position as we like squatting. Its advantage is that the three separate grills can be raised or lowered to fit into various special notches.

Your choice must depend on your needs and life style. For camping and picnics the barbecue must of course be portable, either small, folding or collapsible. Choose a comfortable height if you do not like squatting or bending. A heavy one is all right for the garden, and wheels help to move it around. It must be well-balanced and steady. If it has wheels, there must be proper brakes and wedges to stop it rolling. The material it is made of must be sturdy and long-lasting and preferably rust-proof such as cast-iron, porcelain-enamelled steel, or cast aluminium.

The fire-bowl should hold enough charcoal for lengthy cooking. The distance from the grill to the fire must be variable and there must be adjustable air vents on the side of the bowl to regulate the heat.

Wooden handles are best because they do not conduct heat and thus minimize the danger of burning hands.

A barbecue need not be complicated or expensive. Indeed, you may even make it yourself.

❧ Making a barbecue

Inspired by the Portuguese, we have used a large clay flower-pot. It is best lined with aluminium foil. Push your finger through this and the bottom hole and lift the pot on two bricks to allow for a draught. Half fill with pebbles and cover these with a good layer of charcoal. Place a grill over the top (chicken wire will do). If you are using large enough skewers these can be laid on the edges of the pot without any risk of falling in.

You may use a biscuit tin or an old metal tray with holes punched round the sides to let in air. If you are cooking for two, a thick foil container, the type obtained from freezer shops will hold a couple of hamburgers or two small skewers. An old wheelbarrow can make a useful mobile barbecue. Punch holes through the bottom and sides and fill with stones and gravel. For a large grill rack improvise with parts from an old discarded oven or refrigerator.

At my hotel in the Seychelles large metal barrels were cut in half lengthwise. They were raised to table height for Creole barbecue nights with girders used to make stands. Coconut fronds made a screen from the sea breeze behind the cooks who dished out spare ribs, slices of sucking pig, sweet potatoes, giant prawns, bananas and strange-looking fish.

You can even build a permanent structure in the garden. James F. Marks gives detailed instructions on how to do so in *Barbecues*. Use fire-bricks, which do not crack easily, and build in a spot which normally has enough wind to keep a fire alive but which does not send all the smoke straight into the eating area or through the French windows.

Useful accessories

Only a few tools are really indispensable, some are useful, but most are only fun. I have been barbecuing happily for nearly 20 years with only a grill, a spit and skewers. Fish slices, brushes and forks have come from my everyday kitchen but I must admit I have occasionally wished I had some tongs handy.

A spit is required for cooking large joints, whole chicken or a very large fish. The best ones are made in heavy chrome-plated steel sturdy enough to hold a heavy joint. Although a battery-operated electric one turns automatically and allows the meat to cook unattended, turning occasionally by hand is part of the pleasure.

The grill must be rust-proof, preferably in chrome-plated steel. The bars must not be too far apart or small morsels will fall through. Hinged double grills and baskets are especially good for holding and turning over meat and particularly fish, easily. The grill must always be well oiled before you begin to cook or the food will stick.

Skewers. Many types are sold. For kebabs, buy long ones in flattened steel with a sharp point at one end. Their sword shape is said to be derived from the swords of Turkish warriors who used to thread meat on them for cooking on an open fire. It prevents the meat from sliding and twisting around while cooking. Some are also slightly twisted to make slipping even less likely. Two pronged ones may be used for holding larger pieces. Wooden skewers burn but you can improvise with thin fresh green branches from which the bark has been stripped.

Tongs for turning food or moving embers must be long handled and so must *basting spoons* and *brushes* (use bristle not nylon or plastic) to avoid burning fingers. A long *two-pronged fork* may be handy as well as a spatula for turning over small pieces of food.

Thermometers. Some people like to register the heat of the fire more accurately than by hand. A meat thermometer pushed through the centre of the meat will determine whether it is done.

Bellows are seldom necessary in this country but I do occasionally use a round, woven straw fan.

Aluminium foil is invaluable. Use a heavy duty one, preferably for wrapping foods to cook or to keep warm, as well as for lining the fire bowl for extra reflected heat and for keeping it clean. It may also be spread out over the grill and used as a hot plate (with holes pricked in if you like if the food is not too fat).

For cleaning barbecue and equipment use a metal brush with detergent and hot water.

❧ The charcoal fire

To build the fire, place dry twigs over a loose pile of crumpled paper. Cover with a pyramid of charcoal and set the paper alight. We sometimes use gas from a cylinder to get the fire going. Otherwise several kinds of fire-starters are available. Candle stubs are useful. Small meta solid tablets work well and do not leave an odour. There are also electric starters and a liquid fuel which you sprinkle over the charcoal and let it soak in before you try to light it. But you must not use petrol or paraffin; they are dangerous and give a bad smell and a bad taste. Once the pyramid of charcoal has ignited and started to burn evenly, rake it and spread it out over the surface you need for cooking, taking care not to disturb the firebed. It will be ready for cooking when it has reduced to glowing ash-covered embers, usually after about 20 minutes.

A common mistake is to use too much fuel but you will soon learn to estimate how much you need. For small grills it is enough to cover the area taken up by food, two layers deep.

If you are grilling meat for three people you may need no more than

14 briquet lumps. If you are spit-roasting, which takes a long time, you will of course need more – as much as 40-45 lumps. Even then you start with a few and add more, as you need them. Keep coals in reserve at the side so that they can warm up before being added, a few at a time. Putting on too many cold pieces at once will lower the temperature and cause a lot of smoke.

To save remaining fuel for another occasion smother it with old ashes or throw it in a metal bucket of water.

A refinement is to put a layer of gravel in the fire-box under the charcoal to aid ventilation. (Grease and ashes can be washed off with liquid detergent and the gravel can be used again.)

❧ The art of cooking on embers

Whether you have an elaborate barbecue or an open fire the principle is the same. Cooking is done over the gentle heat of glowing coals or wood embers and you start to cook only when the fire has burned down and the smoke has gone, and a light powdery grey ash covers the glowing coals. Flames will dry out and scorch the food outside and leave it uncooked inside.

You must find out for yourself what heat you require for different types of food and regulate your fire accordingly. Therein lies the art. The cooking time depends on the thickness and type of food, its distance from the fire and from other foods, the quality of the charcoal, the size of the firebed and weather conditions.

To regulate the heat you can lower or raise the grill. Otherwise, for a hotter fire, push the coals together, and for a lower heat, rake them apart. Shaking the white ash off the embers makes them hotter as does more air. If there is a strong wind use wind breaks to shield the fire, and if there is not enough breeze, fan the fire or open vents.

For very slow cooking, such as a large roast, use gentler indirect heat. Do not place the food directly over the fire but a little to the side. Or in the style of the gypsies, make a ring of burning coals around it. Let the joint stand for about 10 minutes before carving.

For grilling you need an even temperature. Test the heat by putting your hand above the coals at the distance where you will place the food. If you cannot leave it longer than 3 seconds it is probably too hot. If you can leave it for almost 4 seconds, it is medium hot, and it is warm if you can leave it for 5 seconds. Move pieces already cooked away from the centre of the fire to make way for less cooked pieces from the periphery. Use a little water – squirt it with a syringe if you like – to put out any flare-ups which result from dripping fat.

Trust your own taste and judgement. You can only learn by experience.

❧ Aromatics

If glowing embers give food a splendid taste, aromatics can make it superlative. Branches or sprigs of herbs thrown into the fire, when the food can catch their perfume and retain it, are a special refinement. Dried herbs, which burn too readily and whose perfume is quickly lost, must be used just before the food is ready. Fresh herbs give out a more powerful and long lasting scent. As their moisture and their oils create a cloud of smoke they must be thrown in a little at a time when the meat or fish is almost done. Delicate herbs such as wild thyme and marjoram can be used generously, strongly perfumed ones such as rosemary, sparingly.

Vine twigs or prunings give a specially delicate taste. They will burst into a crackling flame at the touch of a match. A few handsful of these alone will suffice for a quick grill. Dried fennel stalks make a good bed on which to grill fish such as sea bass and red mullet; other dried herbs may be added with the stalks. Damp hickory chips at the last stage give a smoky flavour. Pieces of garlic and orange peel in the fire also give a delightful aroma.

H. D. Renner in *The Origin of Food Habits*, places gastronomy in culture somewhere between painting and perfumery – as a 'visual and nasal' art. The smell of roasting meat together with that of burning fruit wood and dried herbs, as voluptuous as incense in a church, is enough to turn anyone into a budding gastronome.

In many regions it is considered good to flavour meat with the food the animal has grazed on, such as the wild thyme whose small purple flowers made the mutton spicy, the laver weed, seaweed and salt grasses which gave the marsh lamb a distinct iodine tang, the fruit peels and berries of those fed in the orchard or on the moor or the mint which kept the young lamb happy in the warm valley.

❧ To smoke food

Though smoke generally gives an unpleasant taste to food, the one produced by the damp shavings or sawdust or damp branches of aromatic woods such as oak, alder, hickory, poplar or fruit wood (never resinous woods) imparts a delicious flavour. There are many smokers on the market and there is one you can improvise on p.283. But it is possible to obtain the special smoky flavour by grilling the food first, then smothering the embers with damp sawdust or shavings or damp branches or leaves or herbs plucked from the countryside. If you cover the food with a biscuit tin or similar container or tarpaulin, the elusive scented smoke will permeate it better.

❧ Marinades

However fragrant the aroma provided by burning herbs, it is a fleeting one. For meats to be truly impregnated with flavours, they must be steeped in a marinade for some time. These aromatic baths, usually a mixture of oil and wine, vinegar or lemon juice, even cider and beer, with herbs and seasonings, flavour and tenderize meat and also prevent foods from drying out on the grill.

The tougher meats and those whose own flavour is not the very best benefit most from this treatment, particularly the smaller morsels cut up as kebab which retain all the flavourings.

Fish needs it the least and is enhanced more by herbs in the belly. Milk is sometimes used with smoked fish and sour cream with fresh fish. Honey may be added to lemon or vinegar for a sweet and sour taste. Vermouth, cognac, armagnac, whisky, port and Madeira, all give a magnificent flavour if the fish is coated with them before being wrapped in foil.

There are several classic marinades and many variations. The whole range of herbs, spices and peppers as well as garlic and onion, lemon zest and celery leaves find a place in one or the other. Their use is often a matter of tradition and culture; the better known combinations such as fish with fennel, rosemary with pork, mint with lamb, tarragon with chicken are certainly good, but it does not mean that others should not be tried.

The method: Put the meat, chicken or fish in a deep bowl so that it is covered completely by the marinade. Turn occasionally and leave covered for at least 1 hour or as long as 2 days in a cool place or in the refrigerator. The longer you leave it the tastier and the more tender it will be.

Meat should not be chilled when it is cooked or it will be overdone on the outside and undercooked inside. Take out from the refrigerator 1 or 2 hours before you are ready to cook and drain it well as dripping oil will cause the fire to flare up and smoke.

Moisten with the marinade occasionally, using a brush or spoon, to prevent the food drying out.

Except with fish salt is not usually included in the marinade as it may draw out the juices and dry out the meat. Add it when you are ready to cook or at the end of the cooking.

A glaze may be brushed on to meat or chicken joints about 15 minutes before the end of cooking time to give the food colour and lustre. Recently a mixture of clear honey, lemon juice and soya sauce with a sprinkling of powdered cloves has become popular. It should not be put on too soon as it will caramelize and burn.

❧ Basting and barding – a protection from drying

The heat of a fire, far or near is a harsh form of cooking. Everything except fat meat needs moistening with fat or the result will be dry and hard.

Pure fat, melted butter or oil (better still a mixture of $1/3$ butter and $2/3$ oil), or a marinade may serve to baste meat, fish and vegetables. Use a long-handled spoon to baste a large joint and where the juices fall into a tray pick up only fat on top of the gravy. Use a brush for smaller pieces cooked over the fire when drippings are likely to cause flare ups. If you are in the countryside with wild herbs growing around it is pleasant and attractive to use a few sprigs with which to brush the fat.

It is customary to bard certain lean meats and game and the breast of poultry. Cover with thin strips of bacon or pork fat tied with string. Depending on the size of the meat and the cooking time much or all of the fat will melt away lending a distinctive taste to the meat.

In France lacy caul is commonly used instead of strips of fat. Caul fat is a fatty membrane enveloping the intestines. It acts as a self baster when used as a wrapper. Soak it in lukewarm water for 2-3 minutes until it loosens up. Rinse and lay on a dry cloth and carefully open it up. Cut the best parts into rectangles 12 cm by 18 cm (5 in by 7 in).

❧ Wrapping in leaves

Leaves are the most natural protection for lean and delicate morsels on a fire. Papaya, palm and banana leaves and wetted corn husks are used in countries where they grow. Banana skins make an excellent moist case and lettuce and cabbage leaves can also be eaten. Vine leaves, used for a few delicacies and traditionally to wrap up quails and red mullet, lend a distinctive sharp savour.

❧ Cooking en papillote

Food can be wrapped in damp paper to prevent it from burning or drying out on the fire. Brown paper and newspaper are commonly used though they do not improve the taste. At the start of the twentieth century greased parchment paper became very popular for cooking delicate, quickly cooked foods en papillote. This retained the aroma and juices until the parcel was opened out on the plate.

Foil is more convenient to use and makes it easier to twist edges in to a tightly closed seal. The food inside is steamed in its own juice rather than grilled, and though it has none of the characteristic taste of food cooked over coals, it is remarkably successful with fish and seafood, chicken breast and thin slices of veal, which tend to dry out. With it comes the advantage of adding other ingredients or stuffing. It takes a little longer to cook than food put straight on to the fire and only slightly longer than in paper. Grease the foil so that the food does not stick to it.

To make a papillote, cut the paper or foil into a shape large enough to contain the piece comfortably; hearts are traditional but a circle or a square or rectangle will do equally well. Place the food on one half and fold the other half over it. To fasten the package, hold the edges together and turn them over twice, like a hem, then twist to make an airtight seal. The parcel must be a little baggy to allow for puffing up with the heat.

But you may wrap up the food in any way you like as long as it is properly sealed in.

APPETIZERS AND VEGETABLES OVER THE FIRE

Rather than wait for the meat to be ready, start with tid-bits which take a short time on the fire. They are called amuse gueules by the French because they are fun. Use a large bed of embers. A wrapping of bacon keeps small things with no fat moist and tender.

ટ Salted almonds

Take almonds, blanched or in their skins, sprinkle generously with sea salt and moisten with water. Put them on a piece of foil placed over the grill. Shake the foil to turn them until they are crisp and begin to colour.

ટ Garlic Provençal

Put a whole head in the ashes for 8-10 minutes till it pops and the skin splits. Peel off the skin and sprinkle with a little salt.

ટ Prawns

Only large fleshy prawns are worth putting on the grill. They are best left unpeeled, or if peeled, left for half an hour in a marinade.

For a garlicky marinade mix olive oil and lemon juice with several cloves of crushed garlic, salt and pepper and some finely chopped parsley or fresh tarragon. In the Seychelles I discovered a *Creole marinade* of grated ginger with crushed garlic and chilli pepper beaten into coconut oil. For other marinades see p.200.

Place in an oiled tightly meshed double grill or thread on to skewers and turn over a gentle fire for about 5-6 minutes, basting frequently with the marinade oil or melted butter. Serve with lemon wedges. You can try this with crayfish too.

⁊ Stuffed prunes in port

Stuff pitted prunes (the California variety will do well) with half a shelled walnut. Soak in a little port and water to cover for half an hour until the liquor has been absorbed.
Wrap in a thin slice of bacon and grill until crisp.

⁊ Stuffed olives

Stuff green pitted olives with blanched almonds. Wrap each in a narrow thin slice of bacon and grill till crisp.

⁊ Oysters, scallops and mussels

The simplest way of eating shellfish is to place the cleaned and rinsed shells (see p.275) straight on to a hot grill. When they open they are ready to eat. Provide salt, pepper, bread and lemon juice.
The shellfish may also be removed from their shells and grilled on skewers – with mushrooms in between if you like. Dust with salt and pepper and sprinkle with lemon and oil, then roll in fine breadcrumbs (as added protection) before you thread on to skewers and put them on the fire. Baste frequently with oil or melted butter.
Serve on toast with melted butter and lemon wedges.

To make angels on horseback thread oysters, mussels or small scallops (cut larger ones up) on to skewers, alternating with pieces of streaky bacon, or wrap each one up in a thin rasher before skewering. Grill over a gentle fire turning twice. Allow 5 minutes for mussels and oysters, 10 minutes for large scallops or 5 minutes if they are cut in two. For other recipes see pp.275-7.

⁊ Grilled cheese

Cheese slices. Use a hard dry cheese (goat cheese is particularly good, preferably the small whole 'crotins'). Put slices (floured if a little moist) on a well-oiled grill not too near the fire. Throw in some herbs such as rosemary, wild thyme and sage, which will give a delicate perfume to the cheese. Let it become soft and slightly coloured.

Crème de Gruyère. A French alternative to Welsh rabbit (see p.261) can be prepared in advance and packed in silver foil ready to put on the fire at the same time as a piece of toast. Mash and mix with a fork 3 Petits Suisses, 2 tablespoons of softened butter and a handful of grated Gruyère. Add a pinch of paprika and one of nutmeg. You might also like to try a sprinkling of dried mint or finely chopped fresh basil. Wrap in a well-oiled piece of foil. Put it on the fire until it melts and spread on toast while still hot.

Cheese in vine leaves. If you happen to be near a vineyard cut thick slices of a good melting cheese such as Gruyère, Emmenthal, Bel Paese, Cheddar or Fontina, and wrap each one up in four or five leaves. Put the packages over a gentle fire until the cheese has melted and absorbed the distinct tang of the leaves. Serve on slices of bread.

⁊ Raclette

A Swiss way of melting cheese in front of an open fire derives its name from the French verb 'racler', to scrape. The fromage à raclette, which is made by mountain farmers in the Canton of Valais, can be obtained here at the Swiss Centre and in some specialist shops. Evan Jones describes the ceremony of melting and scraping it in *The World of Cheese.*

'Poise half of a Valais cheese on a rock, or brick or a log before the flickering heat of a fierce fire (not glowing embers) and deftly scrape the cheese with a large knife on to heat-resistant plates as it melts into a creamy, bubbly mass.'

The pale gold sizzling lava is a pièce de résistance accompanied by new potatoes, white onions and sourish gherkins.

⁊ Toasted bread

For a nation that makes so much toast at home we make surprisingly little outdoors; yet the best toast is made on the fire. It is a perfect bed for serving many small items of food.

Hold a good thick slice with a toasting fork or grill tongs close to the fire, turning over once so that it is crisp and nicely browned on the outside but still soft inside and able to soak up any juices better.

In Italy bruschetta is the peasant's and hunter's evening meal. Cut a farmhouse loaf into thick slices, place on a grill and toast both sides to a golden colour but do not let the centre dry out. Rub with a peeled and bruised clove of garlic. Sprinkle with salt and freshly ground pepper and a trickle of good olive oil. Eat while hot and crisp.

You may also add a squeeze of lemon and some finely chopped garlic. Try sprinkling with mint, thyme, penny royal aromatic herbs. Or eat with a crisply grilled piece of fat bacon.

In Catalonia they use garlic, oil and tomato pulp.

❧ A hot garlic or anchovy loaf

A French loaf wrapped up in foil takes minutes to warm up in the ashes of a barbecue. If it is to be the only hot accompaniment to a cold meat luncheon you can heat it over a small bunch of burning twigs. Flavour the bread with garlic or anchovy before setting out.

Crush 2 cloves of garlic; chop or pound 5 or 6 anchovy fillets. Mash either or both together with about 125 g (¼ lb) unsalted butter. Add coarsely ground pepper. Cut a French loaf into slices but not right through so that the loaf still holds together. Spread the butter between

the slices. Close. Wrap in foil and put over a fire or in the ashes for about 15 minutes, turning over once, until crisp and browned.

For an alternative anchovy sauce with oil with which to brush the slices, see p.88 where it is used with prawns.

ஃ A Lincolnshire special called 'roofs'

'Freshly baked rolls are split and the soft inside is taken out. They are then liberally buttered and filled with chopped hard boiled eggs mixed with anchovy paste, butter and pepper. The halves are then put together and baked till very hot and crisp. Wrap them in aluminium foil and put them on a gentle fire.'

(MRS LEYEL)

ஃ Sausages

Sausages are popular with children. Not many English ones are worth bothering about but elsewhere it is a different matter, especially in France and Italy where a wide variety of good fresh sausages are made with almost 100% meat and with additions such as onions, sweet peppers, pistachios, spinach, truffles, garlic and spices. French saucisses and saucissons, andouillettes, boudins and crepinettes are excellent cooked in foil in hot ashes, grilled over glowing embers or cut up into pieces and skewered, as are Moroccan merguez and Italian, German and Polish varieties.

You may cook the long sausages such as andouillette and boudin whole. Roll up in a coil and pierce right through with a skewer to hold firmly. Prick in a few places only and brush with oil. Place on a grill. These require about 6 minutes on each side while smaller sausages require 2-3 minutes only per side.

BARBECUED VEGETABLES

Any of the vegetables and salads described can be taken out to serve at a barbecue, but there is something satisfying about cooking vegetables on the same fire as the rest of the meal. Not least is the richness of flavour they acquire when they are thrown in the ashes or turned over glowing embers.

It is fashionable to thread bits of vegetables such as onions, peppers and tomatoes with meats on the same skewer. It makes an elegant presentation with refreshing variety, even though they do not all cook at the same rate, and some will be overdone while others will still be only partly cooked. If you are cooking them for their own sake, do them separately in the way which suits them best.

All vegetables can be cooked in foil. Wrap cauliflower, runner beans, carrots, peas, onions (cut up into small pieces where necessary) with butter, salt and pepper in a leak-proof packet and leave them for 30 minutes on the grill. Cook them separately or make a mixed bag.

There are some well-tried combinations such as ratatouille (see pp.100-101) which is excellent done in foil, and courgettes and aubergines au gratin for which the vegetables are sliced or cubed and the cheese (Cheddar will do) grated.

But this type of cuisine is more for the camper who hankers for indoor favourites. Those who are getting away from the dining room will prefer the barbecue specials which they do not make every day.

Cook one or an assortment of vegetables giving each the time it requires, starting with potatoes, and adding the others in order of their cooking time.

≥● Potatoes

Potatoes can be speared on a spit or laid on the grill, or they can be put straight in the ashes as they are. But it is less messy and much more popular to wrap them, well scrubbed, in foil. They need 1-1$\frac{1}{2}$ hours on the grill depending on their size, less amongst the hot embers.

You may make an incision and slip in half a clove of garlic before you begin to cook.

Serve cut in half with plenty of butter, salt and coarsely ground black pepper or with thick cream or sour cream and a sprinkling of chives.

Another excellent sauce makes it a meal in itself. Mix some grated cheese – Cheddar or Gruyère for instance – with a little softened butter and some fresh cream. Add black pepper and press the paste into cuts in the hot cooked potato.

≥● Yams and sweet potatoes

They acquire a wonderful flavour when cooked in foil like potatoes for about an hour. Serve with butter, salt and pepper. You may also boil them at home until only partially cooked, then peel them and brown them over the fire.

〜 Onions

Put them, unpeeled, on a spit, over a grill or in hot ashes. In 25 minutes they will still be crisp. Leave them 45-50 minutes if you like them soft. Or you can peel them and cook in foil with a little butter, salt and pepper.

You may also grill the onion cut in thick slices. Brush with oil or melted butter and cook until crisply done.

〜 Turnips

Turnips take about 30 minutes to be done in foil.

〜 Corn on the cob

The corniche in Alexandria where we used to promenade by the sea is forever associated with the enticing smell of roasting corn cobs. Vendors squatted behind little braziers at regular intervals along the sea front, busily fanning the embers to reinforce the breeze or to pass the time.

If you want to cook them in the Egyptian manner, remove silk and husks and turn over a gentle fire for 15-20 minutes until they are well browned with black spots outside and milky tender inside. Serve with salt and coarsely ground black pepper and plenty of butter.

Another method is to pull down the husk, remove the silk and soak the husk in water so that it does not burn. Pull it up again, twist it closed and put the ears on the grill over hot coals for 20-25 minutes turning them occasionally. This way the corn stays pale yellow.

〜 White radishes

The long white radishes now on the market are delicious grilled. Dip in oil and sprinkle with salt and pepper. Turn over the grill for a few minutes. You will not recognize their taste.

〜 Peppers

Grill them as they are, turning them until the skin blisters and is slightly blackened. Peel carefully, remove stem and seeds and cut into strips.

The flesh is soft and flavoursome and better than when it is cooked in any other way.

Serve as a salad with a vinaigrette or tomatoes, or simply with olive oil, salt and cracked peppercorns.

?? Aubergines

The very best thing you can do with an aubergine is to grill it whole in its skin until it blisters and blackens and becomes limp. Peel or scoop out the flesh, mash with a fork and season to taste with olive oil, lemon juice, salt and pepper and if you like, a touch of crushed garlic. Let it cool before you eat it.

Aubergines cut into thick slices. Salting them and letting the juices drain for at least half an hour makes a little difference when aubergines are cooked in this manner. Dip in a mixture of olive oil and a little wine vinegar with a sprinkling of chopped mint and crushed garlic. Drain and cook on the grill for about 15-20 minutes, turning over once and brushing frequently with olive oil. If you dip them in flour before cooking it will give you a good crust.

?? Mushrooms

An old English breakfast, and for that matter evening favourite too is grilled mushrooms and bacon.

Wash them and trim their stalks. Coat with oil or melted butter and turn once over a gentle fire basting again. Cook for 5-10 minutes. Large fat ones can take up to 20 minutes. Sprinkle with salt and pepper. Grill the bacon at the same time.

Champignons grillés à la Bourguignonne. Serve with the same butter with which the local snails are stuffed. Prepare this beforehand and bring it in a cool container. Stir a good amount of finely chopped parsley and a little crushed garlic into softened butter. Season with salt and pepper and beat well.

You may also make a stuffing for the mushrooms by adding some fine breadcrumbs to the butter. Cook the caps on both sides. Put some filling in each and let it melt a bit under the grill.

৵ Tomatoes

Grill them whole turning them on all sides until they are soft and the skin loose. Peel them and serve, lightly mashed, seasoned with salt and pepper and sprinkled with finely chopped fresh herbs and olive oil or melted butter.

৵ Courgettes

Grill small ones whole, large ones cut into slices and skewered, until tender. They need basting with oil or melted butter. Season with salt and pepper when done (5-8 minutes for slices).

BREAD

Several people have told me of experiences in the Sinai desert, by the Red Sea, where a Bedouin offered to cook a fish. He built a fire on some rocks, and while it burnt down to embers, he made a dough with some flour and sea water. Then he pulled a fish from a net in the water, pushed a wooden stick through its tail and cheeks and held it, still wriggling, over the fire between two stones. He brushed some embers away to make room on a fire-blackened stone for the thin flat cake of dough. He turned the fish and bread over once and both were ready at the same time, the fish crisp and brown, the bread puffed out and covered with little black spots.

Unleavened bread is very good, and in many parts of the world it is still the most popular everyday bread. Made with wholewheat, barley, maize, millet and chick pea flours it is baked on the hearth, on a griddle or bakestone or in a frying pan. It is easy and worth trying on a camping trip. Start half an hour before you want to eat.

All you need is flour: use a mixture of wholemeal and plain flour, and just enough water – less than $1/2$ a cup for a cup of flour – to make it stick together. You may add half a teaspoonful of salt and 1 or 2 tablespoons of oil. Add the water gradually and knead vigorously for 8 minutes or until it is a soft elastic dough, then leave it to rest, covered with a damp cloth for at least half an hour.

Put a sheet of metal or a frying pan over a bed of coals which gives an even heat. Take lumps of dough the size of an egg. Pat into flat cakes with the floured palms of your hands and pull the dough thin. Flour the dough so that it does not stick and lay on the smoking hot sheet or pan. Turn over as soon as bubbles appear (in a minute or so) and let the other side cook for half a minute. Then put the bread straight over the fire on a grill. It will puff up immediately. Turn it over. It will be done when both sides are flecked with black spots (2-3 minutes). Brush with melted butter while it is still hot.

Spit roasting

François Rabelais was much taken with the idea of cooking animals on a spit. This passage is from his satire *Gargantua and Pantagruel*:

Thus as they talked and chatted together, Carpalin said, 'And by the belly of St Quenet, shall we never eat any venison? This salt meat makes me horribly dry. I will go fetch you a quarter of one of those

horses which we have burnt, it is well roasted already.' As he was rising up to go about it, he perceived under the side of a wood a fair great roe-buck, which was come out of his fort, as I conceive, at the sight of Panurge's fire. Him did he pursue and run after with so much vigour and swiftness, as if it had been a bolt out of a cross-bow, and caught him in a moment; and, whilst he was in his course, he with his hands took in the air four great bustards, seven bitterns, six and twenty grey partridges, two and thirty red-legged ones, sixteen pheasants, nine woodcocks, nineteen herons, two and thirty coushots and ring-doves; and with his feet killed ten or twelve hares and rabbits, which were then at relief, and pretty big withal; eighteen rayles in a knot together, with fifteen young wild boars, two little bevers, and three great foxes. So, striking the kid with his falchion athwart the head, he killed him, and bearing him on his back, he in his return took up his hares, rayles, and young wild boars, and as far off as he could be heard, cried out, and said, 'Panurge, my friend, vinegar, vinegar.' Then the good Pantagruel, thinking he had fainted, commanded them to provide him with some vinegar. But Panurge knew well that there was some good prey in hands, and forthwith shewed unto noble Pantagruel how he was bearing upon his back a fair roe-buck, and all his girdle bordered with hares. Then immediately did Epistemon make, in the name of the nine muses, nine antique wooden spits. Eusthenes did help to flay, and Panurge placed two great cuirassier saddles in such sort that they served for andirons; and making their prisoner to be their cook, they roasted their venison by the fire wherein the horsemen were burnt. And making great cheer with a good deal of vinegar, the devil a one of them did forbear from his victuals: it was a triumphant and incomparable spectacle, to see how they ravened and devoured. Then said Pantagruel, 'Would to God every one of you had two pair of sacring bells hanging at your chin, and that I had at mine the great clocks of Rennes, of Poitiers, of Tours, and of Cambray, to see what a peal they would ring with the wagging of our chaps.'

There is something magnificent about roasting a whole animal on the spit. It is spectacular and delicious and an occasion that no one forgets. Though it is an unfamiliar practice in England these days, it was once commonplace to cook all kinds of meat in the fireplace and to bring it straight to the table. The spit rested on iron dogs placed at either side of the hearth, and a fire screen soaked in water allowed the cook-boys to turn the spit without burning themselves. The wrought iron spits had claw-shaped prongs to hold the meat, or holes for tying it on. There were fine spits for stringing birds and others that clasped fish so they did not break. Some cook shops had several joints of meat turning on four spits placed one above the other. Customers could choose lean or fat pieces, much or little done, and it was cut up for them and served with salt and mustard on the side of the plate. Beer and a roll completed the feast.

Large animals such as beeves (castrated bulls) were roasted whole in market squares and castle courtyards to celebrate important events. It took from 12 hours to 2 days for the animal to cook through and it was often left to passing citizens to turn the spit. Cooking a whole calf or beeve still requires a civic event such as a City of London Fair, but sucking pig or baby lamb are a marvellous way of providing for a large party. For a smaller company a large joint or bird will do.

Brillat-Savarin claimed that one is born a good roaster, but Escoffier wrote: 'Where roasting is concerned, experience is the surest guide as theory, however precise, cannot replace the eye and the sureness which is the result of practice – one becomes a good roaster with a good deal of attention and observation and a little vocation.'

૨ª The technique of the spit

Some barbecues can carry a large joint and even a small animal on the spit which is usually placed between 10 cm (4 in) and 20 cm (8 in) from the fire, giving a turning circle of 20 cm (8 in) to 40 cm (16 in). Depending on the diameter of the joint and the type of meat, the distance of the spit from the fire may be adjusted so that the meat is at least 5 cm (2 in) away. If it rotates automatically with batteries, it can be left to cook unattended. Push the spit through the centre of the roast and adjust holding forks. Test the balance. If the roast is off centre, remount.

For roasting fowl such as chicken, duck and goose, more than one may usually be fixed together on the spit. They should face in opposite directions so as to even out the weight.

An improvised spit. It is easy enough, provided you have the energy, to improvise.

Here are some suggestions.

1. The best support for a spit is iron stakes with notches to raise and lower the roast; otherwise cut two substantial forked green poles. Drive these upright into the ground at each end of the fire to hold a large iron rod (preferably square) or a strong green branch. This must be about 4 cm (1½ in) thick and long enough to jut about 40 cm (1 ft 4 in) on either side beyond the supports (stakes) to allow for sagging (especially if the piece is heavy) during cooking. Two people will be needed to turn the spit.

To roast a whole animal push the spit pole right through and let it come out at the base of the neck. Pull out the limbs and hold them together on the spit with skewers or fold them back on to the body. Use a wire or a string to tie them.

For a large joint insert the spit through the centre or tie it on. If you leave the bone in, the marrow serves as an inside baster and keeps the meat juicy.

2. You may hold the spit by one support only on one side.

3. One way of cooking a joint in the wilds is to have it free-hanging from a branch by a string, over or beside the fire. It turns by itself and does not require much attention. A small joint need be only 15-20 cm (7-8 in) above the embers and turned occasionally as it becomes golden.

❧ The heat

The heat should be indirect, which means to the side of the animal or joint and not underneath, where dripping juices are likely to cause

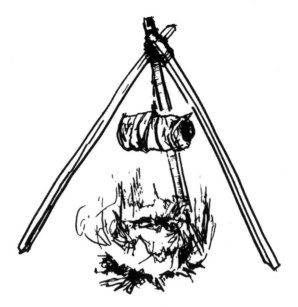

constant flare ups. Direct heat will burn the outside before the meat is cooked through. Have a tray underneath to collect the juices for basting. The food should rotate continuously and needs to be basted more often than is usual in the oven, with the fat that collects in the dripping tray.

There are different views about procedure, about whether it is best to roast at high heat or low, or some combination of the two and as to the importance of searing. But the advantage of first sealing and browning at high temperature to form a crust which imprisons the juices and allows the meat to cook further in these juices seems clear.

Place the animal or joint near the fire (4-5 cm/1½-2 in) and turn it until it is brown all over and has formed a crust to seal in the juices, then move it further away for long slow cooking. Bring it close to the fire again for a crisp crackling surface. Meat must be allowed to rest for this makes it more tender. So it is preferable to time the cooking of a large roast such as a leg of lamb or a joint of beef, to finish at least 15-20 minutes before you start to eat. Keep it warm wrapped in foil.

Seasonings and flavourings do not usually penetrate very far inside a large roast and it is usually necessary to salt and pepper the meat as you carve and serve it.

You may deglaze the pan as you would an oven tray to make a gravy. Remove as much fat as you can with a large spoon. Add a little water or red wine or good vinegar, stir and place the tray over the fire, let the gravy boil up and reduce.

Small animals such as rabbit or hare and birds such as wild duck and pheasant with a dryish flesh need barding to prevent them from drying out (see p.156).

For a large animal start the fire 5 to 6 hours before you want to eat, for a smaller one 1½ hours. It is impossible to give the exact cooking times as it depends on the size and the tenderness of the meat and the amount of fat in it as well as the intensity of the heat.

❧ Whole roast lamb or mutton

Every country in the Middle East could claim it as its national dish and each has its own special way of cooking it.

In Turkey the meat is rubbed with onion juice, salt and pepper and cooked, wrapped in sheets of paper or foil, until it is half done. Then it is uncovered and basted, often with a bunch of feathers or a cloth tied on the end of a stick, and dipped in the drippings which have been caught in a pan. The meat is served sprinkled with cinnamon.

In Morocco it is usual to have two charcoal fires burning on either side of the animal which is held on its spit about 50 cm (20 in) from the ground. The mechoui, as it is called, does not need to be turned but is basted often with melted butter and salted water. Each serving is sprinkled individually with cumin and salt.

In the Middle East mint, sweet marjoram and garlic are all used. Push the herbs with slivers of garlic into incisions made in the meat with a sharp knife.

The meat requires between 2½ and 4 hours (they like it well done in the Middle East but you might prefer it slightly pink inside). As it cooks, the smells conjure up the courtyards of traditional Arab houses with turquoise and cobalt blue tiles, moucharabieh (wooden lattice) at the windows and the clusters of multi-petalled jasmin with whose perfume they habitually vie. They remind me of the story my grandmother told of her childhood days in Turkey when a beggar holding two thick slices of bread was seen standing outside a pasha's yard, where the servants were roasting a lamb. When they told him to go away, he said: 'I am only soaking up the smell'.

In France and Italy too it is not uncommon in the countryside to cook a whole lamb on the spit. The usual way is to marinate it overnight in a mixture of oil, red or white wine, lemon juice, grated onion, crushed garlic, pepper, rosemary and thyme.

In England Fred Carr, for whom Tony Hambro made the spit in the diagram (p.171), regularly entertains 20-30 friends with a young lamb at his house in the country. He buys it frozen at Smithfields where they sell New Zealand and English lamb weighing 13-15 kg (24-30 lb) throughout the year. (Some specialists who supply Arab restaurants have even smaller ones.) The only time you can buy fresh baby lamb at an ordinary butcher is at Easter.

These are Fred Carr's instructions: Let the lamb thaw for at least 12 hours in its gauze covering. Start preparations very early in the morning if you want to eat at lunch time. Put the animal, which comes split down the belly, on the spit, which should be under a metre (about 3 ft) from the ground. Tony Hambro drills two holes on the metal stake for two long sturdy skewers which are pushed through the limbs and hold the animal in position.

Now stuff the lamb with the following (this not only tastes good but makes it look nice): bread crumbs from 1 good loaf of bread, 1/2 kg (1 lb) sausage meat, 1 large chopped onion, 1 chopped apple, a handful each of chopped dates and apricots, a few mushrooms and seasoning. Mix well, put all in the cavity, then sew it up in a neat blanket stich using a large needle and twine.

Prepare an oily French dressing with lemon, salt and pepper and strap a paint brush on the end of a long stick (this will prevent your getting burnt when brushing the lamb).

Keep the fire well back from the animal so that it does not get scorched. You need to keep a really good fire going (not just embers) to create proper heat all the time. You will need layers of logs, 3 or 4 high (about 60 cm (2 ft) long and 5 cm (2 in) in diameter) round the animal in two semi circles, and you must stake up the fire every 15-20 minutes to keep it going.

Turn the spit every so often on the cogwheel and baste regularly. The cooking time will depend on the weather; on a normal summer's day the maximum time for it to be no longer pink but still very juicy is 4 hours. Fred Carr has developed some refinements for even cooking, such as separating the shoulders very slightly from the body by cutting first with a knife, holding them open with a stick, and tying the fore knuckles to the stick.

ò. Sucking pig

A sucking pig was once a popular delicacy in these islands, if we are to believe the poet Massinger, who describes a dish served in the City of London in the sixteenth century:

> Three sucking pigs, served up in a dish,
> Took from the sow as soon as she had farrowed,
> A fortnight fed with dates and muskadine
> That stood my master in twenty marks a piece;
> Besides the puddings in their bellies, made
> Of I know not what.

These days it is an Iberian speciality with a version in every region. Everywhere in Spain and Portugal it is the great festive dish and the sacrificial offering on saints' days.

To roast a sucking pig takes time but it is not difficult. You can now obtain a baby pig, one killed when 2-6 weeks old and weighing 5-7 kilos (10-15 lb), which will feed up to 20 people. A few butchers prepare and set them ready for the spit and freeze them. Defrost completely, then wash it well and rub it with plenty of lemon juice and then oil. Impale it on a spit and cook it about 50 cm (20 in) from a gentle fire with a pan underneath to catch the juices. If you can find aromatic wood to burn, such as juniper, all the better. Heat some pork fat on the end of a skewer and as it melts use it and the drippings to baste the pig. Sprinkle with salt and pepper and cook gently, basting occasionally and turning until it is brown all over. It will take between 4 and 5 hours. Wrap the ears in foil; they are considered a delicacy. For an elegant presentation put a stick in the pig's mouth at the start of cooking and replace it with a large red apple when it is done.

In Sardinia, where roast pig is equally popular, it is split in two lengthways and the halves are cooked on either side of the same fire until the skin is crackling – this way it takes less time (about 2-2½ hours). It is enveloped in myrtle leaves, which grow on the stony hillsides of the island, and left to absorb their bitter scent before serving.

A marinade. Although it is not strictly necessary, here are some suggestions for those who are operating near the kitchen or roasting in the fireplace:

1. Covering the animal with cider overnight gives the pig a very delicate flavour. It is also a good idea to press into a few incisions crushed juniper berries rolled in thyme and coarsely grated pepper. One of my friends inserts slivers of fresh ginger very successfully.

2. Combine a glass of oil, half a glass of wine vinegar, 2 cloves of crushed garlic, pepper and 2 tablespoons or more of fennel seeds.

3. Use a mixture of olive oil and rum.

Soak the pig in one of these and add salt when you are ready to cook.

For those who like a glaze brush with a mixture of honey, ground cloves and oil during the last 20 minutes of cooking.

In the Italian region of Umbria, stalks and leaves of wild fennel are chopped up with garlic and used as a stuffing.

In Rome sprigs of rosemary are put into the cavity.

Another excellent flavour can be obtained from lemon peels and 2 or 3 cloves of garlic. You may use these flavourings for a roast leg of pork which is a simpler matter than a whole pig. It requires 2-2½ hours of slow cooking.

❧ Leg of lamb

For a French gigot with cream, leave a leg of lamb in the following marinade for a few hours: ½ litre (1 pint) dry white wine with 1 onion, coarsely chopped, a few sprigs of parsley, some celery leaves, 2 bay leaves, the juice of 1 lemon, 4 tablespoons of oil, 5 peppercorns and 5 juniper berries. Turn in front of a moderate fire. (Roasting instructions are given on pp.171-3.)

Reduce the marinade in a saucepan over the fire.

Occasionally brush the lamb with oil. When the meat is tender, after 1½-2 hours, stir the juices that have dripped from the meat into the much-reduced marinade. Add a few tablespoons of thick double cream and barely bring to the boil.

Pour a little over each serving.

For a Middle Eastern flavoured roast, mix a few tablespoons of oil with 1 tablespoon of paprika, 2 teaspoons of cumin and 2 large cloves of garlic, crushed, and push under the skin.

❧ Shoulder of lamb with herbs

Ask the butcher to bone the shoulder for you. Open it, sprinkle with salt and pepper and fill with a bunch of fresh herbs such as sweet marjoram, rosemary or thyme, a finely chopped onion and 2 or 3 cloves of garlic, crushed, Roll up, tie or skewer and put on the spit. Proceed as indicated in the roasting techniques (see pp.171-3), turning slowly in front of the fire and brushing with oil from time to time. Allow 1-1/2 hours.

❧ Sirloin of beef or other prime cuts

Dust lightly with dry mustard, black pepper and flour to give a crisp crust. Fold the fat end of sirloin under the lean undercut and hold together with string or a skewer.

Best beef does not need slow cooking to make it tender. Start cooking at a high searing heat in front of the fire and keep the heat high if the piece is small or reduce to moderate if it is large. As a rough guide allow about 20 minutes per 1/2 kg (1 lb) and baste often. If the roast is too lean, tie a thin layer of fat around it. Juiciest when rare, the meat is perfectly tender however briefly it is cooked. Let it rest for 15-20 minutes before serving.

Sauces: A good one to serve with this can be made on the spot. Stir 1 tablespoon of port with 2 tablespoons of red currant jelly and 6 tablespoons of gravy collected from the drip tray.

Another one is seasoned whipped cream with fine shavings of horseradish stirred in (see p.50).

❧ Loin of veal

Ask the butcher to bone the loin of veal. Marinate for a few hours in a mixture of equal quantities of oil and dry white wine with a good sprinkling of black pepper. Roll it up, inserting some sprigs of fresh thyme and rosemary, some slivers of garlic and a few anchovy fillets. Secure with string or skewers. As veal is dry it is best barded (wrapped and tied in thin strips of fat) to keep it moist.

Allow about 25-30 minutes of moderate heat per 1/2 kg (1 lb) for it to be well done and cooked through.

A simple sauce is made by heating up double cream with a teaspoon of dry mustard, salt and pepper. Add the juices of the pan, skimming off the fat first.

૨ Rabbit or hare

The flavour of an animal free to select its own food changes with the seasons. It carries the memory of moist woodlands and sunny fields, the taste of new berries and ripe fruits which may be heightened with the same fruits in a sauce. Season inside and out with salt and pepper, thyme and rosemary.

Coat generously with Dijon mustard. Cover with thin strips of fat and roast for 35-45 minutes until it is tender but the flesh still pink. Make sure that there is a pan underneath to catch the juices.

Sauces: Italian sweet and sour sauce is a legacy of ancient Rome: Boil 4 tablespoons of sugar in half a glass of red wine vinegar until the syrup thickens. Pour out the fat from the pan and add the juices to the sauce.

For another flavour, add 4 tablespoons of wine vinegar to the pan juices after you have thrown out the fat. Then stir in a small pot of sour cream and a few crushed juniper berries.

૨ Chicken on the spit

The chicken must be young and tender. Truss and secure it on the spit. Smear with oil or butter and baste frequently while you turn it beside a good fire for 1-1¼ hours.

One way of preventing breasts from drying out before the legs are done is to bard them by tying thin strips of fat or streaky bacon over them.

A delicious way of keeping the flesh moist and tender is to stuff butter, beaten with herbs, under the skin. Use tarragon or a mixture of cress, parsley and chives. Add 2 cloves of crushed garlic and season with salt and pepper.

For a sauce, pour a little Madeira in the pan when the chicken is ready and stir in a little cream.

Otherwise catch the drippings on slices of bread or toast.

૨ Game birds

Game has always inspired rapturous praise. With the ancients a bird which furnished maybe only a mouthful procured a sort of epicurean ecstasy, and it was said in Rome that the dead may be raised by means of a quail. The Frenchman Vieillot said that the flesh of blackbirds: '. . . so delicate in the time of gathering grapes, acquires at that period a savour which makes it as precious as the quail, but becomes bitter when they feed on the juniper berries, the ivy or other similar fruits'. The small birds with slender beaks, called becaficio in Italy or fig pecker because in the autumn they attack and eat the figs, were, he said, 'In truth, an extract of the juice from the delicious fruits it has fed upon.'

Hunting was unrestricted under Roman law, except that no person could pursue game on another's land without the owner's permission. Today the killing of most types of game is strictly controlled in Britain but laws vary throughout the world. Lilli Gore gives the times of the various open seasons in England in her book, *Game Cooking*, as well as valuable information on the preparation of game, whether feather, fin or fur. It is a good guide for those who have discovered the pleasures of the chase in open country, forest parks and rivers as well as a taste for the distinctive individuality of its produce.

Wild pigeon and duck, grouse, partridge, pheasant, quail are all excellent cooked over coals. If you have shot them yourself and are camping, they should be hung for 2-7 days. The time really depends on personal taste, the size and age of the bird, as well as the weather. Suspend the bird by the middle of the tail feathers. When the body gets loose and full is the time to consider eating. Each person knows when the flesh of a game bird has reached the degree of flavour he likes. If there is no time for hanging, as was the case of a friend who shot a protected bird by mistake on safari in Africa and had to pluck and bury the feathers quickly before roasting it on a hasty barbecue, the flesh is not as gamey but more like poultry.

Pluck the birds, singe if necessary, cut off feet at first joint, wings at the second and neck close to the body. Draw them carefully, wash the cavities with cold water and then truss them. You may leave the heads on and pull off the skin from the neck and head and push long beaks into the body on the side.

Most game is not fat and benefits from barding – covering with a thin slice of fat, either salt pork, streaky bacon or pork fat, tied on with a piece of string. This keeps the meat moist and tender and prevents it from drying out. Otherwise baste often with oil or melted butter.

You may flavour birds by stuffing with a small onion, lemon or orange peel, apples or juniper berries or herbs such as rosemary or sage.

Spit a few birds together side by side, facing opposite directions, and secure them in place with long metal skewers, string or wire. Turn over a gentle fire for 10-40 minutes depending on their size, basting if necessary. Serve on a thick slice of bread or toast which has caught some of the dripping, with cress and red currant jelly.

The French catch the dripping in a shallow pan and stir in a little wine or port when they are ready to serve, or sprinkle a little cognac, and flame. Serve on toast with the sauce.

It is sometimes simpler to split the birds in half, flatten them, and barbecue them on a hot well-oiled grill, turning over once. In this case they will require much less time. Brush with oil or melted butter or a marinade to keep them from drying out.

It is common with quail to roast or grill them wrapped in vine leaves. Cover the package further with well-buttered paper or a strip of fat, tied with string or wire.

THE GRILL

This method of cooking briefly, directly over glowing embers, is highly esteemed by gastronomes and gourmets everywhere but it has not been adopted anywhere as passionately as it has in the countries of Islam. For it is as much part of the gastronomic culture of Muslim India and Muslim Russia as it is of the Arab world, where it is the oldest and still the most common way of cooking meat. Almost everyone, it seems, is a master at searing the meat, judging and controlling the intensity of heat and timing.

Through the influence of its Oriental population barbecuing has lately become fashionable in Israel. During the summer months, families take small barbecues in their cars in the evenings or Saturday lunch-time, and head for the parks or the sea front. Steaks have overtaken kebabs in popularity as they require less work. I was thrilled to see the small fires dotted about in the darkness while delicious smells wafting in all directions reminded me of Egypt.

A grill (or grid) is the most useful piece of equipment for cooking over a fire and wire mesh a good enough substitute. If you do not have a grill it is possible to lay meat directly on to the embers.

For perfect grilled meat the cut must be a prime one. It may benefit from a marinade (see pp.155-6), but often it is sufficient simply to rub it with some oil, salt and pepper (there is no time for the salt to draw the juices out) just before cooking.

See the chart on p.293 for a rough guide to cooking times. You must always be sure to remember that the grill should be well oiled and hot before food is. placed on it and that the meat should not be cold. If you are using lean meat brush it with oil or melted butter or the marinade. Use a pastry brush or a small bunch of wild herbs or grasses. Do not baste with a spoon or the dripping fat will cause the fire to flare up. When it is nearly done throw herbs and flavouring into the fire (see p.154) to give it a perfume.

Foil is a useful companion to the grill for cooking en papillote, which gives excellent results, and one heavy sheet placed on the grill, or two thin layers folded together have the same effect as cooking in a pan. For small morsels that would fall through the grill, prick the foil with plenty of holes and lay on the grill.

If you do not have a spit you can turn a large piece on the grill over a low fire for as long as 2-3 hours or right in the middle of hot ashes, wrapped in foil.

If you cook a whole fat piece of meat of uneven thickness on the grill, keep the thin part further away from the heat than the thick part.

❧ Beef steaks

Use lean tender meat. The best is well aged and marbled or flecked with white fat. Use porterhouse, sirloin, fillet or rump steak. Have it cut 2.5-5 cm (1-2 in) thick allowing about 225 g (1/2 lb) for a good portion.

Trim off excess fat which would drip into the fire and cause flare ups and unappetizing smoke. Cut small incisions around the steaks, in the skin or gristle, to stop them curling. Lightly coat with oil and season with coarsely milled black pepper (some people rub the meat with a cut clove of garlic).

A marinade: Although good steak does not really need it the following will help to tenderize tougher meat and give it a fine flavour: for 6-8 steaks mix 1 glass of oil with the juice of 1 lemon, 4 crushed cloves of garlic and some pepper. Soak the meat in it for a few hours. Lay the steaks on a well-oiled grill above glowing hot embers, turn over once and sprinkle each side with salt when it is well browned.

It is difficult to give cooking times since we all have different interpretations of what we call rare, medium and well done and although we care very much about how it is done our tastes vary widely.

Red meat can be cooked closest to the fire. Those who like it very rare, as the French call 'bleu', simply sear it with fierce heat and that is all. For medium rare and well done, sear first on both sides for a minute (see pp.153-4) on the lowest or the hottest part of the grill and then raise the grill or move the meat away from the hottest part of the fire and complete the cooking until done to the desired degree.

Test the steak by pressing with the finger. If it offers no resistance and remains soft, it is very rare. If it meets with a slightly pliant resistance, it is rare. At this stage a light beading of clear rose-coloured blood appears on the upper crust. The juices become clear rather than red when it is medium rare, and when the finger meets a strong resistance it is well done. Finally, make a small cut with a sharp knife: it is the only way to find out if it is done to your taste.

A good way of serving steak is to put it, sizzling hot, on a piece of toast to absorb the juices, with a dab of butter melting over it. For a flavoured butter see pp.227-8.

It will be more tender if you let it rest for a minute.

🔊 Boned (or butterflied) leg of lamb

Ask your butcher to bone or 'butterfly' a leg of lamb so that it lies flat. Remove any skin and fat, sprinkle with rosemary and rub well with oil seasoned with salt, pepper and crushed garlic. Grill it in the same way as a large steak. Give it fierce heat to begin with on the lowest level and sear 5-8 minutes on either side, then raise it to the highest notch and a low heat and cook a further 15-20 minutes on each side. It should be brown on the outside but still pink inside.

Alternatively, leave the fat on and cook the fat side first. Cook slowly and do not sear.

See pp.44-46 and 48-53 for suggestions on sauces.

🔊 Escalope of veal

As the flesh of veal is a little insipid it benefits from flavouring in a good marinade. The Italians, masters at making the most of this, their favourite meat, like the following rosemary marinade: mix 2 tablespoons of vinegar with $1/4$ glass of oil, 1 clove or garlic, crushed, a good sprig of rosemary and some pepper.

Veal needs to be well-done and should be brushed while cooking with oil or melted butter as it does not have much fat to keep it moist. Remember that white meat needs gentle slow cooking.

🔊 Ralph Hancock's grilled veal recipe

The best grilled veal I have eaten recently was cooked by Ralph Hancock on the windowsill of his Knightsbridge flat. Here is his recipe as he wrote it for me.

Veal chops, preferably big and thick.

Marinade:

1 part cooking oil as light as possible – peanut or sunflower are ideal; 1 part old left-over wine (almost any kind will do – I prefer an acid, even sour, red wine with a little cheap sherry); garlic; coarsely chopped and crushed – plenty of this; coarsely ground black pepper and rosemary – lots of these as well. Do not add any salt.

'Marinate the chops for about 6 hours. I always remove the bones and fat, simply to save space in the dish. It helps the process if you prick the meat with a fork. Turn a few times during the marinating to make the penetration even.

'Grill very quickly on a charcoal grill. Just before you put the meat on, throw a branch of rosemary on to the charcoal and immediately add the meat so that it is impregnated with aromatic smoke. Oil the bars of the grill or the meat will stick. Add salt *after* the meat is done, plus a bit more pepper and a squeeze of lemon if you like.'

≥ Côtelettes de veau en papillote

Cooking in foil is well suited to veal which has a tendency to dry out. The preparation may be done at home, and the packets carried out all ready to put on the grill. (See p.157.)

Sauté some chopped shallots or spring onions, and add a few sliced mushrooms, fresh herbs, salt and papper. Place on a sheet of foil, cover with a seasoned veal chop, and tightly wrap up the package.

Cook the packages over a good fire, turning once. They will take a little longer than meat cooked without foil: 15-20 minutes depending on how thick the meat is.

≥ Stuffed veal chops

An excellent Italian recipe.

Slit each chop horizontally almost to the bone to make a pocket for the filling. Push in thin slices of Fontina or Gruyère with some black pepper and a sprinkling of chopped fresh herbs. Rosemary will do well. Lay the chops flat, press the top and bottom together again and beat the edges hard. Lightly coat with oil and sprinkle with pepper, cook directly on the grill or wrapped in foil for 15-20 minutes.

Try also stuffing the chops with a combination of ham and cheese.

❧ Marinated pork chops

Although pork chops are excellent simply coated with oil and sprinkled with pepper before grilling, they are even better marinated in a mixture of oil and vinegar with fennel seeds and a little crushed garlic. (See section on marinades, pp.155-6.) Cook for 7-8 minutes on each side.

Other well-tried marinades include oil, wine or cider with grated fresh ginger, sage, wild thyme, juniper berries, sherry, lemon and grated orange or lemon rind.

As in the above Italian recipe for stuffed veal chops, you may cut through the meat and slip in a thin slice of Gruyère or Fontina with a sage leaf. Moisten with oil, sprinkle with pepper and cook as usual.

❧ Venison steaks

Buy young venison cut from the leg, or cutlets. If it is tough, marinating in oil with red wine and crushed juniper berries will tenderize it as well as enhance the flavour. Grill very swiftly on both sides to sear, then more slowly till well-done, brushing the steaks occasionally with melted butter, oil or the marinade. Serve with a pat of butter, dusted with salt and pepper.

❧ Lebanese kibbeh

One version of this much-loved combination of meat and cracked wheat is cooked over charcoal. It is worth trying, for it is delicious and makes the meat go further when there is a large party to feed. It is easy to make with a food processor; otherwise it needs much mincing, pounding and kneading.

Mince finely (twice if the butcher does it for you) 1 kg (2 lb) lamb with a good amount of fat. A shoulder is good. Soak 1/2 kg (1 lb) burghul (cracked wheat or bulgur) in cold water for about an hour until it is bloated and tender. Drain through a fine sieve and squeeze out excess water. Grate or finely mince 2 medium onions. Pound everything together in a mortar and knead vigorously by hand, or turn to a smooth paste in the food processor, a few batches at a time, adding salt and pepper to taste. You may like to add 2 teaspoons of allspice or cinnamon – it is not orthodox – but many people do. Take egg-sized lumps of paste and shape into flat cakes. Cook over a medium fire until crisp and brown on the outside (about 10 minutes), turning over once. The fat should keep them moist and tender inside.

In Syria and Lebanon people push a lump of fat into the centre of the cakes to lubricate them as it melts during the cooking, or dip them in a pan of sizzling fat just before serving.

Serve with a salad and yoghurt and some pitta bread (see pp.42-3 for suggestions on serving).

❧ Hamburgers

Everyone has a favourite way of making hamburgers but the simplest, providing the meat is of high quality, is the best.

Grate a small onion into 1 kg (2 lb) lean minced beef. Add salt and coarsely ground black pepper and if you like a few sprigs of parsley, finely chopped. Mix well and form into 4-5 large patties. Cook over a medium fire for 4-5 minutes on each side or to your liking.

For an American cheeseburger mix in a few tablespoons of grated cheese such as Gruyère or Cheddar.

Serve hamburgers in toasted buns accompanied by pickles and relishes, slices of onion and tomato. Provide the traditional bottles of tomato ketchup and mustard and Worcestershire sauce (they are very popular at French barbecue parties these days).

❧ Grilled liver

Calf's, pork or lamb's liver is excellent grilled but it must be wrapped in fat or it will dry out.

Season to taste with salt and pepper and use lacy caul fat (see p.156) or strips beaten very thin to cover it. Place on a very hot grill. Turn over after 2-3 minutes and cook 2-3 minutes more until just done and still pink and juicy inside.

❧ Grilled chicken

It is easier to cook a chicken on the grill than to roast it on a spit, and it takes half the time. Here is how they do it in Italy.

Lay the chicken with the breast down and split it open along the whole backbone. Crack the breastbone and pull the chicken out as flat as you can so that it cooks evenly. Cut the wing and leg joints just enough so as to spread them flat. Turn the chicken over with the inside of the carcase facing you and pound it as flat as you can. In France they call this way of cooking by the provocative name 'à la crapaudine' for its shape is reminiscent of a toad.

Put it in a bowl with a marinade made by mixing the juice of 1 lemon, 5 tablespoons of olive oil and some coarsely ground black pepper for at least 2 hours, turning it over once.

Place the oiled grill quite high, 10-13 cm (4-5 in) above the embers. When the fire is ready lay the chicken on it, skin side towards the fire. Grill until the skin has turned golden brown, brushing with oil from time to time. Sprinkle with salt and turn over more than once, leaving it longer on the bone side until the juice coming out of a thigh (when it is pricked with a fork) is no longer pink – usually about 35-45 minutes. Poussins take approximately 15 minutes. Throw herbs or fruit wood twigs into the fire at the last minute for a special aroma. Serve garnished with sprigs of parsley and lemon wedges.

In Greece they pour a sauce of beaten yoghurt over it.

Further east, chicken is usually jointed and sometimes boned. Cooking time over a lower grill is shorter, and in this way legs and drumsticks can be started before the breasts or put where the fire is hottest with the breasts on the periphery. Legs take about 40 minutes, boned breasts 10-15 minutes to cook through.

A very popular Middle Eastern marinade is made with olive oil, pepper and plenty of lemon juice and crushed garlic. Sprinkle with salt when the chicken begins to colour. Serve in pitta bread heated on the fire.

This marinade comes from the Caucasus. Beat a little paprika, a pinch of cayenne pepper and 2-3 cloves of crushed garlic into some olive oil.

For an Indian tandoori recipe see pp.219-220.

ðŸ‚ Chicken breasts en papillote

The best way of cooking boned chicken breasts is in foil (see p.157). Brush generously with oil or melted butter, season with salt and pepper and sprinkle with fresh tarragon, parsley or coriander leaves and a little crushed garlic if you like. They cook in about 20 minutes. Close the foil well so that the juices do not leak out, and turn over once. Turkey breasts or boned turkey meat of any kind will also do very well.

A *stuffing* may be spread on the flattened breasts and wrapped up ahead of time. Here are a few suggestions:

1. Work equal quantities of fine breadcrumbs and softened butter to a paste, season with salt and pepper. Add a generous amount of crushed garlic and enough finely chopped parsley to make it very green, and moisten if you like with a teaspoon or more of cognac.
2. Moisten ground almonds or walnuts with fresh cream and mix with a little crushed garlic, salt and pepper.
3. To spread chicken liver pâté or mousse is a traditional way in France.
4. Add chopped onions fried till soft with sliced mushrooms and chopped parsley.
5. In Italy a purée of peeled, seeded and mashed tomatoes, sprinkled with some finely chopped fresh basil or parsley, is very popular. A thin slice of Mozzarella is sometimes added.

੨੦ Mixed grill

There is no need to feel limited to one type of food. Perhaps the best thing to offer at a barbecue party is a selection of meats, each cooked in the way that suits it best. Cut the portions small so that guests can have more than one choice.

Cargolade. In the Roussillon in France a variety of meats is put on the grill with unusual companions: the small snails which feed on the local vines. Try this with any snails which have been purged and cleaned. Put the hole facing towards the sky and leave them on the grill for the last 5-6 minutes. The usual meats are lamb and pork chops, both thinly cut, pork sausages and blood sausages, all brushed with olive oil. For the flavour of the Roussillon, make a sauce by crushing a whole head of garlic (each clove peeled) and mashing it to a paste with a pestle and mortar or in a blender. Add salt and pepper, then very gradually add olive oil, beating or blending until the sauce has the consistency of a mayonnaise. This can be done beforehand for it keeps well. While the meat is cooking, spread on thick slices of country bread to serve with the meats.

SKEWER COOKING

ॐ Kebabs

Kebabs are the best known foods of the Middle East. This is not surprising since they are part of the street food tradition of the region, and tourists who never get a taste of local home cooking invariably come across a kebab vendor. Even where there is no restaurant tradition to speak of there will always be cafés selling them. There are many varieties. *In Greece and Turkey* the meat is interspersed with tomatoes, onions and peppers with a bay leaf here and there. *In Egypt*, pieces of meat are threaded alternately with minced meat balls. *Iranians* serve

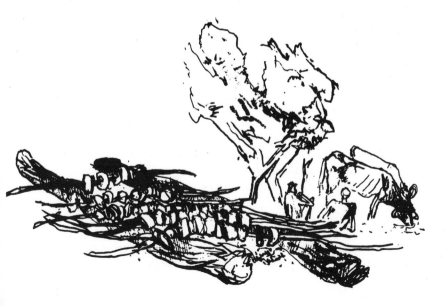

them on a bed of fluffy white rice with a raw egg yolk embedded in the centre. *In Morocco* they are tiny and fiery. Lamb, the favourite meat of the area, is generally used, each country favouring different aromatics.

Use leg or shoulder of lamb. Cut the boned meat into 2-2½ cm (¾-1 in) cubes (Moroccan brochettes are smaller), trim off any skin and excess fat but do not throw the fat away; it can be used to lubricate the meat. 1 kg (2 lb) is enough for five or six skewers. Leave the meat to marinate, covered in a cool place, for at least an hour or overnight – the longer the better.

A marinade: the usual ingredients are oil (I use a light vegetable one) and lemon, onion juice obtained by grating onions or putting them in a liquidizer/blender, and pepper. Other additions which you may like to try are ground cinnamon and allspice or cumin and coriander (1 or 2 teaspoons of each) and a touch of cayenne. Salt is added during cooking.

Just before you are ready to cook, thread the meat on to skewers with a flat wide or twisted blade). A few pieces of fat squeezed between the meat will prevent it from drying out and a piece of onion or a bay leaf will give it flavour. Sprinkle with salt. Although I am not in favour of putting vegetables on the skewer with the meat as their cooking times differ, some people like to. If you do, cut small firm tomatoes into quarters and green peppers into pieces as large as the meat, and thread them alternately.

Cook very quickly over a hot charcoal fire – you do not even have to have a grill; two bricks or stones will do as supports for the skewers. Turn the skewers occasionally, brushing with oil if the meat is lean and has nor bits of fat in between, until it is well browned outside but still pink and juicy inside – usually in about 7-10 minutes.

Serve with a cucumber and tomato salad with plenty of finely chopped onion and shredded white cabbage and lemon wedges. You may slip everything in half a pitta bread which has been warmed up on the fire. The usual accompaniment is tahina (see p.49).

Souvlakia. For the Greek kebab with pork use leg or shoulder cut up in the same way, and marinate in a mixture of olive oil, lemon juice, a good sprinkling of wild thyme, oregano or marjoram, pepper and a few bay leaves.

A gypsy recipe which originates in Hungary uses fillet of beef. Marinate in oil mixed with a good amount of paprika, a sprinkling of thyme, black pepper, a few broken bay leaves and strips of lemon peel. Thread

the last two on to the skewers in between the meat when you are ready
to cook. Sprinkle with salt and place close to embers for 4-5 minutes,
turning over once.

25 Minced meat kebabs

Luleh in Iran, brochettes in Morocco and kofta in the Arab world and
India, are not only the cheapest but also the tastiest kebabs because the
flavourings are worked into the meat. Though lamb is traditionally
used, beef or veal also make good kofta kebabs.

Use fat meat or add some extra fat if it is too lean, to keep them moist
and tender. The secret is to work the meat to a smooth paste. Mince it
twice or ask your butcher to do so, then work it well, kneading with
your hands. In the Middle East people pound it with a pestle and
mortar but for those who have one, a food processor does the job very
well starting from cubes of meat.

Here is my own everyday recipe: for 1 kg (2 lb) minced lamb, add
2 medium onions, grated, one good bunch of parsley, finely chopped,
1 teaspoon each of cinnamon, cumin, and allspice, salt and pepper
to taste.

Work the meat to a paste and leave to rest for an hour. Wet your
hands then take a lump and pat it round the skewer in the shape of a
sausage 10-12 cm (4-5 in) long, or shorter. Press firmly so as to prevent
it from slipping. Turn often over a hot fire for 5-8 minutes. Be careful
not to overcook as they dry out rather quickly.

You may find it easier to pat the meat into plump round patties,
smaller than the usual hamburger, and to cook them on the grill.

Serve with a tomato and cucumber salad in the usual pitta bread if
you like, accompanied by tahina sauce (see p.49) and lemon wedges. Or
put on toast with yoghurt poured over them. An extravagant garnish is
pine nuts browned on foil over the fire.

Variations: To the basic kebab mixture: you may add 4-5 tablespoons of
browned pine nuts, or a handful of chopped pistachios or walnuts and
one of moist sultanas. Shape into plump patties and cook on the grill.

My Moroccan friend, Fatima Ouazzani, makes peppery and spicy
brochettes in the following way: for 1 kg (2 lb) minced meat add 2
grated onions, 2 teaspoons of cinnamon, 2 teaspoons of cumin, salt,
3 teaspoons of sweet red pepper (such as paprika), a large pinch of
cayenne pepper, a good bunch each of fresh coriander and parsley, a
sprig or two of mint, all finely chopped. Work the mixture to a paste,

pat into long sausage shapes on skewers and cook as above. Garnish with sprigs of parsley and lemon wedges.

ɔ&ᴗ Kidneys on skewers

There are several ways of cooking kidneys over a fire. In *The Complete Indian Housekeeper and Cook* Mrs Steel and Mrs Gardiner have them skinned, cut with a sharp knife from the outside round part with a deep, but not too broad, incision and filled with chopped herbs. Cook gently until tender, basting occasionally with oil or butter.

Variations: Split them in half and remove cores and fat, or cut them up into pieces. Thread on to skewers alternating with bits of fat, if you have them, and bay leaves. Cook no longer than 10 minutes, about 8-10 cm (3-4 in) from the fire, brushing with oil or melted butter and turning over once at least. Sprinkle with salt and pepper and serve on hot toast with lemon wedges.

You may also skewer the kidney pieces wrapped in a thin slice of bacon to keep them moist.

ɔ&ᴗ Moroccan lamb's liver brochettes

Kouah, as they are called, are delicious providing the liver is not allowed to dry out, which it will do if not properly moistened with fat. Cut 1 kg (2 lb) liver into pieces and marinate in oil mixed with 1 teaspoon of cumin, 2 teaspoons of paprika, a good pinch of cayenne and salt. Wrap each cube with a thin piece of caul fat or simply thread with alternate pieces of lamb fat. Grill as quickly as possible on a moderate fire until the outside is nice and brown and the inside still pink and juicy.

Sprinkle with wine vinegar and accompany with a salad and bread.

ɔ&ᴗ Italian mixed grills

The Middle East is not alone in cooking small morsels of meat on skewers. Italy has a few dishes of this type; one of its best comes from Spoleto.

For each skewer have a cube of pork, one of boned chicken and one lamb's liver as well as a small lamb chop. Let them marinate in olive oil with a good sprinkling of fresh rosemary and coarsely ground black pepper. Add 3 or 4 juniper berries if you have them and leave to marinate for a few hours.

Thread the meats on to skewers, alternating them with a small slice of streaky bacon and a sage leaf. Cook over medium heat for 10-15 minutes. Sprinkle with salt and serve on a bed of shredded lettuce.

Lombello Arrosto. Cut a fillet of pork into 2 cm (³/₄ in) thick slices. Thread on to skewers alternating with slices of bread cut to the same size and slices of parma ham. Grill on a medium heat for 12-15 minutes until well browned but juicy inside.

❧ Chicken pieces on skewers

Those who have had chicken kebabs in an Oriental restaurant know it either as a splendid dish or as a miserable one, for they can easily become dried out and hard. The main thing is to keep them well oiled and not to overcook. Usually only chicken breasts are used, skinned, boned and cut into 2-2¹/₂ cm (³/₄ in) pieces. Leave in a marinade for at least an hour, longer if possible. Add salt just before threading on skewers and cook for about 6-10 minutes (until cooked) on a medium fire, turning over frequently and brushing with oil or melted butter or the marinade.

Marinades: My favourite is a common enough mixture of olive oil and lemon juice (usually equal quantities) coarsely grated pepper and a little crushed garlic. You can use dry white wine and herbs such as tarragon or rosemary or grated lemon zest.

A delicate taste is given in Turkey with onion juice obtained by grating a large onion or putting it through a blender, and adding pepper and cinnamon.

Yoghurt tenderizes chicken. Flavour it with the spices of your choice – cardamom seeds removed from their pod, allspice, cinnamon, cumin, coriander. I have given a recipe for tandoori and tikka chicken in the Indian menu, pp.219-220, which uses yoghurt as a base.

The most famous chicken kebabs come from Japan. My friend Marion Maitlis brought back this recipe. Marinate bite-sized pieces of chicken for two in a mixture of 4 tablespoons of soya sauce, 4 tablespoons of mirin (rice wine) or medium sherry, 2 tablespoons of oil and 2 tablespoons of sugar for a few hours. You may vary the balance of flavours by adding a clove of garlic and a piece of ginger, both crushed in a garlic press to extract their juice, and some grated orange or lemon rind. Thread on miniature skewers, alternating with small pieces of green pepper, spring onion and mushroom (you may add halved chicken livers), and cook for 8-10 minutes, turning and brushing frequently with the marinade.

Minced chicken unlike minced meat is not part of the butcher's trade, but it is now easy to make at home with a food processor. Mince raw chicken flesh very finely. Mix in a little grated onion and finely chopped parsley and season with salt and pepper and a sprinkling of cinnamon. Work well and press into a sausage shape on skewers or pat into little flat cakes. Brush with oil or melted butter and cook briefly over medium heat, turning over once and basting frequently. Serve with lemon wedges. Minced turkey may also be used in this way.

An Italian way with birds is to thread them with alternating slices of fat bacon to lubricate them and sage leaves to give them flavour.

৯ Country birds or crazy birds

These only look like birds. That is why Italians call them so. In Britain they are called 'olives'. Make them with tender cuts of beef, veal or pork.

Cut slices of meat into strips about 4 cm (1½ in) wide and a little over 6 cm (2½ in) long. Beat them flat and on each piece lay a slice of ham and a sage leaf. Sprinkle with pepper and roll up. Thread these on to skewers with alternate pieces of bread and streaky bacon.

Brush the meat and bread with melted lard or oil. Grill over charcoal, turning the skewers slowly until the meat is cooked and the bread and bacon nicely browned.

৯ Stuffed brochettes of beef

For a taste of Provence cut thin slices of tender beef (fillet, rump, sirloin) and flatten them, being careful not to make any holes. Cut into strips about 4-5 cm (1½-2½ in) wide. Make a stuffing with breadcrumbs from 4 slices of dry bread. Sprinkle with a little oil, enough to make a stiff paste. Add a good quantity of chopped, mixed fresh herbs – parsley, chives, chervil (only a touch of thyme), 2 or more cloves of garlic, crushed, salt and pepper and if you like a few tablespoons of grated Gruyère cheese. Mix well with your hands. Press a little paste on the end of each piece, roll up and thread on to skewers. Cook gently, turning a few times and brushing with oil until done – about 10-12 minutes.

❧ Neapolitan kebabs

Flatten small thin slices of pork or other meats. Season with salt and pepper, sprinkle with raisins or sultanas (soaked in water until plump and drained) and a few pine nuts. Roll up tightly and thread on skewers close together. Cook for 10-12 minutes, brushing with oil or melted butter to keep the meat moist.

FISH AND SEAFOOD

My fondest memories of Portugal are associated with the smell of sardines cooking. Most of the summer nights were spent walking on the beach, waiting for the fish to be pulled in with large nets, and watching it being auctioned in the market place. As the bidding continued, dozens of little fires were started along the sea front in clay braziers shaped like flower-pots. We watched the fishermen clean and wash mountains of sardines, and simply lay them on small grills fixed on the top of the pots, without oil or butter or anything else. Within minutes they were ready. We were offered an endless but irresistible supply of crisp 'sardinhas' with a sprinkling of salt and pepper and vinegar on thick slices of bread, accompanied by a tomato and pepper salad with onion rings and black olives.

Grilling is a most delicious way of cooking any fish, but not all of them can be dealt with as summarily as sardines. Depending on size, plumpness and oiliness, each type of fish needs a particular treatment. Most fish need frequent brushing with oil or melted butter or a marinade to prevent them from drying out, unless they are very oily, like sardines. They can also be floured or rolled in breadcrumbs and then smeared with oil or melted butter, which forms a handsome crust that keeps them moist.

ॐ To prepare the fish

Thoroughly rinse and wash. Draw out the innards through the gills or by slitting the belly. Do not take off the head. It is not always necessary to remove scales as they practically melt in the fire and there is sometimes an advantage in leaving them on. But if you want a charcoal-grilled skin, push the scales up the wrong way with the blunt edge of a knife.

For large and medium fish make a few incisions diagonally in two or three places on each side in the thicker part, with the point of a knife, so that it cooks more evenly. The cuts allow a sauce or marinade to penetrate and prevent the bare skin from bursting.

❧ To cook the fish

A very large fish may be roasted on a spit or cooked on a grill. A double grill or basket makes it easier to turn over without breaking or damaging the skin. Otherwise use a spatula and be sure you oil the grill, or the skin will be torn off taking some flesh with it.

If the fish is very large (more than 1/2 kg/3 lb) place it 15-20 cm (6-8 in) from the fire. If it is medium size place it 12-15 cm (5-6 in) away. Splitting the fish in half through the back cuts the cooking time and gives the smoky taste to a larger surface. If you like a crust roll the fish in flour.

The cooking time varies depending on the size and type of fish – from about 15 minutes for a 1-1.5 kg (2-3 lb) lean fish to 45 minutes for a 5 kg (10 lb) oily one (the oilier the flesh the longer it takes). Judge the time according to the fire. Give the first side longer than the second, or turn over a few times if the fish is firm enough, brushing frequently with olive oil, melted butter or a marinade.

For fish cooked en papillote in foil see pp.203-4.

For small fish you need a well-oiled double grill to hold them while you turn them over. Gut the fish and wash the cavity. Oil and place 10-12 cm (4-5 in) from the fire. Grill one side, sprinkle with salt and pepper, then turn over on the other side and season this one before serving. As a rough guide small fish take 6-7 minutes, medium ones 8-12 minutes (2-3 minutes longer if oily).

ê. Fish steaks

Large fish with a firm flesh (tuna is particularly good) can be cut in thick steaks. You can use fillets but they must be thick or they have a tendency to dry out.

Sprinkle with olive oil, salt and pepper or leave in a marinade (see pp.199-200) for an hour. Drain, dredge in flour if you want a good crust, then sprinkle again with oil or the marinade. Cook on both sides on a gentle fire, brushing again with the oil or marinade, until it just begins to flake and the crust to brown.

Serve with lemon wedges and a sprinkling of chopped parsley.

ê. Eels and elvers

Jane Grigson has written some fascinating things about eels and elvers in *Fish Cookery*.

Clint Greyn, who has cooked them at Clevedon on the Severn, where fishermen sometimes give them away free as part of the catch that they do not usually sell, has added the information that for grilling it is best not to skin them.

Buy eels live and kill them by chopping off the head. Cut the rest into 4-5 cm (1 1/2-2 in) pieces. Marinate in olive oil and vinegar seasoned with salt and pepper, or simply rub with salt. Thread on skewers or place on an oiled grill over a medium fire, brushing with oil and turning often until the flesh separates easily from the bone. Serve sprinkled with olive oil mixed with lemon juice or wine vinegar.

Bay leaves threaded on the skewer alternately with the fish give it a delicious flavour and so do embers from a burnt out bundle of vine prunings.

Clint has found that a mild soya marinade or sauce (see below) also suits eels admirably.

ཉ Marinades and sauces

Though steaks and cubed fish benefit, it is not usually necessary to marinate whole fish at all. The delicate taste is too precious to mask, and skin and scales act as a barrier to the fire. But aromatics in the basting oil give it a subtle perfume and turn the marinade into a sauce. Use olive oil, gently flavoured, to sprinkle the fish, inside and out, and brush frequently during the cooking.

A herb oil. Season with salt and pepper and beat in some chopped herbs such as rosemary, fennel, thyme, bay, tarragon, basil, oregano, marjoram, parsley and coriander leaves. If you let them macerate for a few days the flavour will have infused even better. Prepare a jar and add a crushed clove of garlic if you like.

A spice oil. Flavour the oil with spices such as cumin, coriander, paprika and cayenne – a pinch of the last and a teaspoon each of the others for 150 ml (1/4 pint) of oil. Add salt to taste.

A sharp oil. Oily fish do better with a sharp taste to cut the richness. Add lemon or wine vinegar in the proportion of a vinaigrette or in equal quantities.

A delicious speciality of Orleans is grilled herring served hot with a peppery vinaigrette. Split the fish in half and grill till just flaky. Pour the sauce over it while it is sizzling hot.

A classic Japanese marinade is a mixture of equal quantities of soya sauce and mirin, a sweet rice wine, for which you can substitute a medium or dry sherry, and vegetable oil. You may please your fancy and add to taste: sugar or honey, fresh root ginger squeezed in a garlic press, lemon juice or vinegar (2 teaspoons of each may be right with 2 tablespoons of each of the main ingredients) and a crushed clove of garlic.

Try it with salmon, halibut, turbot and bass.

Harra – a peppery sauce. I shall never forget the hot spicy taste of the sauce which was painted on a large fish for me by a man at Sharm el Sheikh. A few tables and chairs were set around a fire where a variety of fish were being cooked. They were brought wriggling from the sea by a young boy who ran into the water and picked one from a large basket for each order. We had chosen a large one because of our ravenous appetite and it seemed to take hours to cook. Its name sounded like 'loukoz', and when I asked again, the man replied with a mock Jewish intonation: 'Family name Berkovitz!'

'Loukoz' is the Arab name for bass, and I have tried to recreate the sauce from memory. Put all the ingredients in a blender: 150 ml (¼ pint) olive oil, a small onion, 2 cloves of garlic, the juice of one whole lemon or more, salt, pepper, 1 tablespoon paprika, 1 tablespoon cumin, ¼ teaspoon cayenne and one good bunch of fresh coriander leaves.

A flavoured butter prepared in advance (see pp.227-8) makes an excellent sauce as it melts over a sizzling hot fish cooked with little or no embellishments. The most appropriate is one combined with fishy things such as soft poached fish roes or the coral, eggs and creamy parts of prawns, crayfish or lobster. Smoked salmon bits may also be used. Caviare makes a very grand sauce and mashed anchovy fillets a strongly flavoured one. The amount you need will depend on what you choose and the intensity of flavour, but the principle is the same. Pound to a paste, soften a good amount of unsalted butter and beat in the fishy paste, a little at a time.

You may add condiments to taste: lemon juice, a little French mustard, black pepper, paprika, a pinch of cayenne, salt if necessary, fresh grated horseradish. Tomato paste gives a fine colour.

Beurre meunière, the most common butter sauce, can be made on the spot. Cook some butter in a saucepan until it is slightly brown, then add a squeeze of lemon juice.

Thick double cream, seasoned with salt, coarsely ground black pepper and lemon juice, and heated up in a pan with a sprinkling of herbs such as tarragon, parsley or chives, makes the easiest sauce and also the most delicate.

৯ Fish with only its natural flavour

A fish can be cooked as it is with its scales on. Put it straight on to the grill with no oil or butter or anything. Do not slash the fish; simply put the thickest part on the hottest part of the grill, and turn it over a few times until the flesh is done. The scales will coalesce and keep the flesh soft and juicy, and the salt deposit which they contain will intensify the tangy flavour of the sea. Make a little cut with a knife to see if it flakes.

≥▲ Fish flamed in aromatic herbs and spirits

The method is worthy of sea bream, bass, salmon, salmon trout and red mullet, but any other fish will gain in flavour.

Clean, wash and score the fish in two or three places. Stuff the cavity with sprigs of fennel, parsley, thyme or rosemary and roll it in flour. Season with salt and pepper and sprinkle with olive oil. Grill on embers, preferably using a double grill, for 3-5 minutes on either side then turn over again and cook both sides until the flesh has only just become opaque and flaky. Brush frequently with oil. (Turn only once if there is a risk of breaking the fish.) Lay on a bed of dry fennel branches or bay leaves, or a mixture of dried rosemary, fennel and thyme, which may be placed in a serving dish or on a rack. Top the fish with additional herbs. Pour a little heated cognac or other spirit such as marc, armagnac or calvados over them and ignite.

Alternatively, if the twigs are moistened slightly you will get a good smoky flavour.

Prawns are especially good grilled in their shells then laid on a bed of dry fennel twigs. Ignite Pernod in a spoon and pour it on the twigs.

If you have no herbs but a good supply of spirits, heat some up, throw it on the fish as you serve and ignite.

≥▲ Masgouf

At night the banks of the river Tigris in Iraq sparkle with the twinkling lights of little fires. The seductive smoke of a burning camel thorn bush, plucked from the desert, mingled with the aroma of roasting fish entices passers-by. The fish, split open as they come out of the river, are held upright with stakes like a fleet of double masted sailing boats encircling the fire, flesh side towards it to absorb the smoke.

Fried onions and tomatoes, highly spiced with curry and pepper, bubble in pans on the side of the fire. When the fish are almost cooked by smoking they are laid skin side down over the glowing ashes into which the bush has crumpled. The sauce is spread on the browned flesh and gentle pricking allows it to seep in.

❧ Fish wrapped in leaves

The best way to cook red mullet is in vine leaves, a method that also suits other fish and gives a distinctive sharp lemony flavour.

Scale carefully and wash. The entrails are considered a delicacy and should not be removed. If you have time marinate the fish for an hour in olive oil with bay leaves, parsley, thyme, chives and cracked peppercorns; otherwise it is enough to rub inside and out with garlic-flavoured olive oil. Sprinkle with salt and pepper. Wrap in vine leaves and grill on a low fire for 7-8 minutes, turning over once.

If you are in a vine-growing region pick as many vine leaves as you can keep for later use. Blanch for a minute in boiling water, pack in a jar and cover with brine.

Banana leaves and lotus leaves are also good as a wrapping – for all kinds of fish.

❧ Cooking in corn husks

Good for small and medium fish. De-silk the husks and soak them in water for a few minutes and tie them up at the silk end with the fish inside. They can go straight into the bed of coals. Turn them over once. All they need is 15 minutes for a medium-sized fish.

❧ Steaming in seaweed

A most delicious way of cooking on the beach. Wrap the fish in layers of wet seaweed and place on a grill over a gentle fire. Cockles, mussels and crustacea are also excellent cooked in this way. A fish weighing about 800 g (1¾ lb) is done in about 20 minutes, smaller fish, prawns and shellfish, in much less time.

❧ Fish grilled with salt in the Japanese way

The Japanese cook sea bream in salt alone but most other small whole fish can be treated in the same manner. Clean, wash and scale the fish. Sprinkle very generously with salt inside and out (Peter and Joan Martin suggest 2 per cent of the fish's weight in salt in *Japanese Cooking*) and leave for 30 minutes. Wipe the fish dry just before grilling and sprinkle again with salt (especially tail and fins) for a white powdery finish. Cook on an oiled grill for 5 minutes on either side or until golden.

Fish kebabs or brochettes

Large fish, skinned and cut into cubes, and smaller ones, cut into slices, make good kebabs. Salmon, turbot, sword fish and tuna are best , but other firm fish such as monkfish, cod, halibut, sturgeon, grey mullet and mackerel can also be cooked in this way.

Cut the fish into cubes or slices 4 cm (1½ in) thick. Marinate in a mixture of olive oil and lemon juice with salt and pepper, a little grated onion and finely chopped parsley for an hour – fennel, oregano, rosemary or marjoram may also be used. Other marinades are given on pp.155-6, 158, 209, and 213-4.

Thread on to skewers or reeds with a baby leaf between each piece. Turn over a gentle fire, brushing from time to time with the marinade, until only just done – about 8-10 minutes.

Tuna en brochette – with bacon fat to lubricate – is very good.

Barbecued lobster

Cut the lobster in half with a sharp knife and a hammer or meat mallet. Split it from end to end starting at the head. Remove the stomach and the intestinal vein but not the green liver (the tomally), which is delicious, nor the pinkish red roe or coral in the female.

Brush the flesh with melted butter or oil and sprinkle with salt, pepper and lemon juice.

Grill the lobster shell-side down 15-18 cm (6-8 in) above the source of heat for about 20 minutes, until it is almost done. Turn and grill the flesh side for 1 or 2 minutes more. Remove the claws and drop them for 2 or 3 minutes into the embers.

Serve sprinkled with melted butter and a squeeze of lemon. Or make a sauce by mixing 1 tablespoon of mustard with 1 tablespoon of oil and 2 tablespoons of melted butter; add a little salt, cayenne pepper and/or paprika and some finely chopped parsley.

Take a nutcracker with you to crack the claws.

Fish en papillote

Cooking in foil with seasonings and aromatics suits nothing so well as fish, especially since foil has replaced old-fashioned oiled paper.

The fish cooks in its own juices. Nothing is lost and herbs, wines and flavourings are most effective. There is no risk of drying out and the more fragile fish are not damaged.

Big fish like turbot, salmon, bass, sea bream and John Dory can be cooked whole or split in half and each piece wrapped separately. Medium ones like trout, red mullet and mackerel are wrapped individually as are fillets and steaks.

You must have a large enough piece of foil to enclose the fish loosely, and brush it well with oil or melted butter so that the skin does not stick.

Clean the fish and slash the skin diagonally in the thicker part if left whole or cut into 2½ cm (1 in) steaks or fillets. Place on the foil, season with salt and coarsely ground black pepper and sprinkle with a chopped fresh herb; parsley, chervil, tarragon, or bay leaf for the more delicate flesh, rosemary, thyme or marjoram for the stronger tasting fish. It is a good idea to fill the cavity with butter and herbs for extra flavour. A few tablespoons of breadcrumbs will absorb and hold the juices.

You may moisten with dry white wine, or try any of the following: salmon is worthy of champagne, and a drop of pastis or vermouth goes well with trout (so does the juice of a piece of fresh thick cream go extremely well with either. White wine vinegar and ginger squeezed through a garlic press), while a few tablespoons of cider suit mackerel. Sometimes a teaspoon of Dijon mustard is an advantage as is crushed garlic for those who like it. And of course there is the usual squeeze of lemon. The art lies in flavouring subtly so as not to mask the delicate taste of the fish.

Fold the foil round the fish making a loose parcel, with the edges tightly closed by folding and twisting into a firm seal (see p.157).

Put on the grill near the fire (58 cm/23 in away). Allow roughly 5-7 minutes each side for steaks and medium fish such as trout and up to 45 minutes in all for a very large one, turning over once.

Pass round some lemon wedges and let everyone open their own parcel. Some people might like to pour a little heated spirit over the fish and set it alight.

Variations: Parcel the fish with sliced mushrooms or a few sharp gooseberries if it is mackerel.

An unusual stuffing for foiled fish: fill the fish with a sprinkling of raisins or sultanas and pine nuts or coarsely chopped walnuts and hazelnuts or some flaked almonds. These are best toasted first on a piece of foil over the grill. This is not as strange as you might think. It is popular in the Middle East as well as Sicily and south of the Mediterranean, and worth trying with a variety of fish such as sardines, mackerel and trout. I have even added chopped dates successfully.

BARBECUED FRUITS

It is sometimes fun to take advantage of a lingering fire to give the fruits of the season a different savour. You may prepare those that are to be cooked in foil at home and wrap them up ready for the fire.

❧ Caramelized apples

Stick hard eating apples on the end of a skewer and hold them very close to the fire, turning them, until the skin blisters and comes off easily (about 8 minutes). Drop in a bowl of sugar and return to the fire until the sugar melts and caramelizes.

❧ Apples in foil

You may use large tart apples or dessert apples. Wash and core them and place each on a piece of foil large enough to cover them well. Fill the centres with sugar and a dusting of cinnamon or flavour if you like with a small piece of vanilla pod. Dot with butter. Wrap up well in the foil so that the package is leak proof. Put on a hot grill for 40-50 minutes or until they feel soft, turning over once.

You may put the apples straight into the ashes if you wrap them in a double layer of foil. They will need less time, about 25 minutes.

As an alternative, put a few raisins and sultanas in the centre or some apricot sauce (see p.52).

❧ Bananas

Bananas cook very well in their skins. A Creole way is to slit them open and press in a teaspoon of sugar, another of rum and a sprinkling of cinnamon. Put them on the grill for 10 minutes, turning once.

❧ Stuffed pears

Carefully core 4 large pears from the base. Fill them with a mixture of 50 g (2 oz) ground almonds, 2 tablespoons of sugar, 1 tablespoon of butter and 1 large egg yolk worked to a paste (you may add 1 or 2 drops of pure almond essence if the almonds do not have much taste). Wrap each one in foil so that the package is leak proof. Put on a hot grill for about 30 minutes, or until they are soft, turning over once.

❧ Mixed fruit skewers

Thread on to skewers alternate pieces of fruit such as quartered peaches, halved apricots, 2½ cm (1 in) unripe banana slices, chunks of pineapple, orange segments, apples and pears cut into wedges (sprinkled with lemon juice so that they do not darken), pitted plums or cherries. Cook over a medium fire, turning for 5-10 minutes. Sprinkle with sugar and let it caramelize over the fire.

A very attractive alternative to the caramel is to brush frequently with a mixture of 125 g (¼ lb) of melted butter, 1 tablespoon of sugar and 1 teaspoon of cinnamon or powdered ginger or the seeds from a cardamom pod. Or squeeze lemon or orange juice into the melted butter.
Serve with a little of the basting sauce poured over.

❧ Oranges with rum

Peel large oranges, removing the pith. Cut in slices and re-form, sprinkling with very little brown sugar and cinnamon. Wrap in two layers of foil (to avoid leakage), with a sprinkling of rum, and put on the fire for 10-15 minutes.

GRAVEYARD BANQUETING IN CHINA AND BARBECUING IN HONG KONG

Feasting at the graveside is the happiest part of ancestor worship in China. I learnt about the late spring picnics in honour of ancestors, which villagers call hek saontu (eating on the hill), from the sinologist Hugh Baker. In the New Territories of Hong Kong these events are financed by the income from trust land set aside by the ancestors. Whole pigs are brought already boiled, or roasted and glazed to a beautiful brown, and when the family clan is 1000 people strong it may be as many as 17 pigs, as well as cooked chickens and ducks, squid, duck eggs and green yolked '100 year eggs' preserved in ashes and lime.

When the ancestors have extracted the spiritual content from the offering, the worshippers can eat it. After the ritual ceremony, they either take it home or cater on the spot. The cooked meat is chopped up into morsels and stir fried briefly with vegetables and flavourings in woks set up over fires between the graves, while people squat on the grass around large wooden serving tubs waiting to help themselves in little porcelain bowls.

Though the Chinese do not generally much like sweet things, they bring little cakes made out of almond and lotus paste and glutinous flour stuffed with chopped peanuts, coloured in lurid reds and pinks, and often leave them on the graves for the birds.

Another traditional occasion for bringing out food is the outing to watch the full harvest moon on the 15th day of the 8th lunar month, when special sweet and savoury 'moon cakes' with a duck egg inside are given away as presents and passed around as an expensive currency. The little brown pies are taken to the top of mountains, out to sea, or on the lakes where a perfect view of the moon is assured.

For the Dragon Boat Festival on the 5th day of the 5th lunar month people take a pudding of glutinous rice and chicken, cooked in lotus leaves and tied with multi-coloured thread, to eat during the Dragon Boat races.

Ritual and ceremony apart, taking out food simply for the pleasure of eating it in the open is not part of Chinese life. It is more usual to purchase it ready cooked in the street. Popular foods available from stalls are squares of bean curd which can be smelt four blocks away when they are fried, green peppers cut into four pieces, each stuffed with glutinous rice and bits of fish. There is also beef and offal such as coloured intestines and tripe, steamed or boiled with aniseed flavouring. In Hong Kong there are those extraordinary floating kitchens called sampan, as large as a small car, that specialize in seafood. They pull out live crabs, prawns or fish from a tank and cook it in front of you, usually steaming it with fresh ginger and spring onions, and serve it in a soya sauce with a hint of sugar accompanied by black beans and cooked peppers.

It was on a trip to the Seychelles islands, where the most popular meals at the hotel were the creole barbecues, that I discovered grilled meats with a Chinese flavour. A look into the kitchen having revealed a giant drum of Heinz Sweet and Sour Sauce, I took myself to the island restaurants which advertised local foods. These were a mixture of French and African with Indian and Chinese overtones. The Chinese fishermen who have settled in the islands since the last century brought to many dishes their ways of flavouring, most notably to the spare ribs and morsels of pork and the fish which people grill outside their corrugated iron huts.

Though barbecuing is not a traditional Chinese method of cooking the delicate mixtures of soya sauce and sherry, sugar, minced ginger and garlic, vinegar and sugar make excellent marinades and sauces, while the traditional mixture of honey and water makes an excellent glaze for grilled foods.

With the influence of Western culture, barbecuing has recently become very fashionable in Hong Kong, and not only with the rich. On Sundays there are queues of people waiting at the bus stop to be taken to the countryside half an hour's ride away, with bundles and bags hanging on poles balanced on their shoulders. They carry chunks of chicken, pork steaks and spare ribs marinating in soya mixtures and the soft sweet yellowish bread rolls introduced by White Russian bakers. And they bring charcoal or wood for the stone pits and the brick barbecues that have been built out there especially for them.

ಒ Marinades and sauces

These more than anything else in Chinese cooking, are a matter of individual inspiration and taste and though the elements do not vary much, the proportions do. Here are a few suggestions which will give a special Chinese fragrance to your barbecued foods. Use them for king-sized prawns (see p.218), for bass and other fish and for pork. Read about marinades pp.155-6.

Soya sauce. Mix 6 tablespoons of soya sauce with 4 tablespoons of dry sherry, 2 teaspoons of sugar, 4 tablespoons of sesame or other oil and a $2^{1}/_{2}$ cm (1 in) piece of fresh root ginger crushed in a garlic press or with the flat of a knife to extract the juice.

You can vary this by adding 4 crushed cloves, $^{1}/_{2}$ teaspoon of cinnamon or $^{1}/_{2}$ teaspoon of aniseed, a sprinkling of salt and 1 dried tangerine peel cut into pieces.

For a garlicky flavour add as much as 5 cloves of garlic crushed.

And if you like the stronger taste of Szechwan, you can have a good pinch of black or chilli pepper.

Sweet and sour sauce. Mix 3 tablespoons each of soya sauce, tomato ketchup and vinegar with $1^{1}/_{2}$ tablespoons of sherry, $1^{1}/_{2}$ tablespoons of sugar and $^{1}/_{2}$ teaspoon of salt.

For a glaze to paint on the food towards the end of the cooking time, mix 2 tablespoons of honey with 2 tablespoons of water, and if you can get it from a Chinese store, 1 teaspoon of five-fragrance spice.

ಒ Spare ribs

There is not much meat on spare ribs so if that is the main part of the meal you may need 500 g (1 lb) per person. Back ribs are meatier. It makes things easier not to separate the ribs, which need long slow cooking (over an hour) on a very gentle fire. Place the whole racks, rubbed with salt, bone side down on the grill for about 20 minutes, then turn the meat side down for 10 minutes until nicely browned. Turn again and continue to cook with the bone side down for another 30 minutes at least, brushing frequently with one of the marinades, then turn a few times until well browned.

❧ Pork kebabs

Cut fillet or leg into 2 cm (³/₄ in) cubes and leave for an hour in one of the marinades (see p.209). Thread on skewers and turn over the fire for 7-10 minutes, brushing occasionally with oil until crisp and brown.

Or cut pork fillet into slices like large flat coins, marinate and put on the grill.

❧ Spicy pork meat balls

To 1 kg (2 lb) of fat minced pork add 3 tablespoons of sherry, 3 tablespoons of soya sauce, 1¹/₂ teaspoons of sugar, salt and pepper to taste, 4 spring onions, finely chopped, and a 2 cm (³/₄ in) piece of fresh root ginger, crushed in a garlic press to extract the juice. Work well together and roll into small round balls or fiat cakes (which are more practical). A basket grill is useful to turn them over. Cook until they are crisp on the outside but still tender inside.

❧ Vegetables stir fried in a wok

If you want to bring a wok along, you can stir fry any number of vegetables to accompany your meats. You can have Chinese lettuce, cabbage, celery, cauliflower, peas, mange-tout, broccoli, spinach, bean sprouts and mushrooms, any or a few of these.

Wash and drain well, slice thinly, cut into little pieces or divide into flowerets, as required. Sauté quickly in very little oil on a high flame until the vegetables are done but still crisp. Do not overcook.

You need season with only a light sprinkling of salt or you may flavour with a little crushed garlic, grated fresh ginger and a few finely chopped spring onions.

You may also add some tinned vegetables such as baby corn, grass mushrooms or bamboo shoots and cook them through.

SOUTH EAST ASIAN SELECTION

Where Islam has taken root at the confluent of India and China, the Arab art of the grill and the skewer has attained a special subtlety in the form of saté foods. Nowhere has an amalgam of culinary tastes and ways come together so successfully to the advantage of the barbecue as in South East Asia. The cooking of Indonesia, Thailand, Malaysia and Singapore, Burma, Laos and Vietnam is full of variety and reflects the mixed cultural heritage of their multi-racial and multi-religious populations. A wide range of regional styles of cooking has combined with the influence of Arab traders and Islamic scholars to produce a variety of interesting sauces and marinades in a region where the basic cooking apparatus is still the open charcoal fire. Dishes bear the imprint of the old civilisations of India and China in varying degrees as well as a touch of the scents of Holland, Spain and Portugal.

Inspired and guided by Rosemary Brissenden's *South East Asian Food* and Alan Davidson's *Seafood of South East Asia*, I have taken the liberty of borrowing and adapting the varied flavourings of the region. People there have been doing just that from each other for centuries. The selection I include is merely an introduction to the local blends of soya sauce and chillies, rice wine, tamarind, fish paste and coconut milk. Those who wish to discover the true culinary traditions of the area must refer to these books as well as to Sri Owen's *Indonesian Food and Cookery* and Phia Sing's *Traditional Recipes of Laos*. The last was written by the man who was in charge of the royal kitchens in Luang Prabang until 1965. He was also court doctor, poet, choreographer and architect. Although *Modern Thai Cooking* by M. L. Taw Kritakara and M. R. Pimsai Amranand does not have much in the way of grilled foods there are some delightful accompanying dishes.

I have drawn on these books and simplified many dishes. The marinades and sauces have many ingredients, none complicated and making them with an electric blender or food processor is a very simple and speedy matter. If you want to make the ingredients yourself as they are prepared locally this may take a little time and effort but it is not impossible. Coconut milk is made by soaking freshly grated or desiccated coconut in water (about 600 ml (1 pint) for 225 g (½ lb)) for twenty minutes and passing the liquid through a fine sieve. Tamarind juice is made by soaking the dried fibrous pod in water and straining. However, creamed coconut and tamarind paste are now available and need only to be diluted with water. Fish sauce and paste can be bought in bottles or packets or substituted with shrimp or anchovy paste. Several types of soya sauce can be found everywhere. The spices are those on the shelves of most supermarkets. I have used nut oil instead of coconut, and peanut oils and lemon rind instead of lemon grass. Medium dry sherry is the nearest thing to rice wine. You can use crunchy peanut butter instead of fried and ground peanuts. Fresh ginger can be found in many greengrocers throughout the year. You obtain the juice by squeezing a piece in a garlic press. For the purpose of a marinade and a sauce, these things will be good enough. Use the measures given as a rough guide to improvise with what is available, combining the ingredients to taste and making them as hot as you like. (Read about marinades on pp.155-6.)

❧ A well chosen platter of mixed saté

Prepare a meat or a fish platter, or both, and make a peanut sauce to be reheated in a saucepan on the barbecue. Accompany by a large salad of raw vegetables cut up and set out in a manner that also pleases the eye and with plain rice (p.86) if you like. Follow with a selection of exotic fruit.

❧ Meat and chicken saté

Use tender cuts of beef (preferably steak), lamb (preferably leg), pork (fillet, leg or chop) or chicken. Remove skin and bones, fat and gristle and cut into 1½ cm (½ in cubes). Thread onto wooden saté or thin bamboo sticks or small skewers. Soak in one of the following marinades for about an hour. Grill briefly on a hot fire, turning often and basting with oil so that the meat does not dry out. To serve, arrange the skewers on a large heated platter. You may pour the peanut sauce over them or use it as a dip. Garnish with lime wedges and, if you like, some finely chopped or minced fresh chillies.

❧ Fish and seafood saté

Prepare a large variety of different kinds of fish and seafood. Chunks of firm fish, cockles, clams, mussels, prawns and cuttlefish can be threaded onto skewers and marinated. Whole fish must be cleaned and gutted but not necessarily scaled. If you want to marinate the fish, remove scales and make a few incisions on the side. Grill quickly, turning over once and basting frequently with oil and the marinade until it is done and lightly coloured.

❧ Marinades

For pork combine 4 tablespoons of oil, 4 tablespoons of soya sauce, 2 tablespoons of honey, 2 tablespoons of vinegar, 1 teaspoon of aniseeds, 2 crushed cloves of garlic, salt and pepper. You may add a little ginger juice by squeezing a piece in a garlic press.

For lamb blend an onion with 4 tablespoons of oil and 4 tablespoons of soya sauce, adding salt and pepper to taste.

For beef mix the juice of $1/2$ a lemon and $1/2$ teaspoon pure tamarind extract diluted in 2 tablespoons of water, with 4 tablespoons of soya sauce, 1 teaspoon of sugar, 3 crushed cloves of garlic, 1 grated onion and salt and pepper to taste.

For chicken (1) combine 4 tablespoons of dark soya sauce with 1 tablespoon of honey, 2 tablespoons of sherry, 2 tablespoons of ginger juice, salt and a pinch of ground chilli or black pepper.
  (2) Or try a spicy coconut milk paste made by adding 75 g (3 oz) creamed coconut to 150 ml ($1/4$ pint) of hot water. When it is soft, beat well to a thick cream. Add 1 teaspoon of pure tamarind extract and the following ground spices: 1 tablespoon coriander, 1 tablespoon fennel, 2 teaspoons cumin, $3/4$ teaspoon turmeric, 2 teaspoons cinnamon, the seeds of 3 cardamom pods and a good pinch of nutmeg and chilli to taste. Beat well and add 1 tablespoon of ginger juice, 1 grated onion and 2 crushed cloves of garlic.

For fish and seafood (1) mix 5 tablespoons of soya sauce with 1 tablespoon of ginger juice, 3 tablespoons of dry sherry, salt and pepper. If you like you may also add 2 crushed cloves of garlic and 2 minced chillies. For a sweet and sour taste, add 2 tablespoons of vinegar and 2 tablespoons of honey or sugar.

(2) Dissolve 50 g (2 oz) of bought creamed coconut in 90 ml (3 fl oz) of hot water. Put it in the blender with 1 small onion, 1 clove of garlic, 2 small fresh red chillies, a little grated lemon peel, and salt and pepper to taste.

(3) Dissolve 1 teaspoon of tamarind extract in 90 ml (3 fl oz) of water. Add 5 tablespoons of nut oil, salt and pepper.

?● Peanut sauce

There are many versions of this peanut and coconut sauce which accompanies grilled meats and fish alike. Spoon it over the skewered pieces when they are ready to serve, or serve as a dip. For this, provide a pile of lettuce leaves to wrap the grilled morsels, and dip them in the sauce before eating.

It is worth making a large quantity at the risk of having some left over. All the ingredients need not be used. Make your own selection to suit your tastes.

Put through a blender:

2 onions, 4-6 cloves of garlic, 2-8 fresh hot red chillies (or more depending on how hot you like it), 1-2 tablespoons shrimp paste, 2 teaspoons ground coriander, 2 teaspoons ground cumin, 1 teaspoon fennel.

Fry the paste in 4 tablespoons of oil in a large saucepan until the aroma rises. Then add:

175 g (6 oz) creamed coconut dissolved in 1/4 litre (1/2 pint) of boiling water in a saucepan, 2 teaspoons of tamarind extract dissolved in a few tablespoons of water, the juice of one lime, 2 tablespoons of ginger juice, 2-4 tablespoons of soya sauce, 1-2 tablespoons of sugar, the grated rind of one lemon, 340 g (12 oz) of crunchy peanut butter, and salt and pepper to taste.

Stir well, add a little water to thin it down, and simmer gently for 6-10 minutes until the sauce is thick and homogenous. Heat it up again when you are ready to serve.

?● A large salad of crisp raw vegetables

Use any of these which are available: cut cucumber, water chestnuts, bamboo shoots, long white radish, celery, fennel and mange-tout into thin sticks or slices. Shred Chinese cabbage and cos lettuce and add sprouts, blanched if you like. For colour you may add carrots, red radishes cut into slices and firm tomatoes cut into thin wedges. For a sharp note you can have tart fruits such as green pawpaw or mango, pineapple, gooseberries or Granny Smith apples finely sliced (dip in acidulated water to prevent tarnishing).

Before serving toss in the traditional dressing: the juice of 1 lemon, 2 teaspoons of sugar, 1 tablespoon of fish sauce (or salt to taste), a pinch of ground chillies or freshly ground black pepper to taste. Try adding a small grated onion or 1 or 2 cloves of garlic, crushed. Or you may prefer a vinaigrette.

Garnish with sprigs of fresh mint, coriander leaves, watercress or parsley very finely chopped or minced fresh chillies or preserved ginger and slices of garlic fried in oil.

❧ Exotic fruit

The best possible conclusion to a South East Asian meal is a selection of exotic tropical fruits such as mangoes, papaya, guavas, pineapple, lychees, and bananas. Serve them in a large flat basket on a bed of leaves.

Otherwise have a fruit salad of the same tinned fruits.

INDIAN PICNICS —
A RELIC OF THE RAJ

In India, eating is a private affair not to be witnessed by onlookers, and it is regarded as improper to eat in the open. Besides, it is often too hot, and flies and wasps, monkeys and dangerous animals are familiar intruders. It is only the poor who have their tables and their pots and pans beneath the sky of necessity.

But there are a few occasions when eating outdoors is socially acceptable and a matter of pleasure. Travelling is one of them, hunting expeditions in the mountains are another. For both, people bring their servants who cook the usual everyday foods over charcoal stoves with all the necessary kitchen equipment. At the pavilions, where large parties spend the night or several days, and where men and women are segregated, the women supervise the preparation of the meals in the open while the men go hunting deer, partridge, quail and rabbit.

Picnics as such are not part of Indian life but a relic of the Raj, an Anglo-Indian inheritance. The British introduced picnics as a form of festivity in India in the seventeenth century in the early days of the East India Company. During the Raj they gave private parties in their gardens and occasionally rode out to a picnic in the cool of the morning. They made themselves comfortable under the shade of a mango tree, spreading out carpets, cushions and mattresses and hanging out mosquito nets from branch to branch. They returned in rickshaws and palanquins, happy with food and lulled to sleep by the swaying of the palanquins and the soulful chant of the bearers.

Denis Kincaid describes Anglo-Indian picnics in *British Social Life in India (1608-1937)* as stately formal affairs with squadrons of horses riding out and: 'Being arrived and alighted a curious cold collation is orderly set forth on large Persian carpets, under the spreading shade of lofty trees, where a variety of wine and music exhilarate the spirits to a cheerful liveliness and render every object divertive.' There is also a description by Macdonal, a literary footman, of how his master Colonel

Dow set off in a large sailing boat with

> . . . a vessel following us with all the necessaries for an empty house, servants, two havaldors or sepoy sergeants, twelve sepoys with their arms, four flanakins, with eight men for each, four saddle horses, with their keepers. We had plenty of provisions for us for two days in the boats. I was greatly delighted and thought it was a pleasant thing to live under the East India Company.

As the boat sailed up the wide creek towards Thana, the gentlemen drank punch together while two musicians played French horns. In those quiet backwaters where an occasional dhow moved softly over the smooth, white water and a warm sea-wind sighed over the reeds stirring the landward leaning palms and sending the white egrets flapping slowly over the terraced paddy fields, it was delightful to recline on cushions while servants filled and refilled one's glass; and the gentlemen's spirits rose and they burst into song; but after a few more rounds of punch they fell asleep .

When the romantic tastes current in Europe spread to Anglo-Indian circles, nature itself became fashionable, as did sham Orientalism. Everyone talked of leaving the stuffy cities for the rest and refreshment of natural scenery, and the profound reflections inspired by it. As in England, every young lady brought her easel and painting materials. And though the idylls were sometimes marred by attacks by monkeys or swarms of bees, the participants enjoyed themselves.

Miss Emily Eden, author of *The Semi-detached House*, describes a party popular in Simla society in her 1839 diary:

> Our aides-de-camp gave a small 'fête champètre' yesterday in a valley called Annandale. The party, consisting of six ladies and six gentleman, began at ten in the morning, and actually lasted till half-past nine at night. Annandale is a thick grove of fir trees, which no sun can pierce. They had bows and arrows, a swing, battledore and shuttlecock, and a fiddle – the only fiddle in Simla; and they danced and ate all day.

The food they served must have been the type described by Flora Annie Steel and Grace Gardiner in *The Complete Indian Housekeeper and Cook*, which they dedicated to 'The English girls to whom fate may assign the task of being house mothers in our Eastern Empire': chaudfroid, croustade, mazarin, kromesquis, game pie, snipe pudding and tapioca jelly.

These days the meals served in the hillside pavilions are a different story. Samosas and pakoris are handed round, dry vegetables are served. Vindalu, the hot delicacy of southern India, is especially popular because it does not have much sauce and because the vinegared curry keeps a very long time if covered with oil in a jar. But most popular are meats roasted on spits or grilled on skewers. The most elaborate the legendary hunter's meal, consists of several animals, one smaller than the other, stuffed inside each other and cooked slowly on the spit.

One type of cooking which comes from the North-West, predominantly Muslim India, and derives its name from the tandoor, the clay oven built out of doors in which it is usually cooked, is especially popular. Similar results can be obtained over a wood fire, and a variety of kebabs cooked on skewers, and grilled fish make a large selection to choose from if you want to plan a barbecue with the flavours of India. (Read about grilling meat and fish on pp.181-2.)

It is the yoghurt marinade which tenderizes the meats, and the mixture of spices which makes tandoori foods and kebabs so good.

❧ King-sized prawns

Peel and de-vein 500 g (1 lb) prawns. Marinate in a mixture of the following, blended to a cream, for at least an hour:

1 small onion, 2-3 cloves of garlic, 2 cm (³/₄ in) piece of fresh ginger, juice of ¹/₂ lemon, 4 tablespoons vegetable oil, 1 fresh hot green chilli or a good pinch of cayenne pepper, salt.

Drain and skewer or place on a grill over a medium fire. Cook 10-15 minutes, turning over once and brushing with oil until slightly browned.
Serve with a sprinkling of chopped fresh coriander leaves or flat-leafed parsley.

Variations: Tamarind juice instead of lemon will give a tart flavour. Pour a teacupful of boiling water on a small sized lump of dried tamarind pulp and soak for an hour. Strain the liquid, squashing the soft pulp out of the fibrous material. Or dilute ¹/₂ a teaspoonful of paste in a little water.

Swordfish, tuna and other firm fish may be flavoured in the same way and cooked on skewers. For other marinades see pp.208-9.

❧ Tandoori fish

A tandoori paste is a symphony of tastes for which you must use your flair in mixing spices and flavourings.

Marinade for a large (1 kg/2 lb) fish or for smaller ones. Blend the following to a paste – spices must be ground, the rest grated, crushed or minced, or put through a blender.

1 medium onion, 6 cloves of garlic; 2½ cm (1 in) piece of fresh ginger, 1 fresh hot green chilli or a good pinch of cayenne pepper (or more to taste), juice of 1 lemon, 1 tablespoon coriander, 1 teaspoon cumin, 2 teaspoons fennel or aniseed, 5 cardamom pods, 1 teaspoon cinnamon, salt and black pepper, 1 teaspoon orange food colouring.

Beat in 150 ml (¼ pint) of either yoghurt or oil.

Clean and scale the fish and make a few diagonal incisions in the skin. Rub the paste inside and out with your hands and leave for at least 2 hours. Roast on a spit or cook on a moderate grill, basting with oil or clarified butter (see pp.227-8) until the flesh begins to flake and the skin is crisp.

Serve with onion rings and lemon wedges and sprinkle with chopped coriander, mint leaves or flat leafed parsley.

❧ Tandoori chicken

It is so hot in the tandoor that a whole small spring chicken takes only 5-10 minutes to cook. It takes longer on an open fire and needs constant brushing with oil or melted butter to keep it from drying out. Whether it is plump or small, cut it into pieces. If it is a small spring chicken allow a leg and a breast for each person. Skin and make a few incisions in the flesh with sharp knife to allow the marinade to penetrate better. Leave it to soak in the marinade for 24 hours.

Marinade for 2 chickens. The mixture is highly individual, but here is a list of usual ingredients to try. Mash them to a paste in a blender before adding the yoghurt (in India a few papaya leaves help to tenderize the meat).

1 large onion, 6 cloves garlic; a 5 cm (2 in) piece of fresh ginger, juice of 1 lemon, 1 tablespoon ground coriander, 1 teaspoon garam masala, 1 teaspoon ground cumin, 1 teaspoon ground turmeric; 6 cardamom pods,

1 teaspoon ground cinnamon, a pinch of cayenne or chilli pepper or to taste, 1 teaspoon orange or red food colouring, 4 tablespoons oil, salt.

Beat with about 225 ml (8 fl oz) yoghurt in a bowl and turn the chicken pieces in this to coat them well. Leave, covered in the refrigerator, turning the pieces a few times.

Cook on the grill (see pp.181-2), basting often with the marinade as well as with oil or clarified butter (see pp.227-8).

Serve with quartered lemons and garnish with onion rings, softened and rendered mild by soaking in cold salted water for about an hour.

This is a beautiful dish to serve. You may vary the shades of orange and red obtained by the combination of spices with varying amounts of red and yellow colouring.

For chicken tikka use chicken breasts alone. Cut them into strips and leave them in the marinade for as long as possible. Thread on skewers and grill, basting often with clarified butter.

❧ Seekh kebab

Use lamb or mutton free from skin and tendons but with a good amount of fat to keep the kebab moist and juicy. The secret is to work the minced meat to a paste so that it sticks well together around the skewer. Mince it twice and work it with your hands or put it through a food processor.

For 1 kg (2 lb) minced meat add the following flavourings to taste (eat the meat raw to test their intensity). The spices must be ground. In India they are usually freshly roasted or fried to bring out the best of their flavour before they are ground.

1 tablespoon coriander, 1 teaspoon cumin, 2 teaspoons cinnamon, a good pinch of nutmeg, a good pinch of mace; a pinch of cloves, 1 teaspoon garam masala, seeds from 3 cardamom pods, 1 large onion (grated), a 2.5 cm (1 in) piece of fresh ginger (crushed in a garlic press), 3 cloves of garlic (crushed), a squeeze of lemon, 3 tablespoons yoghurt, a few sprigs of fresh coriander leaves (chopped), a few sprigs of fresh mint leaves (chopped), a few sprigs of parsley (chopped), 1 or 2 hot green chillies (minced) or 1/2 teaspoon or more cayenne pepper, salt and black pepper.

Leave to stand, covered, in a cool place for 2 or 3 hours.

Take lumps of meat and press into a sausage shape about 2¹/₂ cm (1 in) in diameter around skewers (with a wide flat blade so that the meat does not slide). Place on a grill over medium heat. Cook gently, turning over once (basting with oil or clarified butter (see pp.227-8) is only necessary if there is not enough fat), until they are brown but still tender and juicy inside (see pp.189-90).

Serve with lemon wedges and slices of raw onions softened by sprinkling with salt for half an hour.

Accompany with chutneys (see pp.239-40) and a yoghurt raita (see below).

It requires experience to hold the meat on the skewer as it tends to fall off if you do not work quickly. It is easier and just as good to shape the meat into round cakes (like a small hamburger).

❧ Bhoti kebab (cubed lamb or mutton)

Cut 1 kg (2 lb) lean lamb or mutton into cubes (see pp.189-90). Leave in a marinade prepared with the following ingredients preferably turned to a paste in a blender. The spices must be ground and the yoghurt added last. The quantities of spices are large but the marinade is not too strong.

1 onion, 2¹/₂ cm (1 in) piece of ginger, 8 cloves of garlic, 2 green chillies or ¹/₂-1 teaspoon cayenne pepper, 1 tablespoon garam masala, 1 tablespoon coriander, 1 tablespoon cumin, 2 teaspoons cinnamon, the seeds from 4 cardamom pods, a pinch of nutmeg, a pinch of cloves, juice of 1 lemon, salt and pepper, 150 ml (¹/₄ pint) yoghurt.

Put in a bowl with the meat turning the cubes so that they are well coated. Leave in a cool place to marinate for 3 or 4 hours.

Drain and thread on skewers and cook over a medium fire until all sides are nicely browned, basting frequently with oil or clarified butter.

Serve with lemon wedges softened onion rings, chutneys (see pp.239-40) and raitas (see below).

❧ Yoghurt raitas

To balance spicy Indian grills there is nothing better than a refreshing yoghurt sauce. Beat into ¹/₂ litre (1 pint) yoghurt in a bowl the juice of half a lemon, 2 crushed cloves of garlic, a few chopped mint leaves and a finely chopped fresh green chilli.

Variations: For a spicy raita add one or more of the following to taste, a pinch at a time: 1 teaspoon paprika, a good pinch of cayenne, 1.5 cm (1/2 in) ginger, squeezed in a garlic press to extract the juice, a good pinch of garam masala, a good pinch of cumin, a good pinch of coriander, a few coriander leaves, chopped.

Other ingredients which are ordinarily added to yoghurt for a raita include: grated carrots with chopped almonds, sliced bananas with sultanas, diced boiled new potatoes and roasted aubergine pulp (see pp.54 and 165).

You can turn it into a salad by adding raw vegetables such as 1/2 cucumber, peeled and grated or finely chopped, a tomato, finely chopped, 1 onion, finely chopped or grated, or 4 chopped spring onions and 1 green chilli finely chopped or minced (optional).

For chutneys see 'Provisions' on pp.239-40.

SUGGESTIONS FOR THE TRAVELLER

THE VAGRANT COOK

The British have always been great mariners and adventurers but the food of their expeditions has usually been a matter of sustenance. It is a curious contradiction that in their forays in the wilds in search of nature so many people still persist in equipping themselves with the evidence of their alienation from real and natural foods, the ugliest products of industrialization and urbanization: processed cheese, dehydrated vegetables, tinned meats and fruit squashes. Not many sailors and campers see cooking and eating as a way of enhancing their holidays, of tasting local produce and exploring new ways of preparing it. It is a question of priorities, for those who most protest their lack of time and facilities are often those who spend far longer than they need painting and washing their yachts and fitting out their caravans.

The job of the sea cook even more than that of the caravanner and the camper is one of planning and organization, of calculating quantities and numbers of meals and of deciding what must be done ahead of time. Menus must be worked out with regard to the type of holiday, its length and facilities, and local resources, so that meals may be adapted to eventualities such as delays due to weather conditions or an exhausting day when one is too tired to cook. Make lists of necessities remembering that your provisions can be augmented by fresh local produce.

There are limitations which make holiday catering different from cooking at home. The restrictions are those of space, equipment, fuel and fresh water, and it is often difficult to keep perishables. A pan of boiling water or a frying pan of hot oil are dangerous things at sea, or even in port where a passing motor launch will rock your boat. But there are many advantages for those who travel with their cooking apparatus close at hand, not least that the cook is freed from serving everyday food and following recipes too closely.

The usual repertoire of holiday cooking is based on one-pan specials suitable for a single burner, on quick and easy meals and food that needs no cooking. For a brief weekend trip all that may be needed are picnic meals prepared in advance; if you are camping or plan to run your boat in a sheltered cove, it is from the section on barbecuing that you can draw inspiration, while on the move, or in open waters, sandwiches and finger foods or instant meals are required. For the lazy hours spent around camp or in settled moorings the preparation of the meal is the highlight of the day when everyone joins in the catering and the cook is seldom abandoned to do all the work alone. Then is the time to embark on a sumptuous feast.

PROVISIONS

If you can buy fresh food as often as you like you will need only a few standbys, with your basic essentials of tea, coffee, sugar, marmalade, olives in oil and the usual condiments, herbs, spices, oils, store-bought mayonnaise, butter and alcohols which are necessary for good cooking. If conditions are uncertain you had best take with you as many good things made to last as you have room for.

It is difficult to keep perishables, especially in hot weather; an electric refrigerator is a rare luxury on a boat or caravan, an ice box not always practical. And although the old and simple method of cooling by evaporation is effective, the capacity of a 'wet box' made of porous cement or clay, kept wet in a reservoir or wrapped in wet towels, is limited. So buy little; take fruit and vegetables under-ripe, and check meat and chicken for spoilage.

Stow the provisions with a system so as to be able to find them easily in order of their keeping properties.

You may use stoneware or porcelain preserving jars but soft plastic containers are best as they are unbreakable and easily stacked. Smaller ones are better than larger ones as, if they are open for too long, there is a risk that the food will deteriorate. Tubes are better than bottles for condiments and sauces. At sea mark your jars and boxes with nail varnish as damp will cause paper to come off.

I have been told by a yachting friend that he always uses dehydrated onions and potato powder because of the time saved and the rubbish produced with the fresh variety. Powders and tins are the usual travellers' stocks these days, but it has not always been so. I wonder what has become of the great repertoire of preserved food amassed by this nation of voyagers. Born of necessity, to store the abundance of one season against the scarcity of another and as a result of the gradual separation of country from town, these provisions were nevertheless something of a delicacy; smelling of alcohol and brine, vinegar and spices, swimming in oil, encased in pastry or set in butter or pig's trotters jelly, salted or smoked, dried or pickled. Writers such as

Elizabeth David, Dorothy Hartley, Jane Grigson and Michael Smith have done much to re-establish this part of a neglected inheritance, which also makes nostalgic appearances in specialist foodstores, evoking memories of oiling, waxing, oatchaff and wheatstraw, baking paste and clay, and burying in sawdust.

Hams, swathed in a crust of muslin, used to be given several coats of whitewash for long keeping; fish was salted and hung up to become hard as wood on racks at the yardarm of sailing boats. Roast chickens were preserved whole in salted butter with spices; their legs were stewed for hours with veal bones to provide a liquor which, when reduced and strained, cooled into a hard jelly. This was cut into squares and dried out on a flannel to make an instant broth when dissolved in water. There was hung beef and beef cheese and cooked meats preserved in pots, set firmly with plenty of butter or suet to exclude the air, and sprigs of aromatic herbs laid on top to keep the flies away. Salt bacon, pickled mackerel, soused herrings and potted salmon were taken to sea.

All these ship's stores were infinitely more interesting than the dehydrated and canned foods for which they were abandoned when Britain developed from an agricultural to a manufacturing nation. The canning industry was conceived primarily as a military measure to secure better stores for armies and navies. Napoleon Bonaparte had given it his support by offering cash prizes for the discovery of methods of preserving foods for victualling his armies, which resulted in the none too appetizing *Appert's Method of Conserving*.

Mass production may be of vital importance but it has nothing to do with gastronomy. Although we may not now wish to preserve our meat by burying it in pits or drying it in the wind, it is better to salt and spice it and surround it with fat than to buy it in tins. It is worth returning to some of the old methods of preserving food for they produce delicacies which are hard to better.

૨✿ Oil and vinegar sauces

To keep fresh herbs in oil, finely chop a bunch and cover with olive oil in a jar. This turns into a convenient sauce for pasta with the addition of salt and pepper and crushed garlic. Parsley makes the most common sauce and basil the much loved pesto.

Sami Zubaida flavours a mixture of olive, walnut and nut oils with a piece of ginger, cut into thin slices, and a few sprigs of fresh coriander leaves.

Piri-piri, a hot Portuguese sauce which originates in Africa is made with dried chillies. Fill about a third of a bottle with them and cover with olive oil. You may also add a few cloves of garlic and some lime juice. Leave for a month before you use it for the flavours to be absorbed. It is very strong, so use it discreetly. It makes a good sauce to brush on grilled chicken as it cooks. Two tablespoons are enough for one chicken.

A large quantity of vinaigrette may be prepared in advance for instant use (for basic recipe and variations see pp.44-5).

My friend Ans Hey keeps a jar of vinegar which she fills with lemon slices, garlic cloves and bunches of the herbs which grow wild around the house, and occasionally a strong chilli.

Agro Dolce is an unusual Italian sweet and sour sauce to serve with cold meats and fish. Dissolve 100 g (4 oz) sugar in 300 ml (1/2 pint) good wine vinegar in a pan. Add 50 g (2 oz) ground almonds and 50 g (2 oz) currants or raisins. Other possible additions are cherries, pine nuts and candied peel, and a few mint leaves will give a refreshing flavour.
Bring to the boil and stir occasionally until it thickens.

See the chapter *Cold sauces and relishes* for other sauces which keep well.

ꝴ Butter

Unsalted butter does not keep as well as salted butter, but rid of its sediment it keeps perfectly well for months and does not burn brown during frying.

To clarify butter, heat slowly in a pan until thoroughly melted and frothy, then chill in the refrigerator for a few hours until the thick layers of clarified butter sets firm on top of the undesirable residue. Transfer the butter carefully to another pan leaving behind the residue. Melt the butter again, and when it froths strain the clear liquid through a cloth into a jar. Make a large quantity; it will come in useful.

The French make a variety of flavoured butters which they call beurres composés. They last as long as butter does and can be drawn upon to spread on a sizzling hot steak or grilled fish and to make an omelette.

Herb butter. Beat some unsalted butter with a spoon until it is light and creamy and add any fresh herb that you like - parsley, tarragon, chives, basil, mint, chervil, cress, blanched or not, and finely chopped. Season with salt and pepper and a squeeze of lemon. You can please yourself about quantities, but usual proportions are 2-3 tablespoons of herbs and the juice of a quarter lemon for 75 g (3 oz) butter. With tarragon it is pleasant to substitute Madeira or port for the lemon juice. With basil a touch of crushed garlic is appreciated.

Garlic butter. Add 2 crushed cloves of garlic to 125 g (¼ lb) softened butter. You may like to boil the garlic for a few minutes until its taste has mellowed.

For anchovy butter beat 2-3 anchovy fillets, minced or pounded, with a squeeze of lemon and some pepper into 125 g (¼ lb) butter.

For a mustard flavoured butter simply mix 1 or 2 tablespoons of French mustard into 125 g (¼ lb) butter.

Flavoured butter can include ground bitter almonds, chopped hard-boiled eggs; Roquefort cheese, chopped spring onions or mild grated onions, chopped capers and gherkins. Some people add red or white wine or meat juices, or colour the butter with paprika. Recently, flavoured butters with the strong taste of cayenne, curry powder or Worcestershire sauce have become popular in France.

Whichever you choose to make, press it in a container, cover with paper and keep it cool.

❧ Special mustards

Condiments attain a high degree of importance when facilities are limited. Here are two ways of making special mustards.

For a French moutarde aux anchois, chop and pound 8 anchovy fillets and combine with about 175 g (6 oz) French mustard. Keep it in a little pot.

For an Italian mustard sauce, put a glassful of white wine in a saucepan with a small onion, stuck with 5 or 6 cloves, and a sprinkling of salt and pepper. Strain and stir gradually into about 100 g (4 oz) mustard. It will keep for months in a corked jar. White wine vinegar diluted with water can be used instead of wine.

?❧ Tomato sauce

In Italy many people keep this sauce at home in a jar as an instant topping for spaghetti and as a useful base for various dishes. It keeps a long time if a thin layer of covering oil is replaced every time it is drawn from. Make a large quantity.

Fry 4 large chopped onions in 5 tablespoons of olive oil, stirring till they are soft and golden. Add 1½ kg (3 lb) tomatoes (skinned and quartered) or two large 800 g (1 lb 12 oz) tins of peeled tomatoes and crush them with a wooden spoon. Add a small 60 g (2½ oz) tin of tomato purée, a carrot and some celery leaves, all finely chopped, 5 large cloves of garlic, crushed, a good pinch each of thyme, basil and oregano, two slices of lemon, 3 bay leaves, a small bunch of chopped parsley, salt and pepper and 1 or 2 tablespoons of sugar. Cook slowly for half an hour, stirring occasionally and adding a little dry white wine or water if necessary. Pour into a large glass jar when slightly cool, covering with a thin layer of oil.

You may use this sauce to poach eggs in or to cook ham or gammon rashers or chicken livers previously fried in butter.

If you are by the sea and find clams, make spaghetti alle vongole. Clean and soak the shells. Put them in a large pan with very little water. They will open after a few minutes of steaming. Take them out of the shells, add them to the tomato sauce and heat it through.

?❧ Vegetable pickles

Pickles play an important part in the sensual life of the Middle East. Greek grocers encourage prospective buyers to taste from their barrelled selections and cafés display them prominently in their windows. One childhood memory which evokes particular longing since its delights were debarred from me for reasons of hygiene, is that of the pickle vendor installed on the street with a row of glass jars of the most alluring colours. Those of his customers squatting around him who could not afford pieces of vegetable seemed ecstatic only to soak up the liquor, usually coloured pink by bits of beetroot, with a piece of bread. But we made our own variety and kept a constant supply, as did most other homes, to cut up into little pieces as mezze to accompany a glass of beer or ouzo, or as ready provisions for the picnic basket.

Although this area of gastronomy remains largely ignored in England, many cultures have turned the necessity of putting the July orchard in the January larder, into sheer delight. It is well worth investing in some large pickling jars (used glass jars from the sweet shop will do well) and embarking on this most easy and rewarding activity, which provides wholesome holiday provisions.

A look through Indian cookery books will provide recipes for chutneys and spicy pickles, old English books will give mustardy and vinegary ones, while Mediterranean cookery books will have recipes for vegetables preserved in oil.

I will include only a few of my own favourites. They use old-fashioned methods and have a long enough life for a holiday but will generally not last indefinitely.

৯ Mixed pickles

It is a good idea to pickle several different vegetables together. They give taste and colour to each other and provide a selection to choose from in one jar. Use a mixture of any of the following: turnips, carrots, cabbage, green string beans, cauliflower, cucumber, melon, sweet peppers, small pickling onions. Red cabbage and beetroot will give the pickles a beautiful red colour. Trim or peel and thoroughly wash 1 kg (2 lb) vegetables. Cut into small pieces and pack tightly in jars with 2 or 3 small whole chilli peppers, 3 or 4 cloves of garlic, slivered, and a few celery leaves. Bring to the boil salted water and white wine vinegar in the proportion 1 scant litre (1½ pints) water to 150-300 ml (¼-½ pint) vinegar and 2-4 tablespoons of salt, and pour over the vegetables whilst still hot. With the lesser quantities of vinegar and salt the vegetables taste more of themselves and are much better, but they do not last as long. The pickles will be ready to eat in about a week and will keep for about 2 months in a cool place.

Variations: For a Chinese flavour add 2 pieces of fresh peeled root ginger.

For an Indian one add 2 tablespoons of mixed cumin, coriander, cinnamon and cayenne pepper with a pinch of turmeric for its yellow colour.

Another good alternative is to replace the chillies, garlic and celery with 20 peppercorns, 20 juniper berries, a good pinch of mustard powder and one of cayenne pepper.

৯ Pickled turnips

A Middle Eastern favourite. Trim, peel and wash 1 kg (2 lb) small white turnips. Cut them in halves or quarters. Pack them in a clean glass jar with a few celery leaves, 2-4 cloves of garlic, slivered, and one large sliced raw beetroot, placed at regular intervals.

In a stainless steel saucepan bring to the boil a solution of 1 litre (1½ pints) water, 150 ml (¼ pint) white wine vinegar and 3 level tablespoons of salt. Pour over the vegetables to cover while still hot. Close tightly and store in a cool place.

The turnips should be mellow and pink right through within a week.

✌ Aubergine pickle

Pickles in oil last indefinitely and make an excellent ready salad.

Slice 1 kg (2 lb) aubergines. Sprinkle layers with salt in a colander and allow 2 hours for the salt to draw out the bitter juices. Wash the slices and poach for 5 minutes in about 1/4 litre (½ pint) wine vinegar and a little water to cover.

Drain and arrange in layers in a large glass jar, sprinkling each layer with a little crushed garlic (use 4-6 cloves) and a pinch of oregano (1 tablespoon in all). Cover with olive oil and close the jar tightly.

The pickles are ready to eat in a few days and can be kept for months.

✌ Green pepper pickle

Grill peppers as close to heat as possible, turning them until the skin is charred. Peel, core, seed and slice into thick strips. Put in a jar with a few anchovy fillets and slices of lemon and cover with oil.

PICKLED FISH

One of the things that Egyptian village folk brought back to Cairo from their visits home was 'fessih': fish which had been salted and buried in burning hot sand to dry. Every civilization has developed a way of curing fish to preserve it. It has been salted and hung like clothes in the wind, laid on stones in the sun and smoked over slow fires in sheds and barrels, resulting in a wide variety of tastes much to the advantage of travellers and nomads. Although in the past the rock-hard kite-shaped board of salt cod has gone on many a long journey all over the world, today the problem of cooking it in a caravan or under canvas is that water is usually in short supply and too much of it is required to desalt and freshen the fish. It is better to take along good quality tins of sardines, tuna fish and anchovies in oil to serve as part of a mixed hors d'oeuvre or simply with bread and butter and a squeeze of lemon. It is better still to take fresh or mildly cured fish soaked in a preserving marinade, which also gives it a most delicious taste.

ت Marinated and pickled kippers

My parents keep a constant supply of kippers in oil which they bring out with olives and cheeses for a snack luncheon. This is their recipe. For 3/4 kg (11/2 lb) plump juicy kippers mix the juice of 11/2 lemons and 1 tablespoon of sugar with enough light vegetable oil to cover the fillets in a jar. Sprinkle layers of fillets with the marinade and some chopped onion. Make sure the kippers are properly covered with oil. They will be ready to eat in 4 days and will keep for a long time. For me they are lovely as they are, but you may also use wine vinegar instead of or with the lemon juice as well as cayenne or black pepper.

Salted herrings can also be treated like this but soak them in water to remove some of the salt first.

Kippers marinated in white wine. A popular French method. Clean and bone 6 fat kippers. Place the fillets in a container, sprinkling each layer with a little finely chopped onion, black peppercorns, a bay leaf, thyme and a few drops of wine vinegar (another version also uses a clove of garlic, a tablespoon of French mustard and half a dozen cloves). Cover with white wine and leave to marinate for at least 5 days. This will keep, closed, for many weeks.

ت Soused herring or mackerel

In France dry white wine is used, in England it is malt vinegar or dry cider, and in Denmark a sweet and sour flavour is given to fish by adding a good amount of sugar as well.

Cook the fish whole if they are small, simply beheading and cleaning. Or you may split and pull out the backbones. In England the fillets are rolled up lengthways and packed closely in an earthenware pot; in France they lay them flat on an oven-proof dish.

For 6 fresh herrings or mackerel, cover the fillets with a large onion, thinly sliced, 1 tablespoon of pickling spices, 1 dried chilli, 3 bay leaves, a sprinkling of salt and pepper and 1/4 litre (1/2 pint) dry white wine or dry cider or a mixture of 150 ml (1/4 pint) wine vinegar and the same amount of water. Cover with foil or a lid and bake in a low 140°C/275°F/Gas 1 oven for about 11/2 hours. Let it cool and set in its jelly. It will keep for a week.

For a stiffer jelly to hold in hot weather, make a stock with the fish heads and flavourings. Strain it well and reduce it quite considerably before mixing with the wine.

Serve dressed with a vinaigrette or sour cream mixed with the fish liquor or a horseradish and fresh cream sauce (see p.50).

The fish can be cut into pieces as an ingredient of many a salad with such companions as potato, tomato, apple, beetroot, hardboiled egg and gherkin.

POTTED THINGS AND 'SAILOR SAVOURIES'

The manufacture of potted meats on a commercial scale had its origin in England. They were so named because they were traditionally preserved in earthenware pots with a thick layer of suet or butter set stiff to exclude the air. For three centuries, potted meats were present on the breakfast and tea tables of the genteel and discriminating. Cooks employed in large private households spent much time chopping and pounding cooked meats, poultry and game as well as fish and cheese, with butter and a variety of spices.

During the nineteenth century, potted meats began to be produced in bulk. Many firms went into the business, which became a very important and competitive branch of the preserving trade. The principal raw materials used in the manufacture of 'sailor savouries', as the traditional fare for seamen and travellers became known, were salmon, anchovies, shrimp, lobster, herrings, chicken, turkey, ham and tongue. They were used alone or in combinations such as salmon and anchovy, salmon and shrimp, chicken and ham, ham and tongue.

Now that potted meats are regarded more in the nature of delicacies and their price is accordingly high, it is well worth preparing them yourself. They are easy enough to make in large quantities, especially for those who have a food processor. A delicious ready meal to serve cold, cut in slices or spread on bread, accompanied by a salad or pickle, they also keep for a long time.

❧ Potted meats

Use cooked meat, preferably pot roasted or boiled. Beef, veal, lamb and pork as well as chicken, turkey and game birds, rabbit and hare make good potted meats.

Remove any bones, skin, gristle and fat. Cut it in slices against the grain, finely chop or mince, then pound it well. Add a quarter of the weight in butter (more if the meat is dry) and beat or pound together to a smooth paste, adding salt and pepper and flavourings to taste. The usual spices to add are mace (an old English favourite but not mine), nutmeg, allspice and cayenne. Cinnamon, cumin, coriander, cardamom seeds and cloves are less common but equally good. All must be finely ground. Add one or two of these a little at a time and taste before you add more. You may also add a little dry sherry or port, by the spoonful, (but not gravy or it will not keep as long) and made mustard.

Pack into pots or jars (plastic will do) and cover with melted clarified butter (see p.227) to seal from the air. Press a piece of greaseproof paper on top and close with a lid.

It will keep for many weeks in a cool place, but every time you take some, you must seal the top again with clarified butter.

Serve with pickles and brown bread.

In the old days they liked to mix meats such as veal and tongue or chicken and ham, which gave a marbled effect when it was cut in slices. The combination of flavours is also good.

ᘒ Potted fish

Trout, salmon, char and grayling are old favourites for this popular English conserve, but there is no reason why you should not use any fleshy fish.

Lightly poach in a stock or court bouillon (see p.85) or bake it in the oven wrapped in aluminium foil. Remove skin and bones and break it into pieces. Season with salt and pepper, mace and nutmeg or spices of your choice. Put into small pots and cover with melted clarified butter. Stir it in between the pieces. When it is cool and firm add more clarified butter if necessary to cover the fish entirely with a 1/2 cm (1/4 in) layer. Cover with greaseproof paper or silver foil and a lid. It should keep for weeks in a cool place. Cover with butter again as you use it.

Serve with brown bread and butter, a salad and dry white wine.

ᘒ Fish pastes

Smoked fish pastes are one of the most delicious things to have benefited from the present revival of old English food, and no one should be happier for their return after almost a century of neglect than holidaymakers who have to cater for themselves.

Kipper, finnan haddock, and bloaters should be jugged before they are used. Leave them in a pan of water, which has just boiled, for 5-10 minutes. Drain and remove skin and bones. Smoked mackerel, buckling, trout and salmon are used as they are. Simply skin and bone, then mash and pound the fish with an equal quantity of butter, or put it through a Mouli, or into a blender or food processor together with the butter. Add lemon juice and cayenne to taste; it is better strongly flavoured.

Variations: Try adding a little port, dry sherry or cognac and spices such as ground cloves, nutmeg and black pepper. Add a pinch at a time and keep tasting. Salt is not usually required.

Put the paste into little pots and seal by covering with melted clarified butter (see pp.227-8). Covered with foil or greaseproof paper, it will keep for a few weeks in a cool spot.

For a paste that will keep just a few days, you can use cottage or cream cheese or whipped double cream instead of butter.

‌ Potted shrimps and prawns

Melt 175 g (6 oz) clarified butter in a saucepan. Throw in 500 g (1 lb) cooked and shelled shrimps or prawns, add a good pinch or two of grated nutmeg and cayenne and just a touch of salt. Heat up not quite to boiling point. Pour into little pots, chill, and when the butter solidifies, add a little more melted clarified butter to seal the prawns entirely from the air. This will keep for a few weeks in a cool place.

Serve with thinly sliced buttered brown bread or toast with dry white wine.

‌ Potted prawn spread

Finely chop or mince 500 g (1 lb) cooked and shelled prawns. Add the juice of half or one whole lemon and its grated rind, salt and pepper and a good pinch of nutmeg. Spoon into little pots and cover with melted clarified butter (see pp.227-8).

‌ Potted cheese

Hard cheeses last longer than soft ones, and a good old-fashioned English way of making cheese last even longer is to combine it with butter.

Use matured Cheddar, Cheshire, Stilton or Roquefort. Pound the cheese in a mortar with about a quarter its weight in softened unsalted butter, adding a little brandy, port or red or white wine to taste.

If you wish, add a sprinkling of pepper or cayenne, nutmeg or mace, or a little made mustard and if necessary a little salt. You may also mix in a few chopped almonds or walnuts. Press into pots and seal with a thin layer of melted clarified butter (see pp.227-8).

Cheese in oil

In the Middle East cheese is kept in oil. Fetta and other soft cheeses are cut into cubes and covered with olive or a light vegetable oil in a jar. Yoghurt, left to drain in a cloth until it is as firm as cream cheese, and mixed with a little salt and pepper and dried mint, is rolled into balls and treated in the same manner, to be spooned out as an appetizer with drinks or as part of a light meal.

I recently discovered in the Vaucluse, Picodons marinés, small rounds of goat cheese kept in olive oil flavoured with the herbs of the region. They are quite a delicacy and worth trying with an ordinary chèvre.

Preserved meats (confits)

My father remembers summer expeditions to the mountains of Lebanon where a whole lamb was prepared for the family to bring back to Egypt. It was called kawarma and was treated as a delicacy throughout the winter months. These are his instructions for young tender lamb.

Separate lean from fat. Cut the meat into medium-sized cubes. (You must have lumps not slices so that you can take them out easily.) Salt the meat. For 1 kg (2 lb) meat use 25 g (1 oz) salt and a pinch of saltpetre. Add a teaspoon of cinnamon and one of allspice or one each of cumin and coriander and some black pepper. Leave covered for 24 hours.

Chop up the fat adding the fat of two other lambs (in the Lebanon the tail, usually wobbling with fat, was rendered down) and melt it down in a large pan over high heat. Add the meat and turn the heat down very low. Stir with a wooden spoon and cook until the meat is just done and its juices are no longer pink. Allow to cool before putting the meat, well covered with its fat, into clean glass, earthenware or plastic jars (well washed in boiling soda water).

Spoon out pieces of meat as they are required, making sure those left are still completely covered with fat. Melt some that was taken out and pour it in again if necessary. Serve the meat cold with vegetable pickles and a salad, or heat it up in a frying pan with a little crushed garlic and serve it with potatoes, mashed or whole, and other vegetables.

The French make delicious confits on the same principle with pork, goose, turkey, duck and rabbit. Jane Grigson gives detailed instructions for all of these in *Charcuterie and French Pork Cookery*. They are easy enough to make in large quantities and will keep for a year if it is not too hot, as long as you are careful to keep the meat always entirely covered with fat.

Use boned pork from the hind loin, cut into large pieces and joint the birds and rabbit but do not bone them. For 2 kg (4 lb) of meat prepare a mixture of 50 g (2 oz) salt and a good pinch of saltpetre with a teaspoon of thyme, one of mace, nutmeg or allspice and 1/2 a teaspoon of black pepper. Rub it into the meat and leave it for 24 hours.

Melt down 1 kg (2 lb) fat from the meat augmented by lard in a large heavy saucepan. Add the pieces of meat and cook them very slowly for about 1-2 hours until tender and no juice comes out when you pierce with a knitting needle, but be careful not to overcook or the meat will be hard and dry (the saltpetre keeps it deceptively pink). In the meantime wash some plastic containers with boiling soda water so that they are perfectly clean. Pack the pieces of meat in, leaving 5 cm (2 in) at the top, and pour the strained fat to the brim (it will contract as it sets). Allow to cool and solidify, then press a piece of greaseproof paper down on it.

Serve cold or re-heated.

?? Rillettes

This shredded belly of pork mixed with fat was one of the bright spots of my boarding school days in Paris. It takes time but not too much effort and is well worth the patience. For 1 1/2 kg (3 lb) belly of pork you will need 2 cloves of garlic, salt and pepper, a good pinch of nutmeg or mace, 2 bay leaves and 1/2 teaspoon of thyme.

Cut the meat into pieces. Put them in a large heavy saucepan with the rest of the ingredients and with pieces of rind at the bottom and sides so that the meat does not stick to it and burn. Add 3 or 4 tablespoons of water and cook on the lowest possible flame, turning the pieces occasionally, until all the fat has melted and the meat is cooked but still soft and juicy. It can take up to 4 hours so be careful that it does not reach the point when it begins to fry and becomes dry and crisp and hard. Do not be tempted to raise the flame. Pour everything into a sieve over a bowl. Remove pieces of rind and bones. Chop the meat and pull it into shreds with your fingers and adjust the seasoning. Now mash and pound it with enough of the fat to make a smooth paste. Press into plastic pots and pour over them enough melted fat to cover the meat well. When it has cooled and set, press a greaseproof paper on top and cover with the lid.

Eat it spooned on to a slice of bread. If you want a pot to last for weeks you should melt some fat or clarified butter and pour it in to reseal every time you use it.

≥ Spiced beef

Mostly a matter of waiting, curing meat is as much a gastronomic event as a method of preserving it. This is Jane Grigson's recipe.

'Buy a 2½-3 kilo (5-6 lb) joint of silverside or round of beef, cut and tied for salting. Rub it over with 100 g (3 oz) dark brown sugar, and leave it for two days, turning it several times.

'Mix together 125 g (4 oz) sea salt or pure rock salt, a heaped teaspoon of saltpetre (from chemists, who can order it, if not in the regular stock), and 30 g (1 oz) each crushed black peppercorns, allspice berries and juniper berries. Rub this mixture into the beef and leave for 9 more days, turning it over once or twice a day and rubbing it with the dark, bitty liquor.

'To cook, dab off the bits of spice, or rinse quickly. Place in a close-fitting pot – this is important – with a generous ¼ litre (8-10 fl oz) water. Cover the top with shredded suet. Jam the lid on the pot with a double layer of foil or a flour and water paste. Bake in the oven at mark 1, 140°C (275°F), for 45 minutes a pound. Remove pot and leave undisturbed for three hours to cool down. Take off lid, drain meat and place on a board. Cover with greaseproof and put a 2 kilo weight (or heavy tins) on top. Leave for 24 hours, before carving into thin slices. Serve with avocado and potato salad and horseradish sauce, or with orange and olive salad.'

≥ Salamis and sausages

Salamis and sausages keep very well and make a substantial nourishing meal.

The Italians are the world's best makers of dried and smoked sausages, and the French excel in the fresh sausage which keeps for more than a fortnight at least. (If you are tempted to make your own, Jane Grigson's *Charcuterie and French Pork Cookery* has everything that needs to be known for the making of sausages, blood pudding, salt pork and hams.) A good delicatessen department will also sell Moroccan merguez and Central European boiling sausages as well as English pure pork luncheon sausages.

Elizabeth David gives a few suggestions for hot sausage dishes in *French Provincial Cooking*: A saucisson à la Lyonnaise is simmered in water or red wine and served with a well-dressed potato salad. In Alsace the boiled saucisson is served with a horseradish sauce made by stirring 1 tablespoon of grated horseradish into 150 ml (¼ pint) thick cream seasoned with salt and pepper and a squeeze of lemon juice.

Blood sausage, boiling sausage and saveloys may be cut into thick slices and gently fried in pork fat, oil or butter and served on a bed of fried apple slices or fried onions and accompanied by mashed potatoes.

If they are very good they may deserve this delicious sauce from Normandy: after frying the slices of sausages pour a glass of cider or white wine into the frying pan; let it bubble, then add 1 or 2 tablespoons of calvados or brandy and stir in 150 ml (¼ pint) thick cream. Heat through.

FRUIT CHUTNEYS

Fruit chutneys are one area of Indian culture which has been well and happily absorbed in our own. They have found their place with our cold meats. Recipes vary considerably in strength and fieriness, in sweetness and sourness as well as in the complexity of their ingredients, so follow your preference especially in the flavouring.

❧ A tomato and apple chutney

Green tomatoes are traditionally used, but here you have to grow them yourself. Red ones will do just as well. Skin ½ kg (1 lb) by covering with boiling water and chop them. Peel, core and chop ½ kg (1 lb) tart cooking apples. Put in a heavy-bottomed saucepan with 1 large chopped onion, 4 cloves of garlic, crushed, 2 tablespoons of raisins, 4 prunes, seeded and chopped, 350 g (¾ lb) brown sugar, 1 tablespoon of salt, 340 ml (12 fl oz) wine or cider vinegar, 1 teaspoon each of ground ginger and allspice. Simmer very gently for more than an hour until the mixture has the consistency of jam, stirring often as it begins to thicken and become sticky.

Add a pinch of cayenne pepper towards the end of the cooking time if you like it fiery.

Let it cool before you put it in a jar.

❧ Mixed fruit chutney

Use apples, plums, pears, apricots, peaches – all or two or three, cored, stoned, peeled and cut into small pieces. Put them in a large heavy saucepan. For 1 kg (2 lb) fruit add 2 tablespoons sultanas, 350 g (3/4 lb) sugar, 225 ml (8 fl oz) cider or wine vinegar, 1-2 teaspoonfuls garam masala, 8 large cloves of garlic, crushed, 1 dessertspoonful of salt, 1 teaspoon ground ginger, chilli or cayenne to taste (from 1/2 to 2 teaspoonfuls). Simmer gently for at least 45 minutes, stirring constantly until the mixture is soft, sticky and thickened.

Cool before you bottle it.

❧ Banana and date chutney with tamarind

To extract the sour juice from dried fibrous tamarind pods obtained at Indian shops is a messy and arduous business. The same shops now sell a concentrated tamarind paste which is not as good as the real thing but will do quite well for this purpose.

Dissolve 2 teaspoons of tamarind paste in 150 ml (1/4 pint) boiling water in a saucepan. Add 1 tablespoon of sugar, 1 1/2 teaspoons of powdered cumin and 1 teaspoon of salt. Throw in about 9 dates, pitted and chopped, and a small handful of slivered almonds, then slice into the saucepan 3 green (unripe) bananas. Stir until the liquor has been absorbed, adding a good pinch or as much as you like of cayenne.

Cool before you bottle it.

PRESERVED FRUITS

A good way of keeping fruit ever at hand is to preserve it in syrup or with wines or spirits. It makes the most delicious quick dessert to be served alone in its juice or with cream, yoghurt or cream cheese. Sliced or mashed to a purée, it can also be used as a filling for pancakes and sweet omelettes or as a topping or sauce.

❧ Pears in red or white wine

Peel 2 kg (4 lb) small hard pears, leaving their stalks on. Put them in a large pan with a bottle of wine and 1/2 kg (1 lb) of sugar, and simmer for about 45 minutes until tender. You can also flavour with 4 or 5 cloves, a stick of cinnamon and the rind of a lemon.

Transfer the pears to a large jar. Reduce the syrup and pour it over them. You may add a few tablespoons of a pear brandy or a fruit liqueur such as cassis.

Serve the pears as they are or with cream, yoghurt or cream cheese.

Variations: try other fruits cooked this way: peach halves, sour cherries or apple slices (for these add the juice of half a lemon).

Port makes an excellent alternative to cooking with wine.

❧ Fruits in alcohol – A mixed pot

In the countries where spirits or eaux de vie, alcohols between 45° and 55°, are not too expensive, fruits are commonly preserved in them. Cheaper alternatives are vodka, gin, rum and some brandies. Start the preserve early in the spring and you will be able to take it on your summer travels to savour after cheese or when coffee is served. It is very pleasant and not that extravagant.

Different methods find advocates who discover little tricks for perfecting them over the years. Some start with raw fruit, pricking the tougher skinned varieties with a needle or blanching them first. The preserve is usually ready after 2 or 3 months.

A large pot of mixed fruit will provide an exciting selection. Use peaches, skinned and halved, melon, peeled, seeded and cut into large chunks, apples and pears, peeled and quartered, cherries, grapes and plums, pricked all over with a needle, pineapple chunks, apricots, strawberries, figs and raspberries – whatever are available – all sound and ripe and well washed. Pack all the fruit tightly in a large pot or jar. How much sugar to use is a matter of some controversy and usually varies between a quarter of the weight of the fruit to the same weight. The fruit is less likely to ferment if you use more sugar. There are various ways of combining spirit and sugar. The simplest is to sprinkle layers of fruit with sugar and then to pour the spirit straight out of the bottle over the fruit. But it may be more effective to warm up the alcohol in a saucepan with the sugar until it is dissolved.

Make sure the fruits are well covered with liquor and seal well.

For a preserve which is ready within a month, poach the fruit in very heavy syrup with its own weight of sugar and half the volume of water, until it is slightly tender and rather sweet. Drain and reduce the syrup, then pour over the fruit and cover with alcohol in ajar. In Apt, the centre for fruits confits in the south of France, where I stopped for 'confiseries comme autrefois' (crystallized fruit as in olden times) from the makers, people were queuing to buy small whole fruit by the kilo while they were in the sticky syrup stage. There were very tiny oranges, tangerines, pears, figs and other fruits ready for taking home and soaking in armagnac, calvados, the apple brandy, guillaumin made from pears, kirsch from cherry stones or mirabelle from plums.

🦋 Apple butter

Peel, quarter and core 2 kg (4 lb) apples. Cook them in cider or white wine to cover and 1 kg (2 lb) sugar, to a very thick pulp (about 45 minutes). Pour into jars and seal.

Variations: spicing the apple butter with 2 teaspoons of cinnamon, 6 cloves and a small piece of fresh ginger or to add a few tablespoons of Calvados or brandy at the end of the cooking time.

An alternative, called apple rum, is to cook the apples with sugar and about $1/2$ litre ($3/4$ pint) water for half an hour. Then add 150 ml ($1/4$ pint) rum and cook the paste for a further quarter of an hour.

Spoon out when you feel like something sweet, or use as a sauce for dessert.

🦋 Dried fruit and nuts

The chosen picnic fare for William Cobbett, who toured the countryside on horseback in the early nineteenth century, was nuts and apples. He urges their merits with great fervour in his book *Rural Rides, with Economical and Political Observations*:

> At Gloucester we furnished ourselves with nuts and apples, which, first a handful of nuts and then an apple, are, I can assure the reader, excellent and more wholesome fare. They say that nuts of all sorts are unwholesome; if they had been, I should never have written Registers and if they were now, I should have ceased to write ere this for upon an average, I have eaten a pint a day since I left home.

Nuts and apples were his way of avoiding the exorbitant prices charged by the inn keepers along the road.

Many people who eat to 'fill up' for sustenance would agree with him, and add dried fruits. These have been esteemed from time immemorial by the peoples of the Near East and the Mediterranean countries. Ever since the crusaders brought them back to Europe they have been the special diet of travellers, their instant sustainers and revivers.

There is now a large trade in all types of dried fruits – figs, pears, peaches, dates, apricots, apples, prunes – either whole or stoned and halved or cut into rings. The choicest are the ones dried naturally in the sun. The best figs and sultanas come from Smyrna, the best dates from Persia, Morocco and Tunisia. Muscatel are the finest table dessert raisins. They are produced in the south of Spain, chiefly in the Malaga district. The largest and the ones that retain a bluish tinge are the best. Other excellent raisins come from Valencia, California, South Africa, Greece and Cyprus, and the loveliest currants, rich blue-black and both sweet and acid, from Greece. Sweet Jordan dessert almonds come from the Malaga coast of Spain. Valencia almonds and those from Sicily are also sweet while Barberry ones from North Africa are bitter-sweet.

STREET FOOD

You may be able to find all you need on the spot in the street. Street food has to be discovered. Each country has its own. Where there is no restaurant tradition this is the only way that foreigners will get to taste local food; the alternative is the cosmopolitan cuisine served in hotels. I have always found it irresistible for the alluring displays and enticing smells, as well as for the cries of the vendors which are able to rouse even a dormant appetite.

As a child in Cairo I was fascinated by the cries of peddlers and street vendors, itinerant sellers of all types of foods. I waited for each familiar voice to pass under my bedroom window to allay the boredom of my enforced siesta. Sometimes the cry was accompanied by the rattle of pieces of paper twisted around bicycle spokes or by the clinking of glasses or the clanking of brass plates. One man, called out every day at two o'clock with a plaintive nasal voice 'Aha awaw!' For a long time I wondered what he sold. With the shutters down I never had a chance to see him. When I escaped the siesta and finally saw him, he was selling nothing at all. Perhaps he liked the sound of his cry.

Vendors plying through the streets or standing in the market, carrying their wares on trays placed on tightly coiled cloths on their heads, or in baskets or barrels strapped to their shoulders, were a source of endless fascination. The more perishable the food, the greater the need to dispose of it quickly, the more pressing their cries.

I was impressed by the speed at which they peeled oranges and separated the segments, sprinkled salt on a cucumber and cut a square out of a water-melon before a prospective buyer had made up his mind, eloquently praising the honeysweet virtues of their fruits at the same time.

Each place had its specialities. Outside the open air cinemas sesame bread rings called semit were sold with Greek cheese. The sea breeze on the corniche in Alexandria carried the smell of corn cobs roasted on charcoal. On the beach you had to toss a coin with the vendor to win a sesame crunch or lose it and still have to pay. Anyone who has taken a

walk in Cairo knows the smoky smell of lamb fanned into their face, and that of the mashed white beans that make up falafel, turning brown in sizzling hot oil. And who has not been tempted by the pickled turnips, swimming in brine made pink by beetroot, by the deep fried aubergine slices soaked in oil and lemon juice or by the crisp round fritters soaked in syrup?

The smells of Baghdad are only a little different. They are spicier. Here too pickled turnips are sold in the streets, but they are often sweetened with dates. Boiled chick peas, sprinkled with oil and pennyroyal mint, are offered steaming hot. Carts are laden with a decorative assortment of hard-boiled eggs, pickles in vinegar, beetroots, tomatoes, spring onions, young lettuce hearts and bunches of fresh herbs. The vendor will cut everything up for you into slices or little cubes and drop it into the pouch of a flat round hollow bread. Kebabshi (kebab vendors) sometimes turn their barrow into a small restaurant by providing a few chairs to sit and eat all manner of grilled meat and offal.

In Morocco, meat is cut very small and flavoured with a greater variety of spices. Vendors squat over small braziers on pavements, browning their mechoui together with little spicy sausages called merguez.

A Tunisian street favourite called brik is a meal in itself. Paper thin sheets of pastry, each wrapped in a parcel around a filling composed of an egg and a choice of other ingredients, are deep fried for passers-by.

In Tehran, those who get to the bazaar before 7 a.m. are able to sample calepache. This is a lamb's head rich with creamy brains stewed slowly in a large cauldron together with feet, tripe and stomach. During the fasting month of Ramadan a meaty porridge called halim is the breakfast food which fills the cauldron with breast of lamb and oats sweetened with sugar.

The anthropologist Ahmet E. Uysal writes in an article on 'Street Cries in Turkey' in the *Journal of American Folklore* (1968) that the list of goods sold in the streets and open air bazaars of Turkey from push-carts, baskets and directly off the ground would cover the entire range of human needs. Apart from the usual fruit, vegetables, meat and fish, cooked foods are also available; soups at breakfast time and sweet pastries during festivals. You will also get metaphors, puns, exaggerated descriptions, earthy and salty humour, practical wisdom and frequent appeals to the medicinal properties of the foods. Peddlers enjoy a good deal of licence for insolence and can often be heard pouring outrageous insults on to passers-by or making rude retorts and using words with double meanings. Some set up a lecture platform and demonstration table to attract prospective buyers.

The best of Israeli food is also in the street, a legacy of the Ottomans reinforced by the ways of Arabs and Oriental Jews. It is here that national styles are forged, that young Israelis from different backgrounds form their conception of the food of their land. They have got used to grabbing a cheap snack on their way somewhere at all times of the day, and it is the different foods, which start as the initiative of the vendor and spread quickly into a rash of kiosks, that bring the tastes and ways of the different communities into the common national pool. Often, they are better than the food provided by the trendy restaurants which open one day and close the next. The cactus peeled for you with art, the sesame bread rings sold with the spice mixture zahtar, fish grilled at the harbour, sanbusak and borekas produced at the back of petrol stations and home-made hummus or falafel offered in the market place are the joys of the country which tourists often miss for fear of food poisoning and because they are strange.

For obvious reasons the warmer and the poorer countries are richest in open-air culinary activities. We have little to offer in England these days besides jellied eels and cockles, hamburgers, hot dogs, chestnuts and ice-creams and, for a brief 3 days a year, red mullet and other Jamaican specialities at the Notting Hill festival. When will we have pancakes at street corners as they do in Paris, where you can have a whole meal of crêpes starting with savoury ham and cheese and finishing with sugar and cointreau? It would be so good to stop and buy oysters from a basket and have them opened on the spot and eat them there and then with a squeeze of lemon.

At one time 'frost fairs' were frequent all over the country during exceptionally cold weather. The seventeenth century diarist John Evelyn describes the tents and booths which were erected over frozen rivers. Oxen and sheep were roasted whole (they were called Lapland mutton) and 'hot codlins, pancakes, duck, goose, sack, rabbit, capon, hen and turkey' were sold as well as mutton pies and hot black puddings. In the nineteenth century there were itinerant vendors with baskets, especially at coach-side and railway station. Lord Macaulay describes the hazards of a coach journey (quoted in *The Greedy Book* by Brian Hill):

I travelled to town with a family of children who ate without intermission from Market Harborough, where they got into the coach, to the Peacock at Islington, where they got out of it. They breakfasted as if they had fasted all the preceding day. They dined as if they had never breakfasted. They ate on the road one large basket of sandwiches, another of fruit, and a boiled fowl: besides which there was not an orange-girl, an old man with cakes, or a boy with filberts, who came to the coach-side when we stopped to change horses, of whom they did not buy something.

IMPROMPTU MEALS

One of the best ways of discovering regional foods is to stop at small shops and markets and purchase local specialities for an impromptu roadside picnic or a cheap meal in a city park. In most countries some of the bigger towns have a permanent market, while smaller ones have a street market once a week. In France they are a feast of colour, scent and bustle, with stalls beautifully laid out with shiny fresh fish, cooked meats, fruit and vegetables and a multitude of cheeses, a song of praise for local produce; quayside stalls sell seafood and shellfish ready for eating with only a squeeze of lemon and a piece of bread.

Remember that outside England you are expected to take an interest in what you buy, so take your time, handle the food and ask the merchant how to cook or use it. You might even be encouraged to taste before you decide to buy. For many people, the spur of the moment meal from the market or the little shop is the most exciting, not least because it requires no work. Buying it provides half the fun. A sturdy shopping basket will be useful, a tin opener, a corkscrew and a good knife invaluable. It does, however, need inspiration and taste to assemble good things from visits to the grocer, the baker, the wine merchant and fruit seller. Lay out separate little dishes of whatever has tempted you – radishes, olives, knobbly tomatoes, spring onions.

ૐ Some well-tried combinations to assemble

Parma ham or other raw smoked hams are as good with ripe figs as they are with melon. There are many varieties of figs fruiting in various colours ranging from purple to whitish yellow, the rich golden yellow being the most prized.

Anchovy fillets, tomatoes and olives are excellent arranged on a slice of good bread softened by moistening with a little water and sprinkled with a vinaigrette dressing. A little chopped onion, capers and some fresh chopped basil if you happen to be in Italy make it even better. In Liguria they use hard dry biscuits (galette), instead of bread, in what is called caponata alla Ligure.

All cheese is good with olives and with a thick slice of country bread to break into pieces and soak up the oil or liquor of the olives. In Greece buy Fetta or Halumi; Halumi is good with a squeeze of lemon. In Italy try Fontina with mild green peppers cut into thin strips. Cream cheeses such as Amari in Greece, Petit Suisse in France and Ricotta in Italy can also be eaten with sugar, honey or jam. The blander ones can be mashed with a drop of brandy or spirit. A good English combination is tart apples with a hard crumbly cheese such as Lancashire or Cheddar and fresh walnuts.

Smoked fish – trout, mackerel, buckling, salmon and eel – need no accompaniment other than lemon and bread and butter, except perhaps a little finely chopped onion.

Cod's roe mashed into a paste with olive oil and lemon juice is excellent with hot toast.

Tuna and artichokes in oil are excellent together, tinned sardines good with hard-boiled eggs. Some grocers sell artichoke hearts. You may like to fill them with mayonnaise and chopped up hard-boiled eggs, spring onions or radishes.

Radishes are lovely with bread and butter and a sprinkling of salt.

Salami and bread and butter take a lot of beating and mortadella is good with fennel.

You can make up a little salad with salt herring, cooked white haricot beans, black olives, quartered hard-boiled eggs, thinly sliced onions, which is a meal in itself.

A Genoese hors d'oeuvre combines small raw broad beans, rough salami sausage and salty sheep's milk Sardo cheese. Another Italian favourite is tuna fish piled up on a bed of haricot beans or French beans dressed with oil. So is a plate of prawns with French beans seasoned with olive oil, lemon juice and a dash of salt and pepper.

❧ Hors d'oeuvres and crudités – a ready-made party meal

A well-chosen hors d'oeuvre platter, simply presented with taste and an eye for colour, can also make a satisfying complete meal. The French present a selection of anchovy fillets, pâté de campagne, sliced sausage, raw ham, hard-boiled eggs, prawns, herring titbits, sardines and olives. Coupled with crudités (see p.92), you cannot want for anything else, except perhaps a well-flavoured mayonnaise or an aïoli in which to dip them. (Various recipes for these are given on pp.46-48.)

❧ Antipasto

You can easily assemble a typical Italian antipasto platter.

An antipasto magro is without meats and usually consists of tuna, hard-boiled eggs, tomatoes, boiled potatoes and beetroot – all set out on a large platter, quartered or cut in slices, accompanied by a vinaigrette dressing or a mayonnaise.

A complete antipasto platter consists of slices of Italian salami, mortadella and raw and cooked ham placed on a bed of lettuce leaves with a few tomatoes cut in wedges, sliced fennel, pieces of tuna fish or sardines, a few artichoke hearts in oil or brine, some fat firm radishes and a few ripe olives. A special dressing enlivens the dish. Make this with olive oil beaten with 2-3 chopped and mashed anchovy fillets. Add lemon juice, salt and pepper to taste and capers if you like.

❧ Steak tartare

Clint Greyn suggests this as a dish to make up in France where suitable meat is easily obtainable: perfectly lean beef, free from every bit of fat and connective tissue, absolutely fresh, and chopped rather than minced. A knife to chop up the accompaniments is the only piece of equipment required to make up this ancient Mongolian nomadic classic. Clint makes it up for two on the plate and eats it just as soon as he comes out from the butcher.

For two, 250 g (½ lb) raw minced beef will be enough. Shape it into mounds on two plates. Make a well in the middle and drop an egg yolk into each. Make a ring of finely chopped garnishes – 2 onions, 2 tablespoons of capers, 2 tablespoons of pickled gherkins and 2 tablespoons of parsley – around the meat.

Present with salt and pepper, tabasco if you like, and lemon wedges. Each person can season and mix in the garnish ingredients as he likes. Have a plate of thin slices of brown bread and butter.

ࣈ Using the local baker's oven

Years ago an uncle in Egypt made a habit of buying a good piece of meat and taking it to the local oven when he was on holiday in Alexandria. He ran with it, sizzling and succulent and wrapped in brown paper, to the restaurant where he had invited some guests to a meal, ordering only drinks and salads. He reckoned this was a cheaper and delicious way of entertaining.

There may not be many restaurants left that would allow this, but there are still country places where the local baker obliges customers with the use of his oven and will let them put in a joint of meat to be collected when it is ready. It is worth finding out and making use of this special service for a party in the country. For cooking a whole baby pig or lamb see the instructions on pp.173-6. They will need less time in the oven than on the spit – about three-quarters of the time.

LIVING OFF THE LAND

'What is sweeter than honey?' The answer to this Arab riddle is 'Free vinegar'. Food that you do not have to pay for has a special charm.

In the Seychelles islands I discovered that it is possible to live quite happily on food caught or found growing wild without recourse to the Indian shops. According to local lore, cultivation of the fruits and spices planted in the eighteenth century by French settlers arriving from nearby Mauritius was abandoned when slavery was abolished. The emancipated slaves, preferring to enjoy their newly acquired freedom, refused to work any longer on the plantations. Most things have managed to grow without attention, the multitude of birds obliging by chewing the berries and spitting the stones in appropriate places. It is always easy to wade into the sea and hit a fish on the head without having to go far out beyond the coral reef where sharks might be waiting. And the coconuts fall by themselves.

The flesh of one species of coconut is a translucent jelly when the fruit is less than a year old and still young and tender. It is delicious eaten chilled with sugar and a liqueur such as maraschino or anisette. Apart from its gastronomic virtues this coconut has other attractions; it is believed to be a powerful aphrodisiac. For centuries, since it was washed ashore on the beaches of India and Africa, this fruit, which only grows in the Seychelles, has excited the imagination of generations. If you see the coco de mer you will understand. For the female nut, affectionately called coco fesses (fesses meaning buttocks in French) is like a curvacious pelvis from one side. From the other it is like a belly framed by rounded thighs complete with what looks like pubic hair. The male trees produce nothing you can eat. They grow phallic catkins 6½ cm (2½ in) thick and 60 cm (2 ft) long with a heavy scented pollen. Legends tell of their nightly visits to the coco fesses. When the nut is old, the jelly dries hard like ivory. It is ground to a fine powder by the bonhomme di bois (the herbalist) and by the sorcerer who specializes in love potions and aids for revenge, with bits of wood, strings, animal bones, seeds and old newspapers with photographs of famous lovers.

There are many things besides coconuts which you can pick such as mangoes, pawpaws, guavas, pineapples, yams, breadfruits, sweet potatoes and bananas. With all this natural bounty it is not surprising that the government drive for 'growing your food' in the form of pop songs on the radio and visits from agricultural advisers, was encountering more than a little resistance. Remembering distant days in Sicily where a tall tower in the middle of an orange grove was pointed out as being constantly inhabited by a marksman ready to shoot down anyone bold enough to pick an orange, I was relieved to find that things were different here. In accordance with biblical law, the law decrees that picking food on another man's land is not an offence as long as you eat it on the spot.

Marching armies, like pilgrims and explorers have always relied to some extent on game and food growing wild when they could not seize a sheep from a farmer or ransack a store on the way. Legendary heroes, when resting from conquests, sought diversion in games nearly as formidable and imitative of their combats, which often placed their lives in danger. Diversions far tamer though no less absorbing were obtained simply by picking fruits and vegetables. The loss of the battle of Waterloo by the French has been attributed to wild strawberries. According to the famous chef Pierre Lacam, when the war was well under way in 1815, General Gérard hurrying to the assistance of Napoleon, found Maréchal Grouchy in the village of Sart-a-Wachain, on the route to Namur, eating strawberries. The Maréchal refused to move.

All those who have dreamt of vast empires – Tamerlane, Timur, Genghis Khan, Charlemagne, Clovis, Napoleon – have of necessity wrenched all they could from trees, fields, rivers and skies. For some it was not only a matter of survival.

For Babur, the first Mogul Emperor, who spent 20 years in the early sixteenth century confirming his position in Afghanistan, regaining the Central Asian empire of Tamerlane and finally conquering within a few months half of Hindustan, it was a continuous gastronomic adventure. A robust and valiant warrior, he was also a joyous drinker and a generous one, a lover of poetry, backgammon and food, who recorded everything in his famous diaries. The engaging conqueror, who combined an incessant activity at war with an extraordinary personal vigour, wept with delight on seeing the cattle on the hills of Fargana, the profusion of fruits in the orchards, the grain in the autumn fields, a duck shot during an excursion on a boat, a deer impaled near a roaring fire . . .

Here is an entry for the year 1520 translated from the Turki text by Annette Susannah Beveridge (1912):

Marching next day from that ground, I made an excursion up the valley-bottom of the Barik-ab towards Qurinq-sai. A few purslain trees were in the utmost autumn beauty. On dismounting, seasonable food was set out. The vintage was the cause! Wine was drunk! A sheep was ordered brought from the road and made into kebabs. We amused ourselves by setting fire to branches of holm-oak.

Mulla 'Abdu'l-malik dïwâna having begged to take the news of our coming into Kabul, was sent ahead. To this place came Hasan Nabïra from Mïrzâ Khan's presence; he must have come after letting me know. There was drinking till the sun's decline; we then rode off. People in our party had become very drunk; Sayyid Qâsim so much so, that two of his servants mounted him and got him into camp with difficulty. Muli Baqir's Dost was so drunk that people, headed by Amïn-i-Muhammad Tarkhan and Mastû Chuhra, could not get him on his horse; even when they poured water on his head, nothing was affected. At that moment a body of Afghans appeared. Amïn-i-Muhammad, who had had enough himself, had this idea, 'Rather than leave him here, as he is, to be taken, let us cut his head off and carry it with us.' At last after 100 efforts, they mounted him and brought him with them. We reached Kabul at midnight.

Babur could tell of the most extraordinary and savage exploits and at the same time rhapsodize about the bounty and splendour of nature and its offerings. When he was not conquering, chopping off heads, fighting relatives and protecting himself against intrigues, he was catching fish, hunting deer, eating and drinking amidst the falling petals and fruit blossoms and the flaming fire of autumn leaves. Pomegranates, oranges and grapes were picked, confections were lovingly prepared and there was continuous wine drinking and revelling throughout all the bloody campaigns. From time to time prayers were said to the prophet Mohamad and forgiveness was asked for the drinking of wine.

Babur also described in great detail all sorts of ingenious traps for animals. In one entry he tells of catching a bird:

Another of the curiosities of the Nijr-âû mountains is the lûkha bird, called also bû-qalamûn (chameleon) because between head and tail, it has four or five changing colours, resplendent like a pigeon's throat. It is about as large as the kabg-ï-dari and seems to be the kabg-ï-dan of Hindûstân. People tell this wonderful thing about it: When the birds, at the onset of winter, descend to the hill-skirts, if they come over a vineyard, they can fly no further and are taken.

Nowadays it is the ordinary holidaymaker who is more likely to make use of the local wild produce and discover that it is the best way to get to know a country.

The spoils of the European wilderness may not be as rich or as exotic but they are there and it is worth keeping your eyes open for such an eventuality, as do the children on their walks to school in Flora Thompson's *Lark Rise to Candleford*.

After the first mile or so the dinner baskets would be raided; or they would creep through the bars of the padlocked gates for turnips to pare with the teeth and munch, or for handfuls of green pea shucks, or ears of wheat, to rub out the sweet, milky grain between the hand and devour. In spring they ate the young green from the hawthorn hedges which they called 'bread and cheese' and sorrel leaves from the wayside, which they called 'sour grass', and in autumn there was an abundance of haws and blackberries and sloes and crab apples for them to feast upon. There was always something to eat, and they ate, not so much because they were hungry as from habit, and relish of the wild food.

There are many edibles growing wild, from barks and fruit, tender leafy greens, vegetables and herbs to small game and seafood. Almost every animal and every fish or bird is good to eat.

Wild berries. They are abundant and widespread in woods, hedgerows and fields. Raspberries, blackberries, wild strawberries, gooseberries and bilberries, depending on their ripeness and sweetness, may be eaten off the bush or need only sugar and fresh cream. If they are too acid, a little simmering, with sugar will turn them into an excellent compote. Hawthorn may be cooked with crab apples which are unpalatable raw. Other fruits are less common but you may come across cherry-plums, wild cherries and red or black currants.

I first discovered the joys of wild strawberries in the moist woodlands at the foot of the Italian Dolomites. The flavour and fragrance of this tiny species is greatly superior to the best strains of cultivated ones. They grow wild in many parts of Europe as well as in England, so be prepared for them on your country walks with basket or polythene bag. If you have neither, large thick leaves rolled into cones make good containers.

Eat them as soon as possible. They do not really need washing, but if you must, wash them as swiftly as possible without letting the water soak out the best of their flavour. They are so good that they can be eaten as they are. Dipping their point into a little salt, pepper or a drop of vinegar brings out the flavour and sweetness.

Otherwise, dredge with sugar and if you can afford to be grand, pour wine (claret for instance) or champagne over them and smother generously with fresh cream. Our hotel at Cortina d'Ampezzo served them up to us with that light-as-a-cloud whipped cream they call panna montata. Wild blackberries, raspberries and bilberries received the same treatment.

Sweet chestnuts are fairly common in woods and parks in the British Isles. The nuts are ready by October and November and may be gathered in the late autumn. Split the prickly husks underfoot and take out the beautifully polished brown nuts. Slit the skins and drop them in the hot ashes of an open fire. Do not try to eat horse chestnuts which have thicker and more widely spaced spikes.

There is a large variety of green leaves which you can eat raw in a salad, such as watercress, white mustard, chicory and some unusual types of lettuce. Others must be cooked. Wood-sorrel with cream makes a magnificent sauce for fish, and wild spinach or beet may be cooked in their own juice with water and butter or oil.

Mushroom hunting is one of the most enjoyable ways of passing the time in fields and woodlands after the first rains, but it is important to get a good field guide to make sure you know that they are not poisonous.

Even without a guide the risks are relatively slight, for out of more than a hundred species, very few are poisonous and even fewer fatally so. The Romans believed that although many mushrooms were poisonous, fate led them to eat only the good ones, and Seneca called the field variety a 'voluptuous poison', for the wealthier inhabitants relished them for the danger attached.

To pick mushrooms, twist gently to break them free. Cut off the base of the stem and remove any blemishes. There is no need to peel or wash them unless they are very dirty, and then do so very briefly. Grill them, brushed with plenty of oil or melted butter, or sauté quickly, small ones whole, large ones sliced. Season with salt and pepper when they have exuded their juices after 3 or 4 minutes, and add some herbs if you have them and a little lemon juice.

HOLIDAY BREAKFASTS

Breakfast was the one meal I awaited with anticipation during my six months at a boarding school in Horsham, fried bread, eggs and bacon, sausages, tomatoes and mushrooms, porridge or cornflakes.

Nowadays it is only on holiday that I realize the value of a substantial unhurried breakfast. Though there is no better morning menu than an English one it is possible to improve on the usual list.

Brown bread, butter and marmalade could be varied with croissants or brioche with coffee, tea or fruit juice. Swiss muesli makes an alternative to oatmeal porridge. Or you could offer as the Israelis do, chunks of cucumber and quartered tomato, hard-boiled eggs, pickled fish and bowls of cream cheese or yoghurt with stewed or fresh fruit.

The potted foods in the *Provisions* chapter may be served on toast while a cooked dish of eggs, fish or meat is especially welcome.

❧ Creamed haddock

Lightly poach the haddock. Flake it and add as much whipped cream as you like. Keep it warm and serve with sautéed mushrooms and a little grated Parmesan.

❧ Kippers

Kippers may be grilled for 5 minutes, or gently fried in very little butter for 2-3 minutes, on each side, or simply have boiling water poured over them for a few minutes. Do not overcook. Serve on toast or with thin slices of brown bread and butter and lemon wedges and a little pat of butter melting over them.

You may also flake them cooked or uncooked and stir them into creamy scrambled eggs.

❧ Herring

A Scottish way for very fresh filleted herrings: season with salt and pepper and lemon juice, dip in seasoned medium ground oatmeal and fry both sides until brown. Serve with lemon wedges and a pat of butter.

❧ Fried pork sausages with apples

Stir some Worcestershire sauce into the cooking fat and add a few apple slices when the sausages are almost done.

❧ Bachelor eggs

What Mrs Leyel calls bachelor eggs are poached eggs served with fried ham on toasted muffins. Split and toast the muffins. Fry a round piece of ham for each half muffin, and on each round place a poached egg.

❧ Scrambled eggs

To the eggs in the frying pan add a bunch of herbs (make your own choice), finely chopped, and add a pinch of nutmeg and salt and pepper.

To vary the standard recipe, break 8 eggs in a bowl, add salt and pepper and beat lightly. Pour into sizzling hot butter and stir over a low flame. Just as they begin to set, add 3 tablespoons of grated Gruyère or Cheddar and stir until creamy. You may also add fried pieces of bacon, chopped tomatoes, asparagus tips or sautéed sliced mushrooms.

❧ Fried spiced bread

A tasty version of a schoolchildren's delight is made by flavouring the frying oil or butter with salt and pepper and ground spices. Try a mixture of a few of the following: paprika, cayenne, cloves, cumin, coriander, cinnamon, allspice. Stir sparingly into the hot fat then fry the bread, turning over once.

❧ Sautéed kidneys

Wash and remove fat and membranes of 2 veal kidneys (beef kidneys need soaking for 2 hours in water with a little vinegar). Cut into slices. Sauté quickly in a mixture of oil and butter – for 3 minutes. Season with salt and pepper.

Serve on fried or toasted bread with a squeeze of lemon juice and snippets of parsley.

For a stronger taste you may add a pinch of cayenne and a little mustard (French or English) or some mango chutney.

TRAVELLERS' SNACKS

Travellers with cooking facilities usually find that one full meal a day is quite sufficient. They like to break the rest of the time with little snacks handed out at convenient intervals.

One feature of old English fare which fills hungry gaps admirably is savouries. They were originally served as the sobering end of a dinner party, after an indulgent dessert. Escoffier claimed that their use was contrary to the rules of gastronomy, but he would surely have agreed that they make most appropriate holiday snacks.

Savouries are generally served on toast: spinach with a poached egg on top, chicken and ham with cheese, liver or kidney fried with streaky bacon, anchovies and olives, fried mushrooms, chutney with cheese – old favourites spiced and seasoned with mustard and hot peppers according to tastes acquired in colonial days. They differ from the open sandwich in that they are cooked and served hot.

For cod's roe on toast, melt a little butter in a saucepan and add smoked cod's roe from a jar. Add pepper, mace and lemon juice to taste and a pinch of cayenne if you like.

For chicken livers, sauté a little chopped onion in some butter until it browns. Add cleaned chicken livers and sauté quickly, turning them over until they are brown but still pink inside. Add salt and pepper, a pinch of thyme, one of allspice before they are done and a squeeze of lemon juice or a drop of brandy at the end. Chop up the liver and arrange on fried bread or toast pouring the juices over it.

To make anchovy toast, mix some anchovy paste out of a tube with a little olive oil and vinegar. Spread on toast, sprinkle with pepper and put under the grill or heat in a frying pan.

?◆ Welsh rabbit

Hikers in Wales know this as the cheapest way to fill up. Evan Jones offers more than one story of how this dish got its name in *The World of Cheese*. Welsh wives, waiting anxiously, spied their husbands or sons returning from a hunt empty-handed and set cheese before the fire to melt as a substitute for a dinner of game. Another, for the alternative spelling 'rarebit' is that it was usually served with savouries at a meal's end and originally named rearbits on early menus in the same way as hors d'oeuvres were known as forebits.

There are innumerable versions of Welsh rabbit ranging from the slice of cheese placed on buttered toast and put under the grill to extravagant stewed versions of Swiss fondue.

Use a good melting cheese. A sharp Cheddar is excellent. Gloucester, Cheshire, Lancashire, Leicester, Wensleydale, Derbyshire and Caerphilly are also good. Make it in a heavy casserole of frying pan on a low fire.

Melt 2 tablespoons of butter and add 500 g (1 lb) sharp Cheddar or a combination of 2 cheeses, cut into small pieces. Add 1 teaspoon of mustard (I prefer to use French but you might like English) and 1 teaspoon of Worcestershire sauce, some freshly ground black pepper or a good sprinkling of cayenne. As the cheese begins to melt, pour in ½ litre (1 pint) good beer, stirring constantly, then stir in 2 beaten egg yolks. When the bubbly mixture is light and creamy serve on hot buttered toast.

Variations: Serve over fried sliced apples and it becomes the delicious *Yorkshire rabbit*. If you slip a poached egg on a piece of toast before pouring on the cheese it is called a *Golden Buck*.

For a more sophisticated version, substitute white wine and a few tablespoons of cognac, kirsch or rum for the beer. A few gratings of nutmeg give a happy flavour to the dish and a little light fresh cream is a pleasant addition.

?◆ Croque Monsieur and Croque Madame

As children in France we loved to order these toasted sandwiches for the picture their names evoked.

For Croque Monsieur put a slice of Gruyère, Emmenthal or Fontina with a large slice of ham or two rashers of fried bacon between two medium thick buttered slices of bread. Grill or sauté in hot oil or butter. Serve hot and golden with the cheese nicely melted. A little bit of crushed garlic in the frying pan gives a special flavour to the sandwich.

For Croque Madame mix 2 tablespoons of flour with half a teacup of cold milk in a bowl and stir until well blended. Heat over a low flame, stirring constantly until it thickens. Add 1 beaten egg, a teacup of grated Gruyère, 2 tablespoons of cognac, kirsch or rum, a sprinkling of paprika, salt and pepper and cayenne and stir until the cheese has melted. Serve over hot toast. You may substitute white wine or beer for the milk and you may like to add a little mustard.

❧ Stuffed bread fritters

The French call these pain perdu (lost bread), the Italians, cuscinetti (little cushions).

Cut medium thin slices of bread, white or wholemeal, and remove the crusts. You may toast them lightly or leave them as they are.

For the filling, grate, crumble or mash some cheese; Roquefort for a French taste, Provatura or Mozzarella for an Italian; matured Cheddar and Stilton do very well. Work it with a little softened butter, enough to make it hold together as a paste and stick to the bread. You may flavour the cheese paste with a pinch of nutmeg, pepper or cayenne or add little bits of things like ham or gherkins, chopped up small.

Spread thickly on pieces of bread or toast and press two together like a sandwich. Dip in milk then in beaten egg, or in beaten egg alone, so that both sides are well coated. Lift out carefully and fry in hot oil or sizzling butter, turning over once, until well coloured.

A sweet version is made with slices of bread dipped in sweetened milk, flavoured if you like with vanilla, then in slightly sweetened beaten egg. A topping is not usual but there is nothing to stop you from having jam or apple sauce or anything you like.

❧ Fried cheese

This can be done with Mozzarella, Taleggio or Bel Paese, which are in all the supermarkets, or with Halumi, which is sold in Greek shops. Cut the cheese into cubes or slices. Dip in flour, then beaten egg, then breadcrumbs and fry in a little oil. Drain and serve immediately.

Or you may dip cheese in batter. Mix flour, white or wholemeal, gradually with enough cold water to make a smooth stiff batter. Season with salt and pepper and flavour if you like with a little spirit such as vodka. Leave it for an hour. Stir in the pieces of cheese, cut small. Deep fry by the spoonful in hot oil until golden-brown. Drain and serve at once.

MEAL IN A FRYING PAN

There are many quick and simple meals which are as easy to make at camp as on a boat or a caravan using a frying pan or a saucepan. A few memorable summer weeks spent camping with a group of Dutch artists in the French village of Lacoste, of Marquis de Sade fame, taught me that the possibilities are unlimited.

Sculptors, painters and potters were helping their colleague, my friend of art school days, Ans Hey, to build a house before the winter set in. She repaid them with a constant and plentiful supply of local food, wines and pastis acquired on excursions to the markets held daily in different villages of the Vaucluse.

In between laying bricks, plastering and cutting wood everyone took turns at cooking. The firebed was large and constantly replenished from a stock of firewood. It was covered by a wire mesh grill, the wooden frame resting on a low brick wall, large enough for several pans to sit on at once. Heavy frying pans and large saucepans and casseroles were used as well as spits and skewers. We fried and sautéed, grilled, toasted and stewed. Children were sent to collect wood and herbs and any wild fruits and edible plants they could find. We cooked the most wonderful fish soups I have ever eaten and dishes of the Midi smelling strongly of garlic and wild thyme and the local wine. We made pancakes and fritters, pots of beans and spaghetti. There was little we did not attempt, but some dishes were more suitable and more easily prepared.

SAUTÉED FOODS

Sautéing is the best and simplest method of cooking in a holiday kitchen because it is fast and requires little fat. Fuel is economized and the risk of danger from hot oil and boiling water is eliminated. All you need is a source of heat and a deep heavy-bottomed frying pan.

❧ To sauté meat

Cut thin slices and pound them flat or take large steaks or chops and cook them for a little longer. The principle is the same: sauté quickly in a mixture of butter and oil, searing the meat first so that it remains tender and juicy inside. Turn over once and season with salt and pepper.

To make a sauce, add a few tablespoons of wine or sherry or a dash of cognac to the pan juices with a sprinkling of herbs and perhaps some crushed garlic, or use fresh or sour cream.

For a pepper steak use tender beef and press some very coarsely ground or crushed black peppercorns – about 1½-2 teaspoons for each steak – into each side and cook as above, 3 minutes on each side over fairly high heat for rare meat. Turn the heat down and cook 2 minutes more for medium steaks.

For hamburgers, make as the recipe on p.186 but work the minced meat less. It is best when it just holds together softly. Make plump cakes and give 4 minutes to either side on high heat and 2 minutes more for each on lower heat.

Ꮽ To sauté calf's liver

Cut in very thin slices. Dust with flour if you wish. Sauté quickly in a mixture of butter and oil until coloured on both sides but still pink inside. Add salt and pepper, a squeeze of lemon, a little vinegar or a few table-spoons of Marsala. Cook a minute longer and serve with chopped parsley.

A Venetian version is to soften and lightly colour several sliced onions. Place the seasoned liver slices on top and cook with the lid on until just done.

Another Italian way is to dredge the liver in flour and sauté in butter flavoured with fried crushed garlic and chopped sage.

Ꮽ To sauté chicken

Use boned chicken or quarters (without the wings). Sauté in a mixture of oil and butter for about 5-8 minutes until barely golden on both sides, then reduce the heat, add salt and pepper and let it cook slowly for another 10-20 minutes (legs require more time than breasts), shaking the pan occasionally and turning the pieces over.

You may add a little wine or sherry, port or Madeira, lemon or tomato juice and a herb such as parsley or tarragon when the chicken has already coloured. Add a little cream if you like, just before you are ready to serve.

An Egyptian way is to flavour the chicken with crushed garlic, lemon juice, a cracked cardamom pod and a sprinkling of spices either cinnamon and allspice or a touch of turmeric for colour.

Chicken with vegetables. Fry the chicken briefly on both sides, then add to the pan any of the following: chopped spring onions, sliced or chopped onions, tomatoes, cut into pieces, sliced courgettes, diced peppers, mushrooms, whole or sliced.

Ꮽ Egg dishes

Cheap, nutritious and tasty, much can be done in a frying pan besides the usual omelette and fried, scrambled and boiled eggs.

With ham and a sweet and sour sauce. Fry 4 thick slices of cooked ham in butter or oil. Remove from the pan. Add 1 tablespoon of sugar and let it brown slightly. Pour in 5-6 tablespoons of wine vinegar and let it bubble for half a minute. Return the ham and slip 4 eggs over it. Season with salt and pepper and cook gently until they have set.

With cheese. Fry a small onion or a crushed clove of garlic in a little butter until it colours. Put in slices or cubes of a cheese which becomes thready when it melts such as Provolone, Mozzarella or Fontina or the Greek Halumi. Add a pinch of nutmeg or spread with a teaspoonful of mild mustard. Break 4 eggs over the top and cook until they set and the cheese bubbles. You may beat the eggs instead of leaving them whole.

A Tunisian dish – Chakchouka. Fry a coarsely chopped onion in a little oil until golden. Add a green pepper, seeded and cut small, and fry until soft. Add 3 or 4 tomatoes, peeled and cut in half, seasoning with salt and pepper, and cook gently for a few minutes. Drop the eggs in whole and cook until set. You may also stir the eggs in if you like a creamy texture.

❧ Pasticio

Years ago, walking through a pine forest along the sea front at Forte dei Marmi, we were amazed at the number of families sitting at tables eating spaghetti under the trees. Surrounded by chopping boards, sieves, frying pans and primus stoves, they had evidently prepared it on the spot and must have started early with the sauce. The Italians, I thought, cannot live without spaghetti.

More recently, and very far from Italy, I spent a night by Lake Tiberias in Israel at a site where campers rented huts and did their own cooking. Here too, amongst the kebabs and steaks and aubergine salads, were mountains of spaghetti. Obviously, everybody likes it enough to make it on holiday and even if you have only one burner you can make everything (sauce and all) with one pot and a sieve.

There are many types of pasta. All there is to know about cooking it is to throw it in a great deal of salted and fast-boiling water, to stir well and to leave it in until it is only just tender – with a bite still. It must not be soft, mushy or sticky. Drain quickly.

The simplest way of serving pasta is also for me the tastiest – with plenty of butter, salt and pepper, sometimes topped with grated Parmesan or crumbled Ricotta.

Al olio e al alio, dressed in olive oil with plenty of crushed garlic and finely chopped parsley, is just as easy.

Another quick sauce is single cream with chopped cooked ham, seasoned with pepper and with salt if the ham is not too salty.

Beans

When you are busy and hard up and have hungry people to feed, tinned beans are a godsend. And you can improve on the usual way of heating them up in their tin, with inspiration from Italy. (A famous Tuscan outdoor bean dish has them cooking in a large wine flask, such as a Chianti bottle with the straw removed, in smouldering ashes for about 3 hours.) You can use tinned beans – kidney, butter or haricot – in their natural juice, with the following embellishments, and serve hot as a meal in itself with bread to soak up the sauce.

With bacon. Fry a few bacon slices cut in small pieces in a pan until they brown. Add 2 cloves of garlic, crushed, and before this colours, pour in a large tin of beans with their juice. Season with salt and pepper, cinnamon, ground cloves and mace. Cook gently until the flavours have been absorbed.

With bacon, onions and wine. Sauté 4-5 chopped lean slices of bacon with a large onion, cut in rings, until both are coloured lightly. Pour in 500 g (1 lb) tinned beans. Add salt and pepper, chopped parsley and moisten with a little dry white wine. Cook for about 10 minutes.

With sage and tomatoes. Add chopped peeled tomatoes and a sprig of sage and season with salt and pepper.

With tuna fish. Drain the beans and mix with peeled chopped tomatoes and tinned tuna with its oil. Add a crushed clove of garlic, salt and pepper and 2 sprigs of basil and cook for 10 minutes.

With pork sausages intended for boiling. Cook them, throw out the water and put them aside. Put a little oil in the pan and fry a small chopped onion until it is golden. Add a chopped clove of garlic and barely let it colour. Stir in 2-3 tablespoons of tomato paste, then return the sausages to the pan and add the beans with their juice and some chopped parsley. Cook for about 10 minutes.

For a Middle Eastern meal buy tinned Egyptian brown beans. For a large 500 g (1 lb) tin, add 2 cloves of garlic, crushed. Heat thoroughly and serve in bowls with a hard-boiled egg for each person. Pass round olive oil and lemon quarters, salt and pepper for each person to season as they wish.

Chick peas to eat as a salad. Drain tinned chick peas of their juice and season to taste with salt and pepper, lemon juice and olive oil. Add plenty of crushed garlic or grated onion and some chopped parsley.

ঌ Pan Haggerty

For this filling potato (500 g/1 lb), onion (250 g/½ lb) and cheese (125 g/¼ lb) dish-in-the-frying-pan from Northumberland, slice the vegetables very thinly. Put alternate layers of potato, onion, and grated matured Cheddar or Lancashire cheese in a well-oiled pan, seasoning each layer with salt and pepper. Cover with a lid and cook gently for about half an hour until the vegetables are very tender.

ঌ Sautéed fruits

For a change from eating them raw, you can make a dessert of sautéed fruits. Apples, peeled and cut in rings, pears, cut in halves or slices, or whole bananas can be sautéed in unsalted butter with a little oil to prevent it from burning. Sprinkle with sugar and let it caramelize slightly. Cook until tender, then pour in calvados, cognac or rum and set it alight.

ঌ Fruit fritters

One way of enjoying wild berries such as bilberries and for that matter any other fruit, is to make them into fritters. To make a batter, gradually add 150 ml (two-thirds of a cup) of milk or water to 100 g (1 cup) of plain flour – enough for a thick cream. Add 2 tablespoons of oil and 2 eggs (to add the egg whites stiffly beaten at the last minute is nice but not always practical), a pinch of salt and if you like a tablespoon of sugar. Beat vigorously until smooth. Leave for 30 minutes.

Small berries. Add enough washed and dried berries to make the batter quite heavy with fruit. Drop the batter in hot oil by the spoonful. Turn over once and when nicely browned, drain and sprinkle liberally with castor sugar.

Larger fruit. Apples, cored and cut in rings, apricot halves, pineapple slices, bananas and orange segments can be marinated for an hour in lemon juice with a sprinkling of sugar or Grand Marnier, Curaçao, rum, kirsch or wine. Drain well before dipping each piece in the batter to coat it evenly. If the fruit is too moist for the batter to stick, dust first with flour or fine biscuit crumbs.

〰 Sweet omelette

Make a light omelette in the usual way by beating the eggs and pouring them into hot butter in a pan, but flavour with sugar instead of salt and pepper – 3-4 tablespoons for 8 eggs is about right.

Or make it fluffy like a soufflé if you have a hand beater. Separate the yolks and whites, beat the whites stiff with a pinch of salt till firm, then add sugar gradually. Fold into the yolks. Cook by the ladleful in hot foaming butter, turning over with the help of a plate. Serve at once sprinkled with sugar and if you like a spirit such as kirsch, cognac or rum, which may be set alight in a tablespoon over a flame.

You may garnish with fresh whipped cream, or top with warmed up jam.

Omelette normande. Make an apple sauce: sauté sliced apples in hot unsalted butter for about 7-10 minutes, stirring and turning them over. Add sugar to taste. Moisten with calvados or rum and set aflame. Shake and remove from the heat. Add a few tablespoons of thick cream. Spoon a generous amount over each omelette as it is ready to serve and fold in half. Heat some more calvados or rum and pour over the omelettes. Set alight.

LONG SLOW COOKING

❧ Camacho's wedding feast

The first thing that met Sancho's sight there was a whole steer spitten on an entire elm, before a mighty fire made of a pile of wood that seemed a small mountain. Round this bonfire were placed six capacious pots, cast in no common mould, or rather six ample coppers, every one containing a whole shamble of meat, and entire sheep were sunk and lost in them, and soaked as if they were pigeons. The branches of the trees round were all garnished with an infinite number of skinned hares and plucked fowls of several sorts: and then for a drink, Sancho told above three-score skins of wine, each of which contained above two arrobas, and as it afterwards proved, sprightly liquor. A goodly pile of white loaves made a large rampart on the one side, and a stately wall of cheeses set up like bricks made a comely bulwark on the other. Two pans of oil, each bigger than a dyer's vat, served to fry their pancakes, which they lifted out with two strong peels when they were fried enough, and then they dropped them into as large a kettle of honey prepared for that purpose. To dress all this provision there were above fifty cooks, men and women, all cleanly, diligent and cheerful. In the ample belly of the steer they had stowed twelve tender little sucking-pigs to give it the more savoury taste. Spices of all sorts, that appeared to be bought by wholesale, were visible in a great chest. In short, the whole provision was indeed country-like, but plentiful enough to feast an army.

Sancho Panza beheld all this with wonder and delight. The first temptation that captivated his senses was the goodly pots; his bowels yearned, and his mouth watered at the dainty contents: by-and-by he falls desperately in love with the skins of wine; and lastly his affections were fixed on the frying-pans, if such honourable kettles may accept of the name. So, being able to hold out no longer, he accosted one of the busy cooks with all the smooth and hungry reasons he was master of; he begged his leave to sop a portion of bread in one of the pans. 'Friend', quoth the cook, 'no hunger must be felt near us today, thanks to the rich Camacho. 'light, 'light, man, and if thou canst find ever a ladle there, skim out a pullet or two, and much good may it do you.' 'I see no ladle, sir,' quoth Sancho. 'Sinner o' me!' cried the cook, 'what a silly helpless fellow thou art!' With that he took a kettle, and sousing into one of the pots, he fished out three hens and a couple of geese at one heave. 'Here, friend,' said he to Sancho, 'take this, and make shift to stay your stomach with that scum till dinner be ready.' 'But where shall I put it?' cried Sancho. 'Here,' answered the cook, 'take ladle and all, and thank Camacho's wealth and bounty for it all.'

MIGUEL DE CERVANTES SAAVEDRA
Don Quixote

On holiday the contents of the stewpot are most likely to be pot luck as the availability of ingredients cannot always be guaranteed. It may take at least 3 hours and maybe 5 or 6 for the meat to be tender and the flavours absorbed, but waiting for the stew to be ready is one of the pleasures of camp life. You will need a large heavy pot or casserole with a close-fitting lid, otherwise you can seal the lid on with a stiff flour and water paste. Stand it firmly on a grill over a constantly replenished fire, smoored (covered with sods) to remain aglow for hours, or in a pit (see pp.284-5).

You may also use a hay box (see p.286): simmer the stew on an ordinary fire for about 20 minutes, then wrap it up in something warm and put it in the hay box for 7-8 hours or overnight.

Meats cooked long and slowly with vegetables in a pot tend to be homely dishes, but you can make them as grand as you like by putting wine, cider or beer in the pot instead of water. For a stew, a great deal of licence is allowed and you can improvise with the following recipes. Make a large amount. If there are not many of you it will do for more than one meal. Serve in soup bowls over a thick slice of toasted bread, to eat with a fork and a spoon.

❧ A French daube

Fry 5 streaky bacon rashers in a little oil. Remove from the pot and sear a whole 2 kg (4 lb) piece of beef (brisket will do) on all sides. Return the bacon, put the meat on top and surround with 5 peeled tomatoes, 2-3 chopped cloves of garlic, a dozen button onions, some finely chopped parsley and the stalks, a teaspoon of thyme, 2 bay leaves, a handful of quartered mushrooms, salt and pepper. Add half a bottle of red or dry white wine and enough water to cover.

There is nothing to stop you from adding other vegetables such as celery, carrots, leeks and little turnips cut into pieces. A slice of lemon or orange gives a delicate perfume.

Put the lid on tightly, seal if you like with a flour and water paste and cook very gently for 4 or 5 hours or more depending on the method. Before serving, adjust the seasonings.

Serve in bowls with potatoes, boiled separately or cooked in the ashes (see p.163), and a thick slice of French bread, lightly toasted on the fire. You will be happy to have anything left over next day.

For a Boeuf bourguignonne cut the beef into bite-sized pieces and dredge them in flour. Fry the diced bacon in a little oil with the vegetables until they brown before sautéing the meat. Add wine and flavourings as above and cook for several hours in a closed pot.

੨੩ A Flemish carbonnade

Use 2 kg (4 lb) of a cheap cut of beef. Trim off the fat. Leave whole or cut in pieces of any size. Cut 2 large onions in slices. Fry them in a little oil until browned and take them out of the pot. Then sear the meat on all sides. Add 2-3 tablespoons of flour and let it brown. Return the onions to the pot with 2 bay leaves and a few parsley stalks. Cover with a bottle of beer (strong ale, pale or brown), bring to the boil, remove any scum and then add a pinch of nutmeg, a teaspoon of allspice, 3 cloves, 2 tablespoons of vinegar, salt and pepper and 2 teaspoons of sugar.

You may also add a few sliced carrots and 2 crushed cloves of garlic.

Cook for several hours until the meat is very tender. Taste and adjust seasonings.

Serve with French bread cut in thick slices, lightly toasted over the fire and spread with butter and French mustard.

Serves 10-12 people.

੨੩ Boeuf à la mode

This makes an admirable hot pot. Use the recipe on p.80, but without the calf's feet, which provide the jelly for the cold version.

🍃 Hunter's chicken

2 small chickens, 2 tablespoons flour, 4 slices bacon, 3-4 tablespoons oil or butter, 3 cloves of garlic (crushed), salt and pepper, 1 bay leaf, ¹/₂-1 teaspoon thyme, basil or marjoram or all three, a few sprigs of parsley, ¹/₄ litre (¹/₂ pint) dry white wine, 2-3 tablespoons tomato purée, 225 g (¹/₂ lb) mushrooms.

Make this in a large heavy pot,
   Cut the chicken into quarters, remove the skin if you like and dredge with flour. Chop the bacon and fry gently in oil or butter and remove on to a plate. Fry the chicken pieces in the same fat and brown lightly all over. Add the garlic, salt and pepper and herbs and cover with white wine. Stir in tomato purée and add the mushrooms cut in two or four if they are large. Cover the pot and simmer ³/₄-1 hour in the ashes or over a low flame.

🍃 An Irish stew

Use mutton or lamb – about 1 kg (2 lb). Trim off all the fat and cut in largish chunks. Peel and slice 1 kg (2 lb) onions and 1 kg (2 lb) potatoes. Alternate layers of each in a large pot, starting with potatoes, sprinkling each with salt and pepper, occasionally with a pinch of nutmeg or thyme. Cover with water and simmer, with lid on for at least 2-3 hours, until the meat is very tender and the potatoes melted. Serve with hot toast or put it in the bowls before filling them with stew.

STRAIGHT FROM THE WATER

As everyone knows who has tasted it, a fish just out of the water is quite different from the one bought from the fishmonger.

The ancient Romans, who idolized fish as much as the Greeks before them, were particularly fond of cooking them live. To indulge in these refinements of pleasure they constructed fish ponds on the roofs of their houses and built canals bringing river water into their dining rooms. The fish swam in tanks under the table and it was only necessary to stoop and pick them out the instant before eating. The greater sensualists sharpened their appetites by watching them agonizing in boiling water or on the grill. There was no better stimulant than an expiring mullet, blushing red in its agony and turning lighter shades during its passage from life to death. Our own sensitivities allow us greater pleasure in the more sporting activity of fishing and looking for shellfish on the wet sand when the tide has gone.

Though we do not now wish to see a fish die in its sauce, it is certainly at its very best when freshly caught, and no one must miss an opportunity of tasting it still smelling of the sea or just out of stream or lake.

If you are on a fishing holiday, cruising in a boat or camping near a fishing port or on the beach, you may not fulfil the dream of many yachtsmen to furnish all the meals by means of your own fishing prowess, but you can at least purchase good fresh fish from local fishermen or at the quayside market. Amaranth Sitas writes in her book *Kopiaste* published in Cyprus: 'Fish tastes better if caught with a spear or prongs because it is killed instantly. Second best is fish caught by angling or in snares, and last when caught by trawlers or nets because then the fish dies of suffocation.' I am unable to confirm that, but certainly it is only by the water that you can taste fish and shellfish at its very best, absolutely fresh.

Collecting shellfish and crustacea can easily become a passion, and the excitement lies as much in the hunt and the rituals of preparation as in the food itself. Although sometimes, as with winkles, it is more an absorbing distraction than a matter of good eating, nothing is more agreeable than a platter of gathered shellfish and other seafood including clams, cockles, mussels, scallops, crabs and prawns. They are treasures that you find in clusters strewn across the sand just after the tide has gone, or simply feel when you wade barefooted into the water. You can prize them off a rock as with sea urchins or dig them out of the sand with shovels, rakes, hoes or trowels, or you can hammer them out of their homes in rocks. Razor clams leave holes in the sand as a clue to their presence and crabs hiding in shallow pools can be caught at low tide. Poke around with a stick and use a rake to pull them out of the swaying seaweed where they lurk.

❧ Dealing with shellfish

There is only one danger when you gather your own: polluted water. Not all shellfish, or mussels, are edible; some are even poisonous, so you must seek advice from locals. Make sure that you never collect them in parts of the sea that may be contaminated by sewage. Always wash them well in several changes of clean fresh water and leave them in a bucket of clean sea water for at least 6 hours or overnight so that they disgorge any sand. Remove beards with a knife or scissors and discard those too heavy, too light, broken or open. Make sure that they are all alive by gently forcing them open. If they stay open they are likely to be dead and must be discarded.

Boil cockles and winkles in clean sea water seasoned with pepper, thyme and a bay leaf. Use pins to extract them from their shells with a curling motion so that they do not break.

Purists rightly prefer to eat shelfish alive and raw. Prize them open with a special knife or let gentle heat do it for you. Serve with lemon and slices of buttered brown bread.

If you prefer to cook them, throw scallops, clams and mussels into a bucket of boiling sea water. They will open and be cooked within 5 minutes. Discard those that don't open. Shellfish will also cook on a grill or sheet of foil over a bed of coals in the same time. Serve with melted butter or oil and lemon juice.

In France in the Charente they have a very dramatic way of cooking mussels on the beach which is called an éclade. Place the shells close together pointing towards the centre on a bed of leaves or a wooden plank. Cover with a thick blanket of dry pine needles and set alight. Blow off the charred bits and eat the opened mussels with fat slices of country bread, buttered and sprinkled with salt and pepper.

If you have a frying pan and facilities you can take the shellfish out of their shells, dip them in beaten egg, then flour or fine breadcrumbs and fry them quickly in oil or butter, turning them over once until golden (about 4 minutes). A squeeze of lemon and black pepper is all you need.

For a special treat sauté large scallops in butter with a touch of crushed garlic. Add salt and pepper and a little white wine and cook for 10 minutes. Or pour in a few tablespoons of brandy. Heat it for a few seconds and set it alight.

❧ Mixed seafood salad

Open shellfish as described on p.159. Follow the instructions on pp.280-1 for cooking an octopus and cut it into small pieces. Poach shrimps and prawns for 10 minutes and shell them.

Put everything in a large bowl and dress with plenty of olive oil and about half this quantity of lemon juice. Add salt and pepper, and a touch of French mustard if you like. Leave for an hour or so before serving, sprinkled with finely chopped parsley.

❧ New England clambake

This ancient way of cooking clams and other shells has become an American institution. It takes time but provides a pleasurable occupation for the beach and gives the seafood a tangy fragrance. Start at least 3 hours before you want to eat.

Dig a pit. Line it with rocks. Collect drift wood and start a great roaring fire in the pit. When it has crumbled to embers, cover with a thick layer of wet seaweed. Put all the cleaned live shells on top with prawns and other seafood (in America they also put in potatoes in their jackets, pieces of chicken, sausages and corn in the husk). Cover with another layer of seaweed, then a thick layer of sand to seal in the heat. To make sure you do not get any in the open shells when you uncover them, put sheets of paper or cloth between sand and seaweed.

You can start eating after about an hour. Have ready bowls of melted butter, salt, pepper and lemon juice to savour the seafood, which will be perfumed by the seaweed.

🐚 Cooking fish in a wet newspaper

Many an angler must have treated his catch in this manner: wrap the fish in several sheets of wet newspaper and put it close to a roaring fire or over dying embers to cook slowly and gently, protected by the steam of the wet newspaper. As an added refinement you may sprinkle the newspaper with vinegar.

🐚 Crabs

No crab can ever be as good as the one, fresh from the boiling pail, which you have just pulled out of a shallow pool.

Fill a large pot or a clean metal pail with fresh sea water and add enough salt to float an egg. Bring it to the boil over a fire and throw in one or more crabs at a time. Let the water return to the boil, then simmer for 10-15 minutes if the crabs are small (less than 500 g/1 lb), and 10 minutes more for each extra pound. It is hard to estimate their weight but the time does not matter too much.

To eat you will need a sharp knife, a nutcracker or a mallet to crack the legs and claws, and thin skewers or long needles to poke out difficult bits. Twist off legs and claws. Turn the crab on its back. Lift up and remove the pointed flap together with the intestinal vein and take out the central body part. Discard the feathery lung sections and scoop out the soft flesh.

Serve in the shell with a bowl of melted butter or some heated double cream and lemon juice, and some bread.

If you want to serve it cold as a salad, dress the chopped crab meat with olive oil, lemon juice, salt and pepper, garnish with parsley and return it to the washed shell.

🐚 Fried prawns

The large ones are best. Fry them in their shells in sizzling oil or butter with crushed garlic, salt and pepper. In the Seychelles I learnt that fresh ginger suits them well. Add a little, grated or squeezed in a garlic press, or use a pinch of dry powder.

🐚 In praise of raw fish

Many people who try raw fish find it so good that they lose their enthusiasm for cooked fish, and it has become the fashion these days to search in old-established cuisines for traditional ways to serve it up. As fish has to be absolutely fresh to be eaten raw, the best time to start is with the fisherman's haul or your own catch while it is still full of the savour of the sea or stream. Although the muddy taste of some fresh water fish such as carp, dace and roach, may be slightly tempered by soaking for a few hours in salted water, they are not the most suitable fish to be eaten raw. Most other fish are so delicious that they need few embellishments.

First you must gut, scale, clean and wash the fish (for instructions see pp.196-7); then you must fillet it with a sharp knife.

The Dutch leave herrings sprinkled in a large quantity of coarse salt overnight. When you are ready to eat, remove the skin with a sharp knife. Split the fish down the centre of the back, lever up the backbone and carefully pull it out; the tiny fine bones will come off with it. All you need is some finely chopped onion and you have the best way of savouring herring.

Marinating in lime or lemon juice is a method which originated in Polynesia and has long been popular in South America and Mexico, where it is called seviche. It has recently become one of the fashionable foods with gastronomes around the world – rightly so for it is delicious. You may treat salmon or humbler fish such as whiting, mullet, herring, bass, bream, anchovies, sardines and smelts in this way.

Cut the fish in pieces or in slices 1.5 cm ($^1/_2$/2 in) to 2.5 cm (1 in) thick, and cover with lime or lemon juice for about 3 hours, by which time the flesh will be opaque. (You may also cut it very thin, like smoked salmon, and leave it to marinate for only half an hour.) Drain and reserve the juice. Use some of it to make a dressing with olive oil, salt and pepper. You may add a sprinkling of chopped fresh herbs such as parsley, tarragon, oregano, basil and dill. A good accompaniment is marinated mushrooms.

For a Latin American flavour add peeled and chopped tomatoes, finely chopped onions, a sliced or chopped fresh hot pepper and a touch of crushed garlic. Spread this on top of the fish served on a bed of lettuce. A squeeze of Seville orange juice may be added to the dressing.

For a Japanese way see pp.144-6.

૨૦ Fish cooked 'au bleu'

This is a good way of cooking trout, carp, pike, roach or porthouse just as soon as it is pulled out of the lake or river. Fill a clean metal pail with

1 part vinegar and 3 parts fresh water. Add salt and pepper and put it to boil on the fire. Then toss in the fish unscaled, gutted quickly while still live and jumping, and simmer for 5-10 minutes until it is just cooked through (and the trout tinged with blue).

Serve with butter and lemon juice and boiled new potatoes.

₹♣ A fry-up

There is not much you can do with very little fish besides a fry-up, and for that you must be on firm land and in possession of a large deep pan.

If the mountain stream has provided a collection of little fish at the end of your line, or if your net is full of a mixed bag from the sea, this is how you deal with an assortment of small fry such as sardines, anchovies, whitebait and smelts:

Dry the fish in a cloth as it is, then roll (toss lightly) in flour. Heat plenty of oil in a deep frying pan, preferably one with a wire frying basket. Fry a few at a time so that they do not stick together, in very hot oil. The smaller the fish, the hotter must be the oil. Whitebait need the oil to be smoking. They will be ready in a matter of minutes. Shake the basket gently if using one, or separate the fish with a fork. As soon as they are crisp and brown drain and serve on paper serviettes to absorb the oil. Garnish with sprigs of parsley and lemon wedges.

That is how the hotel Beau Rivage served us the result of a day's arduous fishing on the beach in Alexandria when we were children.

₹♣ Sautéed fish

Sautéing is the easiest way to cook a fish. Mark Twain describes frying one with bacon in *By the Camp Fire*:

> They came back to camp wonderfully refreshed, glad hearted and ravenous; and they soon had the camp fire blazing up again. Huck found a spring of clear cold water close by, and the boys made cups of broad oak or hickory leaves, and felt that water, sweetened with such a wild-wood charm as that, would be a good enough substitute for coffee. While Joe was slicing bacon for breakfast, Tom and Huck asked him to hold on a minute; they stepped to a promising nook in the river bank and threw in their lines, almost immediately they had reward. Joe had not had time to get impatient before they were back again with some handsome bass, a couple of sun perch, and a small cat-fish – provisions enough for quite a family. They fried the fish

with the bacon and were astonished, for no fish had ever seemed so delicious before. They did not know that the quicker a fresh water fish is on the fire after it is caught, the better it is; and they reflected little upon what a sauce open-air sleeping, open-air exercise, bathing, and a large ingredient of hunger make, too.

To cook fish à la meunière, clean and scale (sole is best skinned), cut it in steaks if it is too large for the pan, season and dust with flour. Sauté quickly in a sizzling mixture of butter and oil or in clarified butter (see pp.227-8). For larger fish, reduce the heat and cook slowly until done (3-5 minutes for steaks and small fish, up to 10 minutes for a large trout). Season with salt and pepper and a squeeze of lemon and serve with sprigs of parsley.

You may also let the butter turn brown (which is called beurre noir) before putting in the fish.

As a luxury and for a sauce, stir some dry white wine with a few chopped fresh tarragon leaves in the pan drippings.

For a garnish, lightly fry slivered blanched almonds or sliced mushrooms in the same butter and pan and pour in fresh cream.

૨ An octopus

One summer I witnessed the demise of an octopus on the Greek island of Scopelos. A group of people were gazing into the sea. One was holding a pole with a white vest fastened on the end which he shook in the water. He pulled it out to a murmur of congratulations, for embracing it was an octopus which looked imploringly at the congregation. An onlooker carefully turned its ink sack inside out, gutted it and removed the eye and beak, then, holding it by its tentacles, beat it against the ground relentlessly. Another rubbed it vigorously with a stone. The entire process to tenderize the flesh took almost half an hour, during which time the others had started a fire. By the time the octopus was cut into pieces and threaded on skewers, the fire had died down to embers and was ready to receive it. As a foreign guest on the island I was not allowed to go without sampling a few pieces.

For those who are interested, octopus is as good boiled as it is grilled, but remember to beat it well; otherwise, however long you cook it, it will still be like rubber. Put it in a large pan of clean sea water and simmer for about 2-2^1/$_2$ hours. Take it out and cut into small pieces.

Dress with plenty of olive oil and lemon juice, adding a little French mustard, salt and pepper and leave to absorb this for 2 hours before serving.

Very tiny baby octopus like squid (cleaned of intestines and ink sacks) are delicious fried in oil with chopped onions or a little garlic, salt and pepper. Cook over a brisk heat for 10 minutes. Sprinkle with parsley and lemon juice.

ℰ Bouillabaisse

If you are near the Mediterranean you must make this soup which accommodates whatever you can find. There is no better way to sing the praise of the produce of the sea, and you would be well advised to go armed with a copy of Alan Davidson's *Mediterranean Seafood* which is a mine of information on all its edible marine life.

Bouillabaisse belongs to Marseilles and has the flavour of the Mediterranean. With aïoli and pastis, it is a main ingredient of the local 'douceur de vivre' without which you can never fully enjoy the blue of the sea and the sky, the mauve of the rocks, the pale pink and ochre houses, the forgotten ports and the game of petanque. As is to be expected from the Midi, local opinion is divided as to how the best bouillabaisse is made. Alan Davidson gives a simple and excellent version:

'Buy fish as follows:

(a) a rascasse or two, depending on size

(b) some other fish with firm flesh such as monkfish, gurnard, weever or star-gazer eel or moray or conger

(c) some delicate fish such as whiting or flatfish

(d) a few small wrasse or the like

(e) an inexpensive crustacean which might be squille or a petite cigale.

'Have 2 kilos (4 lb) in all. Gut and scale the fish, cut them in pieces where necessary and wash them.

'Now heat a wineglassful of olive oil in a large cooking pot and brown in this a large onion, finely sliced, and 2 cloves of garlic. Add ½ kilo (1 lb) of peeled and chopped tomatoes (or a corresponding amount of tomato concentrate) followed by about 3 litres of water (preferably boiling) and the fish from groups (a) and (b) and (d) and (e). Those from group (d) are intended to disintegrate in the cooking, adding body to the soup. Season with salt and pepper. Add chopped parsley and a pinch of saffron, a piece of orange peel, a clove, a bay leaf and a sprig of thyme. Pour a wineglassful of olive oil over all. Bring to and keep at a vigorous boil for 15 to 20 minutes. Add the fish in group (c) towards the end of this period, allowing just enough time for them to cook.

'When all is ready lift out the crustaceans and the fish which are still whole and serve them on one platter. Pour the broth over pieces of garlic-rubbed toast in soup plates (straining it in the process if you wish). Serve rouille alongside.'

For the rouille: Pound two cloves of garlic and two sweet red peppers in a mixer, add a chunk of bread, soaked in water and squeezed, and mix well. Then add 2 tablespoons of olive oil and beat in some fish broth, about $1\frac{1}{2}$ wine glasses full for a thick sauce.

❧ Rice for the open sea

Seychellois fishermen, who spend their days between the 60 islands of the Indian ocean archipelago, bring only long-grain rice and a heavy pot with a lid for the traditional midday meal. When they begin to feel hungry they boil up some sea water in the pot over a fire, throw in an equal volume of rice and when the water begins to be absorbed they lay a few fish, whatever they have got in their nets, on the top under the lid, to steam for the last few minutes while the rice cooks.

Arroz a la marinera Alan Davidson gives this Spanish recipe in *Mediterranean Seafood* for a paella-type rice and seafood dish which is a little more elaborate. The small round-grain rice and the larger quantity of water give the dish the soft mushy quality of Italian risottos. 'You will need:

$\frac{1}{4}$ litre ($\frac{1}{2}$ pint) olive oil, 700-750 g ($1\frac{1}{2}$ lb) rice (if possible Valencian), plenty of paprika, 2 onions, chopped, 4 tomatoes, peeled and chopped, $\frac{1}{2}$ kilo (1 lb) in all of angler-fish, squid and cuttlefish prepared and cut into chunks and strips, $\frac{1}{2}$ kilo (1 lb) in all of Norway lobster, prawns and mussels, (or substitute any fish and seafood available) just over 2 litres of fish stock.

'Heat the olive oil and add the pieces of angler-fish, squid and cuttlefish. When these are golden add the chopped onion and tomato and paprika. Continue to fry all this for a few minutes, taking care not to burn the paprika.

'Next add the rice and twice the quantity by volume of fish stock. (This will work out at just over 2 litres or $3\frac{3}{4}$ British pints). Three minutes later add the Norway lobster, prawns and mussels (cleaned but whole). Continue cooking for about 20 minutes until the rice has absorbed all the liquid.'

๛ Hot smoking

Hot smoking is an idea that should appeal to anglers for it cooks fish in 20 minutes and gives it a most unusual smoky flavour. I was introduced to it by Maggie Black who invited me to a lunch of smoked delicacies and proved that most things are enhanced by this method of cooking. It is quite different from cold smoking, which takes hours and days.

Little smokers for taking on a picnic have been appearing on the market in recent years, but the enterprising can make their own with a metal box, a baffle plate and a grill.

To smoke fish, spread some wood dust at the bottom of the tin hickory, elm, apple, ash, all these are excellent. Put the baffle plate over it, then the grill. Slash the fish diagonally so that it does not curl and season if you like with salt and pepper and lemon juice and put a sprig of herbs in the cavity. You may find this superfluous beside the strong perfume of the smoke from the smouldering wood dust. Lay the fish on the grill. If it is too big to fit in you can cut it into steaks. Shut the lid and light the fuel, methylated spirits or meta tablets, in the burner underneath. The fish will be ready to eat in about 20 minutes. Trout and mackerel are especially good treated in this way.

PRIMITIVE WAYS OF COOKING

২৯ Pit cooking

Kafupi Petrides, a painter who lives on the island of Evia in Greece, wrote to me about her occasional oven: 'I dig a hole in the earth or sand, line it with large stones and make a good fire on them for about half an hour. When it has died down completely I wrap fish or meat or game which I have seasoned with salt and pepper, rigani or bay and garlic, lemon juice or wine, as the case maybe – in a large piece of foil and put it in the hole, cover it completely and heavily with the earth or sand and leave it to cook for 2$^1/_2$ to 3 hours . . . .'

However primitive it might seem, this is an excellent and satisfying way of cooking still practised all over the world in the countryside. Greeks call it klephti or robber cooking, and in Sardinia cooking in a pit is also known as brigand cooking. For in this way animal thieves can cook their stolen sheep or calf, pig or donkey undetected. In the Middle East it is used mainly on festive occasions but some villages in Libya still make large communal pit ovens to hold the food of all the households as well as that of occasional travellers.

There are different ways of cooking in a pit: over a fire or when it has died out, or with the fire on top, over ground.

Make a pit as large as you like to accommodate one item or a variety of foods; 60 cm (2 ft) deep and 90-120 cm (3-4 ft) across is a good size. Make a fire at the bottom and let it burn down to embers for about an hour. Grape wood gives the food a special taste. Place a wire mesh or other grid a few inches above the embers, supported by metal rods and bricks or stones. Place the food on the grid, wrapped if you like in layers of paper or foil for cleanliness (this will result in a steamed effect). Cover first with branches, reeds or such things and then with grass or hay.

Cooking without a fire takes longer but the result is food of particular tenderness. Line the bottom and sides of the pit with medium-sized stones and smaller ones or shingle in between. Build a large hard wood fire on top of the stones and let it burn for at least 2 hours so that the stones may store enough heat. Let it die down, then brush or rake off the embers and bits of charcoal. Cover the stones with a bed of grass or better still with aromatic leaves such as vine or beech and a few sprigs of any herbs that happen to grow around. Lay the food to be cooked (meat, fish and vegetables, seasoned to your liking) over the leaves and cover with a second thick layer of leaves. Pile small rocks, stones, earth or sand on top of the leaves to weigh them down and to retain the heat. If you have a tarpaulin or canvas lay this on the leaves first.

You may also wrap the food in paper or foil with the seasonings of your choice. In the latter case it will cook in its own steam.

Cooking time depends on the type and size of the food; it is difficult to give correct times and necessary to uncover and test if it is done. As a rough guide everything takes at least half as long again as in a normal oven. I have not tried it myself but that is what my friends say. Overcooking in this way never seems to harm the food.

The brigands' way is to have the fire on top of the food (no doubt so as to put the animal out of sight as quickly as possible!). Put a metal sheet placed on a ridge half way up the hole to hold the wood.

An improvised oven in the ground

All you need is a large tin with a lid and a metal sheet.

Dig a hole in the ground large enough to contain it. If the ground is wet, dig it larger and line it with flat stones. Light a wood fire in the hole. When it has burnt to embers push them to the sides of the hole and put the tin in the centre. Cover with the metal sheet or a piece of wood. For a more even heat, shovel some embers on to the metal sheet and let them burn on top of the hole. You can bake a cake or a large joint or the stews on pp.271-3.

A built-up oven

For a large permanent camp it is worth building a more elaborate kind of oven. F. Marian McNeill gives instructions for this in *The Camper's Kitchen*:

The materials required are bricks, turves, stones or clay, with two pieces of sheet-iron or tin, about three feet square.

'With the bricks or other material build round three sides of a square the same size as the sheet-iron. When it is about nine inches high, insert one piece of sheet-iron, and continue building until the two sides are about eighteen inches high. The back, however, must be a little lower than the sides, so as to provide a draught. The second piece of sheet-iron is placed on the top, and is supported, of course, only by the sides.

'The fire is lighted on the lower shelf. The space below serves as an oven for joints, puddings, or cakes, whilst soups, stews, vegetables, etc., are cooked on the top of the stove.'

❧ A reflector oven

A useful arrangement for cooking in front of a camp fire is a reflector also described by F. Marian McNeill. This consists of a shallow open-fronted box or screen, preferably of aluminium, with a sloping roof, and a shelf supported on ledges in the middle. The food to be cooked is placed on the shelf, and heat from the fire is reflected down from the top and up from the bottom in addition to the direct rays. With the concentrated heat from every direction, the food cooks evenly and quickly. The reflector can be made to fold, and with hinge-pins and rivets of aluminium wire, is rustless. To get the best results, the metal should be kept polished, and when not in use it should be protected with canvas.

❧ A haybox

A haybox is an old-fashioned method for long slow cooking which works very well. Some friends cook their meal in their car boot in this way when they go out for the day.

Line a wooden or strong cardboard box tightly with a thick blanket or insulating felt or pipe lagging and fill with hay or straw or newspapers. Transfer a boiling pot straight from the fire to the box or wrap food in foil then in a towel and bury in the hay. Cover with more hay and lagging and secure the lid. If the food is boiling hot when you put it in, it will continue to cook slowly for many hours.

❧ Cooking in clay

In England this is known as a gipsy method of cooking hedgehogs but it will also do very well with fish, birds and any little animal. The advantage is that you do not need to pluck or skin; spikes, feathers, fur and skin all come off with the clay, leaving the flesh perfectly clean, and cooked in its own juices. Remove head, feet and entrails and clean the cavities and if seasonings are at hand, stuff with herbs, a small onion and a slice of lemon and a sprinkling of salt and pepper. Cover with wet clay, coat after coat, to a thickness of 4-5 cm (1½-2 in) and bury in hot embers. When the clay cracks it should be ready. Depending on size it may take between 1 and 3 hours. Remove from the fire and break open.

❧ Fish baked in clay

If you can find fine sticky clay (it may be with a red or a bluish tinge) it is worth trying this method of cooking fish which really seals in the flavour. If it is not already wet, work it to the consistency of a stiff dough. Encase the fish live if you can, stunned to keep it from wriggling. Otherwise simply gut the fish through the mouth and put a sprig of herbs or a slice of lemon in the cavity for flavour. Do not cut the belly or mud will get inside and do not scale the fish or remove the head; leave it as it is. Simply cover it completely with a layer of mud pie clay about 2½-4 cm (1-1½ in) thick and place it on hot embers. There is much controversy over the length of cooking time: some cooks advocate 15 minutes only for a medium-sized fish and 15 minutes per ½ kg (1 lb) for a large one, while others believe that a 1½ kg (3 lb) fish needs 2 hours. I have not tried it and my informants were equally divided but each said that when the clay cracks the fish should be done. Remove from the fire and break open the shell. Scales, skin, fins and tail will come off, remaining stuck to the clay, leaving the steaming white flesh full of juice and flavour.

EQUIPMENT

Everyone seems to agree on the perfect spot for a picnic or at least those who have put their choice on paper do. It should be green, with green ground and leafy trees for the sun to shine through, small paths, hidden recesses, gentle hills and above all water: a rushing stream, a smiling lake or a bubbling cascade. Some like to sit on the grass and eat with their hands to commune more fully with Nature and be part of it all. Others like to lord it over her by spreading a table-cloth and bringing out their finest china, cut glass and silver. My parents bring a folding table and chairs for the sunshine hours they spend under a tree on the Heath a few minutes from home.

The necessary equipment for outdoor eating is a matter of taste. There are no rules. Lady Harriet St Clair quotes a celebrated German cookery book in her own *Dainty Dishes* with suggestions for a shooting breakfast: 'Gentlemen usually prefer eating this about the middle of the day, in the open air, with their fingers in order that they may lose no time; so it is not generally necessary to send knives or forks or tablecloths, but you must take care, in order not to make them angry that the luncheon is there at the right time and place.'

H. D. Renner in *The Origin of Food Habits* is another advocate of using fingers especially for gnawing bones: 'Many things are allowed outdoors which are not inside. One is gnawing bones.' He says, 'The meat is tastiest near the bone and can be smelt at the same time as eaten which exerts a far more intense effect as on the plate. The action of gnawing prolongs the pleasure and you can still recollect the pleasant feelings for a long time after by taking an occasional sniff at your fingers.'

It is quite possible to eat in a very elegant manner without knives and forks. Flat pitta bread is used in the Middle East to scoop up morsels of food and to dip into creamy pastes or soak up the last of a sauce, and leaves of all kinds make excellent plates and spoons. In the areas where they grow banana and lotus, leaves are commonly used; around the

Mediterranean it is vine leaves, but it is easier and nicer to wrap the food up in lettuce leaves of the soft round variety which do not break when you roll them up.

To carry the food, the traditional lidded wicker baskets with handles on two sides are useful. Large old-fashioned ones like a suitcase, good for large parties can be found in a few stores, but a small ordinary basket may be all you need, or a metal or plastic box.

Whether you have a large cardboard box as a hamper in the car or only a back pack, it is important to organize food and supplies to save space and make transport easier. Equipment must be light and not bulky. Containers must be leak proof especially if they contain liquids. Screw-on tops are best for these. Reinforce the closing if necessary with heavy masking tape. Use heavy duty freezer polythene bags and cling wrap. Wrap anything that bruises easily in soft paper before packing and breakables such as bottles in a cloth.

Make a list of what you need: deep plates or bowls to avoid spillage; plastic cups, ground sheet, rug, corkscrew, tin opener, sharp knife, matches, cutlery, large plastic bags for rubbish and dirty crocks, salt, pepper, sugar, condiments, sauces and relishes (Mrs Beeton's choice was 'a stick of horseradish, a bottle of good mint sauce well corked, a bottle of salad dressing, a bottle of vinegar, made mustard, pepper, salt, good oil and pounded sugar . . . and ice'.) Please yourself.

Useful tips. Serve foods from the moulds in which they have been cooked or the bowls they have set in. Don't bother to turn them out. Small individual timbal moulds are attractive to present but a larger mould is more practical for transport. For easier serving, things may be carved or sliced and re-formed into their original shape and wrapped tightly in foil. Otherwise bring a good carving knife and a wooden board.

Keep perishables in the coldest part of your car and insulate food boxes with damp newspaper if it is very hot. Bottles may be cooled in a running stream but must be placed securely or tied to a tree. Or leave them for a while in a windy spot wrapped in a wet towel.

Keeping things hot or cold. It is possible and easy to carry safely a varied and elaborate feast.

Technical progress has gone far in providing us with all manner of containers for keeping things hot or cold, crisp and fresh, without letting them spill, crush or crumble. You will find them in any camping department. There is a wide range of portable vacuum and insulated containers: bags, boxes, chests, buckets, beakers, tumblers, jars, jugs and serving dishes in all shapes and sizes to keep solid and liquid foods hot for up to 4 hours or cold for 8.

If ice packs are put inside, foods can be kept really chilled for a whole day. These packs, which may be rigid or flexible, contain a gel substance that stays colder than ice for a very long time. Two packs used together are doubly effective. They must be left in a freezer compartment overnight until their contents solidify. Some packs can also be used for keeping things hot and must be put in boiling water for 10 minutes, but they are only effective for an hour or two. Plastic insulated boxes usually have a tray on the lid to hold the packs. In an insulated bag frozen packs should be laid on top of, but separated from the food; hot ones must be put at the bottom.

Whatever the container and however many items, these must be frozen or chilled and kept in the refrigerator till the last minute or packed very hot straight out of the oven. Rinse the container before filling it. Stuff cloth or paper in between the items to prevent air pockets which make it less effective.

A version of the old haybox (see p.286) will also keep things hot for a long time.

❧ Stoves and other cooking equipment

The problems of cooking in a caravan or galley or at camp are governed by cooker capacity and the necessity to economize on gas and by limited working space. They are easily overcome with a little thought and ingenuity and the right equipment which usually has to be limited to a minimum.

For fuel unless you rely entirely on the open fire you have the choice between a bottled gas cooker, a paraffin-burning stove or an alcohol or met hylated spirits one. With all of these there are usually one or two burners, a grill and occasionally an oven.

Stoves burning paraffin are the most economical, but they must be assembled and the burner pre-heated. Primus stoves are compact and easy to operate but greater care is needed in handling the fuel. Cartridge gas stoves are the most expensive to run but the easiest and best to use, though they do not function very well at low temperatures. Different models have varying capacities, attachments and extras. Mini light and collapsible picnic cookers using methylated spirits and meta fuel tablets may be all you need for a brief cooking or for warming up food.

For a long holiday there is a wide range of gas cookers with two burners and useful parts such as wind breaks, cooker shelf, warming rack and grill pan. Most valuable is one with a fine adjustment from fast burning to the slowest simmer. Rechargeable gas containers can easily be refilled. For average summer-time cooking a 4.5 kg (10 lb) container should last about 10 days.

You will need a canteen of one or more saucepans or frying pans that nest into each other for storage. If you cannot carry much the French army kit and the G.I. canteen are ideal, but their aluminium pans are of necessity light and thin and you must be careful not to burn the food.

If you have space it is well worth taking heavy-bottomed pans (non-stick ones are useful) with fitting lids. High narrow saucepans are best for saving heat and fuel.

A griddle is excellent for making bread (see p.167) and cooking steaks and sausages. The best is made of cast-iron, has a ribbed surface and a stick-resistant matt enamel finish.

A heavy pot or casserole which can be left for hours in hot ashes is useful for stewing.

A pressure cooker or a crockpot, if you have a battery, save fuel and time.

Other necessary cooking equipment includes water carriers, lanterns, food boxes, can opener, corkscrew and the basic necessities of the kitchen: sharp knife, wooden spoon, grater, fish slice, rotary beater, garlic press. Add to these a campfire grill and heavy duty foil and an axe and saw for cutting wood.

Barbecuing chart

The cooking times suggested should be taken as only a very rough guide. In reality timing depends not only on the thickness and type of food, whether it is lean or fat, tough or tender and the distance from the fire, but also on the relative efficiency of the grill, the size of the fire-bed, the quality of wood or coals (this especially varies widely) and their concentration, as well as the weather conditions. The time given is for cooking on both sides. You may prefer to give the first side a longer cooking time.

If the food is wrapped in foil cook for an additional 5-10 minutes. The heat of the fire is measured by the distance of the grill or spit from the bed of embers:

Searing hot	4-5 cm ($1\frac{1}{2}$-2 in)
Hot	8 cm (3 in)
Medium	10 cm (4 in)
Low	13 cm (5 in)

If you cannot adjust the height of the grill easily, simply change the position of the meat from the hottest part – straight above – to the edge of the fire.

For cooking on a spit, the distance should be measured from the fire to the food. To obtain medium heat place the spit 15 cm (6 in) away from the fire so that the meat is about 10 cm (4 in) away. Lower it for searing and raise it for slow cooking.

TYPE OF FOOD	CUT	THICKNESS OR WEIGHT	HEAT	Approximate (generous) total cooking time (for both or all sides)
Beef Best rare or underdone, seared and browned outside.				After 1 minute searing each side and turning once, give the second side a little less than the first.
	Steaks	2.5 cm (1 in)	hot	6 minutes for rare, up to 10 minutes for medium.
		5 cm (2 in)	hot	8 minutes for rare, up to 16 minutes for medium.
	Hamburgers	2.5 cm (1 in)	hot	6-10 minutes.
	Kebab	2.5 cm (1 in)	hot/ medium	5-10 minutes turning frequently.
	Small roast	such as fillet	low	Sear first. Cook 7 minutes per 500 g (1 lb) for rare, 10 minutes per 500 g (1 lb) for medium. Turn occasionally.
	Large joint	up to 4 kg (9 lb)	spit	Sear first. Cook 15 minutes per 500 g (1 lb) for rare meat, 20 minutes per 500 g (1 lb) for medium.
Lamb Pink and juicy in France, well done elsewhere	Chops	2-2.5 cm (3/4-1 in)	medium	Cook 7-15 minutes. Bring closer to the heat to brown for the last 2minutes. Turn once.
	Kebabs	2-2.5 cm (3/4-1 in)	medium	6-15 minutes, turning frequently.
	Minced kebabs	flat cakes or sausage shape	medium	5-8 minutes, turning over once or more.
	Butterfly leg of lamb	6-8 cm (2½-3 in)	low	35-45 minutes for pink inside, 15 minutes more for well done. Turn occasionally.

TYPE OF FOOD	CUT	THICKNESS OR WEIGHT	HEAT	Approximate (generous) total cooking time (for both or all sides)
Lamb (cont'd)	Leg or rolled shoulder	1½-2 kg (3½-4 lb)	spit	1¼-1½ hours (or 20 minutes per 500 g (1 lb).
	Whole baby lamb	10 kg (21 lb)	spit	4-5 hours, turning occasionally.
Pork Should be well done but still juicy.	Chops	2-2½ cm (¾-1 in)	medium	15-20 minutes, turning once.
	Kebabs	2-2½ cm (¾-1 in)	medium	12-15 minutes, turning frequently.
	Spare ribs, whole rack		low	1½ hours.
	Large joint		spit	25-30 minutes per 500 g (1 lb) plus 25 minutes extra.
	Whole suckling pig	7 kg (15 lbs)	spit	3½-4 hours, turning occasionally.
	Sausages		medium	8-12 minutes, turning frequently.
	Boudin andouillette		medium	20-25 minutes, turning frequently.
Veal Needs to be well done but not dry.	Chops	1½-2 cm (½-¾ in)	medium	8-10 minutes, turning once.
	Fillet thinly sliced	½ cm (¼ in)	medium	6-8 minutes, turning once.
	Rolled loin or shoulder		spit	25-30 minutes per 500 g (1 lb), (about 1½-2½ hours).
Kidneys Browned outside, juicy and rare inside.	Calf's, sliced or cut in half lengthwise; or lamb's, whole or cut in half lengthwise		medium	5-10 minutes, turning once.

TYPE OF FOOD	CUT	THICKNESS OR WEIGHT	HEAT	Approximate (generous) total cooking time (for both or all sides)
Liver Browned outside, pink inside.	Calf's, lamb's or pig's, thickly sliced		hot	4-6 minutes, turning once.
Chicken Must be a young and tender one.	Boned breasts		medium	10-15 minutes, turning once or more.
	Legs or drumsticks		medium	25-35 minutes, turning occasionally.
	Wings		medium	10-15 minutes, turning once or more.
	Kebabs		medium	5-10 minutes, turning frequently.
	Whole, split open		medium	30-45 minutes, turning occasionally. Give longer to the bone side.
	Whole	(3-3½ lb)	spit	1½-2 hours.
	Livers		medium	5 minutes.
Poussin	Split open and flattened		medium	20-30 minutes, turning occasionally.
	Whole		spit	20-30 minutes turning occasionally.
Duckling	Whole	split open	medium/ low	About 40 minutes. Turn occasionally starting with the skin side down.
	Whole	2-2½ kg	spit	1-1½ hours.
Wild Duck	Whole	(1-1½ lb)	spit	30 minutes.
Goose	Whole	small, young	spit	Allow about 20 minutes to the 50 g (1 lb).

TYPE OF FOOD	CUT	THICKNESS OR WEIGHT	HEAT	Approximate (generous) total cooking time (for both or all sides)
Guinea Fowl	Whole	young, (under 1½ kg (3 lb), split open and flattened	medium	20 minutes, turning occasionally.
Squab	Whole	split open and flattened	medium	15-25 minutes.
Rabbit	Whole	cut into pieces	spit	45-60 minutes.
	Young		medium	15-30 minutes.
Fish Must never be over-cooked as it dries out.	Large	whole	low	Allow 10 minutes per 2½ cm (1 in) of thickness, turn at least once.
		split in half	low	Allow 10 minutes per 2½ cm (1 in) thickness. (You need not turn).
	Small	medium small	hot/ medium	8-12 minutes.
		very small	hot/ medium	5-6 minutes.
	Steaks	2½ cm (1 in)	medium	6-10 minutes. Turn once (thinner steaks or fillets do not need turning).
		5 cm (2 in)	medium/ low	12-20 minutes.
	Kebabs	2½ cm (1 in)	medium	5-8 minutes.
King-size Prawns	In their shells		medium	8-10 minutes. Turn once.
	Without their shells, skewered		medium	5-6 minutes, turning occasionally.
Lobster	Cut in half		low	15-20 minutes shell side, turning for the last 3 minutes.

TYPE OF FOOD	CUT	THICKNESS OR WEIGHT	HEAT	Approximate (generous) total cooking time (for both or all sides)
Shellfish	In their shells		medium	Until they open.
	Out of their shells or skewered		medium	5-10 minutes.
Snails	In their shells		medium	5-6 minutes.

BIBLIOGRAPHY

BEARD, JAMES, *Beard on Food*, New York, Alfred A. Knopf, 1974. *Barbecue With Beard*, New York, Warner Books, 1976. *Delights and Prejudices*, New York, Simon & Schuster, 1971.

BECK, SIMONE, *Simca's Cuisine*, London, John Murray, 1973.

BONI, ADA, *Italian Regional Cooking*, translation by Maria Langdale and Ursula Whyte, Sunbury on Thames, Thomas Nelson & Sons, 1969.

BRISSENDEN, ROSEMARY, *South East Asian Food*, London, Penguin Books, 1972.

CHILD, JULIA, *From Julia Child's Kitchen*, London, Jonathan Cape, 1978.

DAVID, ELIZABETH, *French Country Cooking*, London, Penguin Books, 1965. *French Provincial Cooking*, London, Penguin Books, 1964. *Mediterranean Food*, London, Penguin Books, 1965. *Spices, Salt and Aromatics*, London, Penguin Books, 1970. *Summer Cooking*, London, Penguin Books, 1965.

DAVIDSON, ALAN, *Mediterranean Seafood*, London, Penguin Books, 1972. *Seafood of South East Asia*, London, Macmillan, 1978.

EKAMBARAM, MANORAMA, *Hindu Cookery*, Bombay, D. B. Taraporevala Sons & Co., 1963.

GARDINER, G. and F. A. STEEL, *The Complete Indian Housekeeper and Cook*, London, William Heinemann, 1904.

GORE, LILLI, *Game Cooking*, London, Penguin Books, 1976.

GRIGSON, JANE, *Charcuterie and French Pork Cookery*, London, Penguin Books, 1970. *Fish Cookery*, London, Penguin Books, 1975. *Good Things*, London, Penguin Books, 1973. *Mushroom Feast*, London, Penguin Books, 1973.

HARGREAVES, BARBARA, *The Sporting Wife: Game and Fish Cooking*, London, H. F. & G. Witherby, 1976.

HAZAN, MARCELLA, *The Classic Italian Cookbook*, London, Macmillan, 1980.

JAFFREY, MADHUR, *Invitation to Indian Cooking*, London, Jonathan Cape, 1976.

JONES, EVAN, *The World of Cheese*, London, Macmillan, 1980.

KRITAKARA, M. L. and M. R. PIMSAI AMRAMAND, *Modern Thai Cooking*, Bangkok, Editions Dunag Kamol, 1977.

LEYEL, MRS C. F., *Picnics for Motorists*, London, George Routledge & Sons, 1936.

LEYEL, MRS C. F. and HARTLEY, OLGA, *The Gentle Art of Cookery*, London, Chatto and Windus, 1925.

MABEY, RICHARD, *Food for Free: Guide to the Edible Wild Plants of Britain*, London, Fontana, 1975.

McNEILL, F. MARIAN, *The Camper's Kitchen*, London, Alexander MacLehose & Co., 1933.

MAGASAWA, KIMIKO, and CAMY CONDON, *Eating Cheap in Japan*, Tokyo, Shufunotomo Co., 1972.

MARKS, JAMES F., *Barbecues*, London, Penguin Books, 1977.

MAHER, BARBARA, *Cakes*, London, Jill Norman and Hobhouse, 1982.

ORTIZ, ELISABETH LAMBERT, *The Book of Latin American Cooking*, London, Jill Norman, 1981. *The Complete Book of Japanese Cooking*, New York, M. Evans & Co., 1976. *The Complete Book of Mexican Cooking*, New York, M. Evans & Co., 1967.

OWEN, SRI, *Indonesian Food and Cookery*, London, Prospect Books, 1980.

RODEN, CLAUDIA, *A Book of Middle Eastern Food*, London, Penguin Books, 1970. *Coffee*, London, Penguin Books, 1981.

ST CLAIR, LADY HARRIET, *Dainty Dishes*, Edinburgh, 1866.

SING, PHIA, *Phia Sing's Traditional Recipes of Laos*, London, Prospect Books, 1981.

SINGH, BALBIR, *Indian Cookery*, London, Mills & Boon, 1971.

SINGH, DHARAMJIT, *Indian Cookery*, London, Penguin Books, 1970.

SITAS, AMARANTH, *Kopiaste*, Limassol, Cyprus, 1968.

SMITH, MICHAEL, *Fine English Cookery*, London, Faber & Faber, 1977.

SYSONBY, LADY, *Lady Sysonby's Cookbook*, London, Putnam, 1935.

TEZUKA, PROFESSOR KANEKO, *Japanese Food*, Tokyo, Board of Tourist Industry, Japanese Government Railways, 1936.

Other books

BATTISCOMBE, GEORGINA, *English Picnics*, London, The Country Book Club, 1951.

BRILLAT-SAVARIN, JEAN ANTHELME, *Gastronomy as a Fine Art*, London, Chatto & Windus, 1889.

HARTLEY, DOROTHY, *Food in England*, London, Macdonald, 1954.

HILL, BRIAN MERRIKIN, ed., *The Greedy Book: A Feast for the Eyes*, London, Rupert Hart-Davis, 1966.

KINCAID, DENIS, *British Social Life in India 1608-1937*, second edition, London, Routledge & Kegan Paul, 1973.

RENNER, H. D., *The Origins of Food Habits*, London, Faber & Faber, 1944.

INDEX

Potted:
  cheese, 235-236
  fish, 234
  meat, 233-234
Poussin, 296
Prawns:
  fried, 277
  grilled, 158, 218, 297
  king-sized, 209, 218, 297
  potted, 235
  salads, 85-89, 99, 248
Preserving, 225-243
Prunes:
  grilled, 159
  with meat, 52, 77
  purée, 52
Purées:
  fruit, 51-52
  vegetable, 54-55

Quail, 179-180
Quantities, xvii
Quiches, 68-69
Quinces, 115

Rabbit:
  confits, 236-237
  potted, 233-234
  roast, 178, 297
Rabelais, François, 168
Raclette, 160
Radishes:
  crudités, 92, 248
  white, grilled, 165
Raised pie, 71-72
Raisins:
  with courgettes, 24
  with fish, 204
  with roasts, 78
  in salad, 102
  types, 243
Raitas, 222
Raspberries:

fool, 109-110
macerated, 107
purée, 8, 114
tarts, 113
Ratatouille, 100
  tart, 67
Raverat, Gwen, 32, 119
Red currant jelly, 52
Red mullet, 201, 202, 204
  See also Fish
Relishes, 53
Renner, H. D., 154, 288
Rice:
  to boil, 88, 145-146
  with fish, 88, 145-146, 282
  salads, 88, 102, 145-146
Roach, 279
  See also Fish
Roes:
  in butter sauce, 200
  in caviare mousse, 121-122
  taramasalata, 57
  on toast, 248, 260
Rolled sandwiches, 4
Rolls, 162
'Roofs', 162
Rouff, Marcel, 10
Rouille, 282
Rousseau, Jean Jacques, xii, 28

St Clair, Lady Harriet, 132, 288
Salads:
  dressings for, 44-46
  fish and seafood, 13-14, 85-88,
    145-146, 248-249, 276
  fruit (sweet), 24, 106-109
  meat, 79, 83-84
  vegetable, 14-15, 24, 31-32,
    92-103, 214-215
Salmon:
  cold, 85
  in fish terrine, 89
  grilled and flamed, 201

NOTES

NOTES

NOTES

NOTES